Conflict, Migration, and the Expression of Ethnicity

Published in Cooperation with

THE CENTER FOR INTERNATIONAL DEVELOPMENT
AND CONFLICT MANAGEMENT
University of Maryland, College Park

Conflict, Migration, and the Expression of Ethnicity

EDITED BY

Nancie L. Gonzalez
and Carolyn S. McCommon

Westview Press

BOULDER, SAN FRANCISCO, & LONDON

A Westview Special Study

Copyright © 1989 by Westview Press, Inc.

Published in 1989 in the United States of America by Westview Press, Inc., 5500 Central Avenue, Boulder, Colorado 80301, and in the United Kingdom by Westview Press, Inc., 13 Brunswick Centre, London WC1N 1AF, England

Library of Congress Cataloging-in-Publication Data
González, Nancie L. Solien, 1929–
   Conflict, migration, and the expression of ethnicity / by Nancie
L. González and Carolyn S. McCommon.
      p.   cm.—(A Westview Special Study)
   Bibliography: p.
   Includes index.
   ISBN 0-8133-7620-3
   1. Ethnicity.   2. Emigration and immigration—Social aspects.
3. Ethnic relations.   I. McCommon, Carolyn Sue.   II. Title.
GN495.6.G66   1989
305.8—dc19   88-10655
                                                                      CIP

Printed and bound in the United States of America

The paper used in this publication meets the requirements of the American National Standard for Permanence of Paper for Printed Library Materials Z39.48-1984.

10   9   8   7   6   5   4   3   2   1

CONTENTS

1

CONFLICT, MIGRATION, AND THE EXPRESSION OF ETHNICITY: INTRODUCTION

Nancie L. Gonzalez

The three topics joined in this book are not new in anthropology. Each has a large and respectable literature, much of which has become classic, even outside the discipline. The contributors, however, share the conviction that we still have much to learn about the inter-relationships among them -- how conflict both produces and is a product of migration, and how ethnic phenomena are interwoven with both. It is not our intent to define the slippery concept of ethnicity; indeed, most of the authors recognize that different investigators and theorists have used and will continue to use it in quite different ways (see Cohen 1978, Royce 1982, Riggs 1985). Like the concept of culture itself, ethnicity is a theoretical construct that we use to help us understand and explain certain kinds of things, events and behavior that we observe in the field.

Similarly, conflict and migration may also be variously defined by different investigators. Although we hope the case studies included here will shed light on all three, we warn the reader at the outset that we do not pretend to offer a unified theoretical treatment of them; rather, each author presents a situation in which the data seem illuminated by using these three conceptual variables -- sometimes following the lead of other investigators, and sometimes in novel formulations. The following is an attempt to set forth some of the "common understandings" about these concepts as they are used in this volume, together with a glimpse of how each presentation is related to the others and to the whole.

Ethnicity as an Ethnographic Category

Probably the social groupings most frequently observed by ethnographers working in complex societies are those bound together by a common language, religion, domestic values, and kinship -- in other words, by the ethnographic characteristics by which anthropologists have long recognized and described human cultural variation. Once we termed the ethnographic units we discovered "peoples and cultures," and laypersons called them "tribes" or "nations," but with the rise of multinational states and their incorporation of once-autonomous peoples within their political folds, "ethnic group" has become the more customary designation of such units by both anthropologists and others.

Most ethnographic observations have been focused on small, local units at relatively simple or lower levels of sociopolitical integration, although in recent years anthropologists have more and more contributed to studies of global sociocultural systems. In the latter endeavor, it is now commonplace for anthropologists to study various kinds of constituent groups in plural or pluralistic societies, as well as macrolevel phenomena associated with nations, states, and international institutions and organizations that crosscut the latter.

Only Burns and Diskin here deal with the kinds of societies that have traditionally been considered grist for the anthropological mill. In all the other papers, the "ethnic" subjects are named for the country from which they have migrated or derived -- Salvadorans, Guatemalans, Greeks, Turks, and in the case of the Palestinians in Lebanon and in Honduras, by the name of a non-existent country whose "citizens" are nevertheless bound together in diaspora in their dream of regaining lost territory and of creating a nation therein. There is virtually no concern over whether we are dealing with ethnic groups or categories, with boundaries or content, although all the contributors seem to agree that there are ethnic phenomena involved.

Most of the authors are not bothered by this problem of ethnic "apples and oranges," although Mandel properly cautions us against both the "laundry list" way of defining an ethnic group and against the danger of reifying ethnicity -- making it into an objective entity that is somehow "out there" waiting to be studied. Anticipating Mandel, I believe it is fair to say that most of the present authors have used a folk, rather than an analytic definition of ethnicity in thinking about their subjects. In one sense, it is a professional "folklore," deriving principally from anthropology; but political scientist Rubenberg, coming from a different tradition, tends to think of ethnicity in another light -- ironically, she alone refers to Barth's notion of "primordial" ethnic attachments, although she also believes that in the case of Lebanon, factors other than ethnic rivalry catalyzed the conflict. Indeed, a primary conclusion that can be drawn from all the papers, is that the *definition* of both self and group in ethnic terms is enhanced, if not actually generated, by the conflict/migration/conflict situations in which the subjects of our papers have found themselves. This is not how early anthropologists accounted for the origin of ethnic phenomena, although ethnohistorians have now demonstrated that some groups, such as the Miskitu may indeed have originally been the product of local conflicts and migrations brought about by the expansion of Europeans into the New World -- itself a process involving all three concepts (Helms 1971).

This discussion continues to beg the questions of how we define ethnicity, how we know it (or its symbols, or its boundaries, or its scope, etc.) when we see it, and how we treat and evaluate it in relation to other variables. For most of the authors, ethnicity is treated as a given; it is not itself the primary focus of their analyses. In each case it tends to be seen and accepted in emic terms, i.e., as the people being observed define themselves and others. Except for instances in which the author is self-consciously dealing with the *concept* of ethnicity, this is how most anthropologists handle it in their descriptive works. Thus, the papers vary in whether they deal with relationships, symbols, or stereotypes. Most include at least a cursory review of both "internal" and "external" definitions of the group's ethnic identity. Durham's contribution picks up from the questions raised here and by Mandel, giving us further thoughts on the definition of ethnicity than are found in the papers themselves, which concentrate more on how ethnicity is expressed under the circumstances described.

Development

More important to most of the authors have been the contexts within which the ethnic variable has been played out in their observations. "International development" is one such, and is the fourth dimension of the discussion for which these papers formed the background. It is often assumed, especially by economists and "development specialists," that commercial and industrial development, even on a small scale, will be a panacea for the world's ills. Education of the masses is often justified as a means of fitting them for jobs in that sector -- either on the production lines of factories or fields, or in white-collar and service oriented positions. It is also thought that improvement of the industrial sector in the less developed countries will stem the tide of international migration as people leave or are forced off their traditional plots.

But some of our papers (Gonzalez, McCommon, Mandel) suggest that the development process itself may encourage emigration, often because its benefits are unequally distributed, or because newly acquired literacy and access to knowledge about the larger society through the mass media increase the sense of relative deprivation felt by some sectors of the population. Their dissatisfaction may lead to local conflict, which in turn may become an additional push factor, as in El Salvador.

Migration then, aside from itself being an important context within which to examine the ethnic variable, has often been linked with development, as well as with conflict -- less often have the three been considered together, as different aspects of a single, ongoing, worldwide process. It was my hope to bring together papers that would provoke discussion along new lines -- to show that conflict and migration influence each other, and that both are in many ways the product of development, as may be ethnogenesis itself under certain conditions.

Migration

The last two decades have seen a significant change in the unit of analysis typically chosen by ethnographers. Often the communities we study today are found in cities, along highways, in refugee camps or in "model villages"; they are, in fact, made up of emigrants from the rural tribes and villages we formerly haunted. They may even have become parts of cities and towns in the U.S. and other industrial nations. In effect, we have followed our informants as their lives have been changed by national and global pressures that inevitably today reach into the most remote places.

Sometimes those who leave home have been eager for the bright lights; more often they are attracted by better wages, easier workloads and public services available in cities. Once there, they find themselves members of a plural or pluralistic society, and either in defense or in pride, accept the status of "ethnic group." Sometimes this becomes merely a euphemism for lower class (Friedlander 1975, Gonzalez 1969, Mandel *infra*). In the new setting, however, they are likely to become tied to the larger social whole in ways different than those they had known in their home settings. Individuals may find themselves drawn, because of job or educational opportunities, to personal attachments outside of their original kin and identity group. New non-traditional marital arrangements link families in new ways, breaking down the rigid social and cultural boundaries that characterize more isolated peoples. Cross-cutting ties develop as the newcomers become absorbed in multiple activities and groupings. This, in turn, creates the context for what we call "situational" ethnicity, in which individuals identify with one ethnic group for some purposes or under certain conditions, but with others or with only the national culture when that suits them better.

There are fads and fashions in scholarship, as in other things, but even when the world at large saw urbanization and industrialization as the keys to a better life for more people, anthropologists tended to be cautious, and not merely in an effort to save the rural, more isolated communities for their own research, as has frequently been charged. They saw too clearly that rural-to-urban and temporary international migration rarely benefited "their people " in lasting ways, and that it often led the migrants to cultural and ethnic suicide (Gonzalez 1988, Rubinstein 1983, Seeger 1981). Where we erred was in not realizing that ethnicity as a principle and as an organizing force may rise again anywhere, even when most observers have thought it dead, or when its bearers had not previously thought of themselves as "ethnics."

The migratory process, whatever reasons motivate it, seems first to enhance the sense of solidarity among those who migrate, who are often united by the bonds of kinship, community, and ethnicity, as well as by class. Symbols of ethnicity, such as language or linguistic style, dress styles, dietary preferences and religious behavior serve as reminders of their origin to the migrants themselves, while at the same time marking these people as outsiders in the sheltering locale. They help to establish who are "we" and who are "they." It matters little whether the migrants have all shared these symbols earlier in their lives, for they now serve to bind them together, perhaps in new ways, and to shield them from an often hostile receiving society. Many Palestinians in Honduras are more self-consciously Palestinian there than they ever were at home, and sometimes flaunt "Arab" customs that they have learned from books.

International migration has many faces. For some, it is primarily a psychological frontier; the aim is to find the economic wherewithal abroad to maintain an old way of life at home that seemed to be slipping from their grasp. Sometimes the money sent home by migrants allows those left behind to keep the home fires burning -- at least for a time. The migrants may or may not return to share in the benefits made possible by their sacrifice, and sometimes, as Mandel shows for Turkish workers in Germany, they find they cannot really go home again and expect to be accepted in their former status.

Some migrants at the outset make a conscious decision to abandon an old, unsatisfactory way of life for what they believe will be paradise on earth, and some will swear that they have found it, never thinking again about what they have left behind. For others, migration leads to a new, syncretic existence, one that incorporates two (or more) distinct ways of doing things, two sets of "neighbors," i.e., face-to-face contacts and mutual aid networks, and a declining sense of national loyalty and patriotism for any particular "homeland."[1] The Arabs of Honduras, until recent events in Israel and the West Bank refueled their passions, were an example of such an adaptation. Some of the latter, in addition to maintaining their connections in Bethlehem, compounded the situation by spending a good bit of time and by purchasing property in the United States as well. But still others, such as the Kanjobal Maya, leave home in desperation, knowing that the new life in exile will give them but little if any economic improvement, but fearing for their very lives if they remain in their homeland.

Conflict: Latent, Violent, Armed and Protracted

Work by anthropologists on war and conflict has taken many forms. Several anthologies dealing with various aspects of modern warfare have appeared (Bohannan 1967, Fried *et al.* 1968, Levine and Campbell 1972, Nettleship *et al.* 1975, Foster and Rubinstein 1986), and some attention has been paid to the question of "primitive" war (Turney-High 1949), and to the evolution of war (Otterbein 1970). All of these assume that "war" involves some degree of violence, the use of arms, and a social charter, which distinguishes war from crime, delinquency, and terrorism.

Latent conflict is usually addressed by anthropologists in relation to political processes -- decision-making, dispute management, witchcraft, factionalism, and the like. At the state level, latent conflict has been most often called the "cold war" and has been almost entirely left to the political scientists. There are, however, a few papers by anthropologists in Foster and Rubinstein (1986) that deal with the subject.

To date, few anthropologists have dealt with the issue of *protracted* conflict. One exception is Gamst (1986), who has described centuries of violence in the Horn of Africa. The subject is mostly discussed by political scientists -- many of whom depend heavily upon the concept of ethnicity (Riggs 1985). When anthropologists deal with ethnicity and conflict in modern societies, or in those undergoing pressures from more developed nations or sectors, they have concentrated on resource competition (Despres 1975) and/or on the relationships between conflict and indigenous political systems (Leach 1954, Sahlins 1961) or on the exploitation of traditional peoples by colonial or neocolonial interests (Melville and Melville 1971, Smith 1978, Wolf 1982).

Political scientists, on the other hand, in addition to examining power structures, have lately stressed psychocultural factors in their analyses (Wedge 1986). Ross (1985) points out that social structural theories of conflict fail to articulate how the apparent interests of social groups are converted into organized, collective action. Azar (1986:29) believes that the study of ethnicity and the "drive" for ethnic identity enables us to understand the nature of conflicts generally. He hypothesizes that (a) security, (b) distinctive identity, (c) social recognition of identity, and (d) effective participation in the processes that determine conditions of security and identity, are essential human needs, the denial of which leads to protracted social conflict.

This hypothesis, based on data for some sixty nations,[2] is supported by many contemporary and historical situations, but it seems not to fit the circumstance of many peoples in diaspora from their original homelands. In fact, it seems likely to this writer that international migration acts as an alternative mechanism for coping with the denial of such needs, although it is also apparent that it does not necessarily act as a deterrent to violence in the homeland. The Kanjobal and Salvadoran cases, as well as those of the Palestinians in Lebanon and Honduras, are examples of what I have called "conflict migration," although the last of these differs from the former in that most of the refugees were forcibly removed from their homes.

Nietschmann, a cultural geographer, has also been concerned with the role of ethnicity in armed conflict. In a recent excerpt from a forthcoming book to be entitled *The Roots of Conflict,* he suggests that in 120 cases of armed conflict[3] in the world today, 82% (98) involve what he calls "nations" fighting for their independence or some negotiated territorial or political autonomy within a larger state (Nietschmann 1987:7). He terms this the Third World War, and links it to migration only in that it produces almost all of the world's refugees (p. 12). As in several of our cases here, some *decide* to flee in what they believe to be their best interests; others remain home and engage in active conflict to try to improve their situation.

Ethnicity and Conflict

Conflict of one sort or another seems often to be a trigger in ethnogenesis or ethnoregenesis, whether or not migration is involved. The Miskitu are a fascinating example at the micro-level, their ethnicity having been generated by conflict both historically and during the current Nicaraguan conflict. The Kanjobal Maya in Florida are coping with the new idea that "Guatemalan" may be a more acceptable ethnic designation in the United States than either "Mayan" or "Kanjobal." Yet as Moore suggests, the Guatemalan nation itself suffers from a lack of national symbols by which its people can distinguish themselves and which will enhance their sense of unity and patriotism.

Voluntary emigration is less common, especially today, than is the case of those who flee from their birthplaces as economic or political refugees -- overtaken by conditions or events outside of their control, and which they rarely understand well. Again, our anthropological attention has swung from the nitty-gritty of the daily life of ethnic migrants fleeing conflict situations to the politics and economics of development -- the wily seductress that promises freedom from "tradition" and misery, but more often creates new dimensions and definitions of human bondage, including sometimes a commitment to violence as a way of life. Unfortunately, true development, in the sense of basic improvements in a regional or national economy such that all the people benefit, is itself forestalled when violence becomes endemic and protracted.

The papers in this volume assume that the development process in the contemporary world is likely to exacerbate or create conflict at the local level for several reasons. First, as a more democratic philosophy permeates development discussions and projects, there is the danger that the more privileged and dominant local groups, fearing for their vested interests, will tighten their grip, not permitting fiscal and other reforms necessary for overall improvement of standards of living.[4] This may provoke distress and rebellion among the less-privileged -- especially those whose educational level allows them to perceive and understand the meaning of relative deprivation. The Kanjobal Maya of Guatemala were on the brink of development until their ideas were labeled communist and radical and they were driven from their homelands altogether.

Secondly, the new values people everywhere have come to place upon industrially produced goods have created a perpetual demand for low-paid factory and service workers in virtually all "developed" countries today. Many institutions have evolved that help create and maintain a continual migration or circulation of peoples from the less industrialized to the more highly industrialized areas -- from rural to urban in the Third World, and from less developed to more highly developed countries. Not only did this lead the Germans to invite Turks to their country as "guest workers," but whatever niche the Kanjobal Maya may be said to have found in the United States derives from our desire for cheap agricultural products, picked by a succession of low-paid, often foreign, workers. Discussions of a generation ago about underdevelopment and dependency among the poorer nations failed to predict the current state of affairs in which certain classes of people are relegated to more or less permanent dependency upon wage labor -- wherever they can get it.[5]

Thus, local conflict in a Third World country may benefit its more developed neighbors by directing a flow of migrant labor their way. When the flow is larger than the number of jobs, however, wages are depressed. Although this may trouble some sectors of the receiving society, employers will benefit. But massive unemployment in turn fuels unrest and increases both latent and violent conflict. Thus, both the United States and Germany face potential internal unrest as a result of their immigration policies.

Finally, many modern states, most of which have incorporated multiple "nations," peoples, or ethnic groups, as well as a diversity of groups based on other criteria, have not developed effective ways of resolving or managing fundamental disputes engendered by territorial or economic competition, oppression of some groups by others, or by disagreement over fundamental rights and values by which to live. Such political failure, in turn, may promote protracted conflict -- both latent and violent -- among the groups, as well as out-migration of many of those who find themselves helpless to improve their situation.

The papers in this book not only document the fact that local conflict spawns refugeeism, but several deal with ensuing events in the receiving societies, including the rise of new inter-ethnic tensions when the refugees are defined as unwelcome intruders -- sometimes by preceding refugee groups who fear erosion of their own beachhead (Burns). Although refugees sometimes readily find work in the industrial sector of the receiving society (often at lower wages), most live in substandard conditions and usually are forced to depend for some of their subsistence on various national and international welfare programs. Local citizens may resent the use of national funds to pay for health and educational needs of the newcomers (Burns, Mandel, McCommon). There is a good bit of such feeling in the United States, although it is not fashionable to admit it (Perez 1986).

Some ethnic cleavages have long historical roots that maintain latent conflict and intermittently produce violence, but in other cases, ethnicity may be invented or reawakened as a reaction to outside forces. Anthropologists have frequently dealt with this phenomenon, calling it "nativism," "revivalism," or "revitalization." Durham discusses it in terms of instrumentalism -- ethnic symbols being manipulated for specific ends. Such is evident in both Diskin's and Moore's chapters, as well as in Mandel's and my own. Ethnic revival or ethnoregenesis may occur either in a foreign setting among peoples only distantly bound together, or in a homeland where other allegiances have superceded the ethnic for various reasons. In the case of the Miskitu of Nicaragua, Diskin shows that it may be considered a means of overcoming leveling mechanisms imposed by authoritarian governments bent on redressing class injustices. The urge for self-determination may be underestimated by those polities that stress the "melting pot" as a solution to sociocultural development.

The plight of returning Turkish workers and the new dimensions of ethnicity imposed upon them by themselves and others as a result of their diaspora is a phenomenon not previously addressed in the anthropological literature. The taking on of characteristics of the host society by migrants, who are thereby differently perceived and defined by their compatriots left behind is certainly more common than has heretofore been recognized. Mandel's discussion should stimulate a good deal of further research on this subject. The potential for conflict in the home setting between migrants and stay-behinds should also be considered and explored.

The addition of one paper by a political scientist (Rubenberg) was not merely tokenism. The area she treats is one in which violent conflict, migration, and ethnic cleavages have all been protracted for a very long time. Lebanon once seemed well on its way toward achieving a developed status, and Israel was accorded that early on. Yet development has not brought the benefits expected, and "Lebanon" has become almost a synonym for a chronic state of war. As such, it could not be left out of a discussion dealing with the variables in the title. Due to her having been in the wrong place at a crucial moment in time, Dr. Rubenberg was forced to spend several months in a Palestinian camp in Lebanon in 1982. I know of no anthropologist who has lived for so long a period inside a refugee camp. Her insights are, therefore, unique and a valuable contribution.

The organization of the chapters might have been done in several ways. We have chosen to highlight what might be thought of as three different stages of development in which conflict and migration result. The first, illustrated in the chapters by Diskin and Moore, is that in which the state apparatus, when faced with internal conflict with ethnic expressions, tries to coopt the dissidents by downplaying ethnic differences and at the same time promoting loyalty to the larger whole.

A second stage can be seen in the response of dissidents under such pressure who emigrate to another country. Mandel, Burns and Gonzalez have described several such instances. Finally, such migration may in turn lead to another stage of further ethnic conflict in the receiving society, as in McCommon's chapter on Belize and that of Rubenberg on Lebanon.

In closing, I wish to thank all the contributors. Several of the papers in this volume (Burns, Diskin, McCommon, Rubenberg) derive from an invited symposium sponsored by the General Anthropology Division of the American Anthropological Association at its meeting in Chicago, November, 1987. William Durham was the invited discussant at the session, and his paper is a more formalized version of the remarks he made there. We had an enthusiastic and participating audience, to whom thanks are also due for a fruitful discussion.

Three papers (Gonzalez, Moore, Mandel) were added later because their content and thrust seemed both compatible and complementary to what the original panelists had in mind. We are all pleased that Ruth Mandel who gave her paper in another symposium at the same meeting, consented to join us in publishing this book. Alexander Moore's paper was given a year earlier at another AAA symposium, then expanded for a presentation at the Center for International Development and Conflict Management at the University of Maryland, which is sponsoring the present volume. My chapter on the Arabs of Honduras was written just as we went to press, the field work not having yet been accomplished at the time of the AAA meeting. Clearly, the idea for the symposium was stimulated by my plans for that work, and the paper was in turn shaped by the symposium and its ensuing discussion. It remains a preliminary analysis, as research is ongoing.

NOTES

1. Of course, many migrants may never have felt loyalty for the nation-state in which they happened to be born, reserving such feelings for their kinfolk, their villages, or other more immediate social units.

2. Azar has compiled data from newspapers and other sources that report activities at the state level in some 130 countries. These are stored in the Conflict and Peace Research Data Bank at the Center for International Development and Conflict Management at the University of Maryland (Azar 1980).

3. Nietschmann defines this as "...fighting by organized groups that represent some collective interest, identity, nationality and (usually) territory" (1987:6).

4. An interesting article from the *Carta Seminal*, 4 November 1950, of the local Chamber of Commerce in San Pedro Sula, Honduras, noted that following World War II, prices for items of ordinary daily use such as shoes, cloth, corn, beans, lard and gasoline had doubled and sometimes tripled, while wages had remained constant since the middle thirties. The note was a plea to local business men to raise salaries to prevent widespread misery.

5. This book does not deal directly with the role of land reform or its opposite, the loss of lands through sequestration (as among Palestinians in Israel and the occupied West Bank), ecological destruction of soils (as in desertification), or natural disaster. Flight to the cities and to other countries has obviously been provoked by all of these. Conflict is clearly a part of the first situation, while development may well be a contributing cause of both the first and the second, as in much of the Sahel.

2

REVOLUTION AND ETHNIC IDENTITY: THE NICARAGUAN CASE

Martin Diskin

During the past ten years, five factors have been significant in re-shaping the ethnic identity[1] of the populations of the Atlantic Coast of Nicaragua. They are: the development of a network, now worldwide, of indigenous and indigenist[2] advocacy groups; the success of the Sandinista revolution in July 1979; the decision by the United States to use Indian aspirations for self-determination as part of its effort to overthrow the Sandinistas; the experience of migration and exile for some coastal people; and the changes in Sandinista policy that led to the present autonomy law for the Atlantic Coast. Each of these, in its way, constituted a pressure, an obstacle, or a stimulus, as well as a context in which self-conscious reflections on identity took place. These reflections were partially conjunctural statements made in the face of specific political challenges. They were also responses to general curiosity as to the nature of coastal people's participation in events that received wide publicity. As such, they are part of an ongoing process of emerging ethnic identity.

The Atlantic Coast of Nicaragua, the Mosquito Coast, while remote from the consciousness of most Nicaraguans who live on the Pacific side of the country, has not been isolated from significant world currents. Spanish colonial domination was barely implanted there because of the inhospitable climate and difficulty of exploiting the environment. Two indigenous populations of the Coast, the Miskitus and Sumus, were deeply involved in the maritime conflict between England and Spain in that region (Hale 1987:34-38). In the early 17th century, the Miskitus occupied the coastal littoral and the banks of the large rivers, although the Sumus were apparently the numerically larger group (Incer 1985). The Miskitus, because of their favored location, became the brokers for the British and served as pilots and crews, and helped refit and stock ships with food and water. In return, they received firearms, with which they subdued the Sumu and became over time the dominant group. This interlude with the British lasted over two centuries, during which the British established a Miskitu kingship. King Jeremy I was crowned in Jamaica in the 1680s (Helms 1986:508). Although the matter of whether kingship was an indigenous institution among the Miskitu is under debate (Helms 1986; Olien 1983; Dennis and Olien 1984) there seems little doubt that contact with the British established the Miskitu as a mobile, aggressive, politically astute group.

Although the Spanish were not able to establish their hegemony over the coastal region in what is now Nicaragua, the British presence was largely a maritime one, resulting in little direct settlement, except for a small community in Bluefields. In cultural, terms, the British interlude left many English loan words in the Miskitu language, many English surnames among coastal people, and the use of English among the Creole (Afro-American) population, itself largely migrated from the British insular Caribbean. A more serious threat to British control of the area came from the United States, during its period of growth as a regional power in the early nineteenth century.

The tensions between the British and the United States, the prime contenders for the Nicaraguan Mosquito shore, were resolved with a British withdrawal in favor of the United States. With the 1860 treaty of Managua, in the United States-British negotiations, the British took pains to insist upon the rights of the Miskitu as a formal condition of their departure (Dozier 1985) and Nicaragua was accepted as the legal hegemonic presence on the Atlantic Coast. Nevertheless, these diplomatic and military currents helped structure present day ethnic identities in the area.

These bare details are mentioned because, although this paper focuses on the past ten years, it is obvious that the earlier period is not one of pristine remoteness. In addition to this exposure to international political pressures, since the early 19th century Moravian missionaries had successfully converted most indigenous people of the Atlantic Coast. The Moravians preached a rather ascetic form of religious practice. Moravian worship has become well integrated into community life and the pastor is an important figure in most indigenous communities. Almost all Moravian pastors have origins in one of the coastal ethnic groups, Miskitu, Sumu, or Creole (i.e. English-speaking Black). So, while the Atlantic Coast is a difficult region climatically and access has always been a problem, at the same time, it has been shaped by cosmopolitan influences. The key to understanding its ethnic structure and emerging ethnic identities is the interaction between the greater political context and the cultural structure of the region's groups.

During the 1970s, the Somoza government paid little attention to coastal people. There was sporadic penetration in coastal social life of political parties. The National Guard had a presence there but social tensions were not great and the Guard is not remembered quite as bitterly for its violent behavior as it was in the Pacific part of the country. The significant social and economic actors were transnational corporations, mostly U.S., engaged in lumbering and mining operations.

Indigenous Advocacy

In this atmosphere, a certain amount of ethnically based organizing occurred. CORPI (Consejo Regional de Pueblos Indígenas de Centroamerica, México y Panama) was active in the region. Its activities were not confrontational, but it served as a model for the expression of regional indigenous interests. Not being a threat to economic or political interests, it did not experience any significant repression by the government, nor were its achievements particularly important.

Specifically Nicaraguan indigenous organizations were ALPROMISU (Alianza de Progreso de los Miskitus y Sumus) and SUKAWALA (Sumu Kalpapakna Wahaine Lani or Asociación Nacional de Comunidades Sumus). Both dated from the early 1970s (Jenkins Molieri 1986:183-90). Although the name of ALPROMISU indicates that historical animosities had healed between the Sumu and Miskitu and both groups could be represented by one association, for many Sumus there was still a need to have a specifically Sumu organization, SUKAWALA. Each organization had somewhat different goals. ALPROMISU's original goal was to counteract the damage caused by INFONAC, the forestry project favored by the Somoza government that was bitterly resented by most of the Miskitus of the area (ibid:148-51), although in Jenkins' view its leadership was quickly coopted by Somocista interests (ibid:189-90).

Through these three organizations, (CORPI, ALPROMISU, and SUKAWALA) coastal people developed valuable experience in advocating local causes with the central government. Especially for a growing group of Miskitus, who were reaching high levels of academic attainment, participation in these organizations was a way to operate in a national setting without abandoning their concerns for their people. These organizations also became vehicles for contact with international indigenist groups as well. On the eve of the Sandinista revolution, a group of indigenous organizations had begun to construct an agenda that included cultural rights, education, health services, and to a degree, land questions.

In a dramatic moment in November 1979, three months after the Sandinista victory, Daniel Ortega went to Puerto Cabezas. As a result of discussions held there, MISURASATA (Miskitu Sumu Rama Sandinista Asla Takanka or Miskitus, Sumus, Ramas, and Sandinistas working together) was formed and immediately became the formal representative of the ethnic groups and indigenous people of the Atlantic Coast with a seat on the Council of State, the governing body of the new government. The excitement about the founding of this organization concealed the vast difference in underlying goals held by the Sandinistas and the Indian peoples.[3]

These various Indian groups, although operating on the Atlantic Coast of Nicaragua, were an integral part of a world-wide effort. This effort strove, on the one hand, to create a body of international law guaranteeing the rights of "peoples" rather than merely individuals, and on the other, to elaborate organizational forms to implement these activities. Thus, by the early eighties, there was a large network, some affiliated with the U.N., others with religious bodies, and others representative of the new spirit of indigenous self-assertion, with indigenous leadership and self-management.[4] As MISURASATA developed a more energetic and aggressive posture toward the government, its link with the international network became a major source of support.

The Sandinista Revolution

The victorious Sandinistas, strongly supportive of "organized" groups, thought that MISURASATA would develop coastal support for the Sandinista revolutionary vision. That included extending the same pattern of agrarian and organizational reform as they were developing on the Pacific Coast. But the Atlantic Coast did not suffer from land shortage nor were there the same patterns of exploitation that existed in the other parts of the country. Indeed, the local population was not a classical peasantry at all. The Sandinistas notion of a two class system did not correspond to coastal reality. For coastal people, especially indigenous groups, any extension of Nicaraguan control, Sandinista or other, was to be resisted.

The Sandinistas, culturally similar to all previous governments - Mestizo, Catholic, Spanish-speaking - held rather vulgar views of coastal people. While there was a spirit of service on the part of the Sandinistas in their effort to bring modern agriculture, health, and literacy to the coast, it was often done with the belief that the coast was "counter-revolutionary" because it was not the primary scene of the fierce combat and enormous sacrifice during the insurrection against Somoza that characterized the rest of Nicaragua.

The leaders of the new Indian organization, on the other hand, saw this as an opportunity to work with the revolutionary government to advocate regional autonomy in a more coherent way than had been discussed in the prior period. MISURASATA issued various statements of its goals (cf. Dunbar Ortiz 1984a). Although these were expressed within the context of Nicaraguan sovereignty, to the government they suggested regional separatism, especially statements with regard to land. These were phrased in terms of an "Indian country", i.e. a large block of autonomous territory, rather than a recognition of community tenure forms (MISURASATA 1981). Rather quickly, these differences led to conflict.

The government position assumed preeminence in matters of national sovereignty (defense, justice, control of unclaimed land) and offered the recognition of any traditional form of land tenure, including communal. But community ownership, in the government's view, was related to traditional needs for agricultural and fishing rights, and left a good deal of "unclaimed" or "national land" (FSLN:1981).

During the literacy crusade of 1980, MISURASATA argued successfully to include Indian languages and English in the campaign. Other demands of MISURASATA were not so successful. The demand the government legalize an Indian territory that included most of the Atlantic Coast region and fully one-third of national territory (MISURASATA 1981), was rejected. In 1981, several violent incidents occurred leading to the unfortunate culmination of tensions at the end of the year. Indians who had fled to Honduras attacked villages on the Rio Coco, which formed the border between the two countries. Armed confrontations increased in intensity and frequency and by the end of the year, the government announced a program of forced removal of dozens of villages. The removals and destruction of houses and livestock were said by the government to be to protect the villagers and deny the fighters the resources of the communities. This initiated a period of warfare on the coast.[5]

For the fighters and their families living in Honduras, and for some Miskitus living inside Nicaragua, this was a new aspect of identity, i.e. an Indian "nation" militarily engaging a state apparatus. For the foreign sympathizers with the Indians, this conflict was seen as a classic guerrilla struggle with the guerrillas winning. For many Miskitus living inside Nicaragua, this period was one of increasing privation, as travel was restricted by the government, food production declined, and many communities were occupied by the Sandinista army. The Miskitus were also punished by the actions of their own "warriors" who interfered with transportation, destroyed bridges, made recruits through kidnapping, and forced whole communities to migrate to Honduras (Americas Watch 1986). If the warriors and their ideologues (mostly based outside of the country) were fighting to rid themselves of the presence of the state, at the local level the state became even more present and oppressive.

The United States

For the United States the conflict on the Atlantic Coast was understood as another front in the "contra" effort. The covert war against Nicaragua became public knowledge by early 1982. Shortly thereafter, reports circulated about the CIA training and arming Indian fighters in Honduras. The formal link to the United States provided a prefabricated identity for the Indian fighters. Thus, when Stedman Fagoth testified in the Senate in 1982, he described the Miskitu people as a "democratic, communitarian tribe" (Fagoth 1982:1). By then, he was associated with organizations in the United States that have been identified with the far right (e.g., the Council for Inter-American Security). He described for the Senate certain Miskitu customs such as the selection of a supreme (magna) council of elders that met once a year to legislate for the Miskitu nation.

The United States offered military aid to Indian fighters in Honduras and later, in Costa Rica, on condition that they aid the Contra cause. During the most intense fighting in 1982, 1983, 1984, the Indians were responding to the abuses committed by the Sandinistas and were quite cooperative. Their major spokespersons, Fagoth in Honduras and Brooklyn Rivera in Costa Rica, offered different representations of the Indian struggle. Fagoth stressed the anti-Sandinista anti-Communist element alongside a romantic, idyllic image of Miskitu culture. His message seemed to be; once the Sandinistas were defeated, traditional Miskitu culture (as he defined it) would be an adequate guide for the future. He maintained iron discipline in his personal leadership and many reports stressed his personal violence as a tool of enforcement.[6]

Rivera was not as close to his troops as Fagoth to his, since he spent more time moving in international circles, creating support for his cause. For Rivera, the point of the conflict was not merely the overthrow of the Sandinistas, but the creation of a new arrangement for co-existence with the Nicaraguan government. Rivera's arena included Washington, Ottawa, and Geneva. In the United States, he received support from the Indian Law Resource Center and Cultural Survival in Cambridge, Massachusetts. His Washington contacts included Senator Ted Kennedy and other members of Congress.

Through these means, contact was made with the Sandinista government and in late 1984, Rivera returned to Nicaragua, toured the Atlantic Coast and held conversations with the government in Managua. This, in turn led to four negotiating sessions with the Sandinistas that went until April 1985 in Mexico City. For his audience, congressional liberals and indigenist organizations, Rivera represented an uncontaminated Indian agenda, rather than an Indian Contra front.

Sandinista Policy Change

By mid-1985, several policy decisions had been formulated by the government. First, Indian fighters on the Atlantic Coast were not considered Contras in the sense that the fighters of the FDN (Fuerza Democrática Nicaragüense) were. The Sandinista military commanders of that region understood the Indian struggle as being motivated differently from that of the pro-U.S. contras. Also, efforts were made to negotiate agreements with Indian combatants. The most successful of these was signed in May 1985 with Eduardo Pantin in the town of Yulu. Under this agreement, which became a model for future arrangements, the Indian fighters remained armed, promised not to fight, agreed to protect the territory they occupied, and to maintain free transit for all. In return, the Sandinista army respected the truce, helped move food into the area, serviced the zone with medical attention, and helped with construction projects. At that time, the government announced that his government would help people return to the Río Coco. Finally, of great importance, the government responded directly to MISURASATA's demands and published a draft of an autonomy statute for the Atlantic Coast.

By taking these four steps (Indians not considered Contras, cease-fires signed, return to the village, drafting of autonomy law), the pace and nature of the conflict changed. Reports of Indian attacks from Honduras were less frequent. The zone was more open since the Sandinista troops withdrew from certain areas and did not patrol the places where resettlement was going on. This led to further cease-fire negotiation. Reynaldo Reyes, an Indian fighter, agreed to negotiate, and returned with his men in January 1986. Since then, numerous other Indian fighters have returned, many with armed men, in a similar fashion. At present, there is virtually no fighting on the Atlantic Coast of Nicaragua.

The autonomy document, published in four languages (Spanish, Miskitu, Sumu, and English) was made part of a *"consulta popular"* and taken to all the villages in the region for discussion in village assemblies. A similar procedure took place in the southern part of the coast. Finally, the autonomy statute, modified by public discussion, was ratified on Sept. 2, 1987, by the national assembly. It grants land rights with titles, political representation, a share of natural resource use, as well as a recognition of cultural differences and the right of the Indians to adhere to them.[7] While the autonomy issue is still not definitively settled for many coastal people (cf. Akwesasne Notes 1987 for a treaty proposed by MISURASATA), the public dispute centers around modifying and perfecting the law, rather than armed conflict.

Miskitu Refugees

For many Miskitus, the period of conflict meant moving to Honduras to live as refugees. Some became official refugees under the protection of the UNHCR (United Nations High Commissioner for Refugees) while others sought places to live and farm in the Honduran Moskitia (department of Gracias a Dios). Some began living in camps organized militarily by MISURA, Fagoth's group. Miskitu attitudes toward the conflict, autonomy, and the Sandinistas in general, seems to depend upon how long they were in Honduras. The long standing Honduras residents seemed well installed in rather favorable environments, while those refugees in camps complained of shortages of everything. Other people lived outside the UN camps and were subject to control by the Indian military organizations, MISURA, and KISAN, and were in steady contact with members of the United States armed forces and the CIA (personal observation during a May, 1987 trip to Moskitia).

Some refugees, those who were coerced into crossing the border in April 1986 (Americas Watch 1986), began repatriating themselves almost as soon as they entered Honduras. Later, in recognition of the autonomy plan, the reduction of the level of fighting, and changes in the conduct of the Nicaraguan troops, other refugees in Honduras began to repatriate in increasing numbers.

This turn of events was unsettling for the Contras and their U.S. allies. A new organization YATAMA, was birthed by the CIA, with help from the Honduran Army, under the leadership of Fagoth, Rivera, and other Indian leaders. In speeches, they urged refugees not to return to Nicaragua and to consider how to pressure the Sandinistas more efficiently than before (personal observation). In spite of this appeal, however, Indian refugees returned to Nicaragua in large numbers when an "air bridge" was negotiated between the Nicaraguan and Honduran governments in April 1987 and in even larger numbers once the land bridge opened in Leimus on the Coco River shortly after that.

Discussion

During the last ten years several significant events have helped shape the ethnic identity of coastal people. Once the newly organized coastal people's impulse for change through political activism became linked to a U.S. sponsored war, it became necessary for Indian leaders to articulate the nature of Indian society. This was done both for their U.S. sponsors as well as for their own unity. These efforts served to help mold an explicit sense of ethnic identity of all the participants.

The Indian ethnic protestations were seen as an effort to obtain certain prerogatives from the state by arguing their prior right to determine their cultural identity, as well as their territorial base. In this debate, the U.S. military presence served to jeopardize the existence of the Sandinista state. Another effect of the link to the U.S. was to strengthen the Indian position, especially within the U.S. and among countries allied to the United States. This support produced its share of contradiction, however, for United States support assumed the validity of Indian cultural and territorial rights in Nicaragua, but not for Native Americans within the U.S.

Two general positions emerged among Indian activists both inside and outside of Nicaragua. One held that the path toward Indian liberation and autonomy implied the destruction of the Sandinista government. This was in effect the position of Fagoth. He organized the most effective and well-equipped military force. He maintained close liaison with the United States and Honduran military and freely traveled to the United States developing support and raising funds.

The other position, identified with Brooklyn Rivera, cited Indian autonomy as the reason for hostilities against the Sandinistas. But it recognized that a combined diplomatic-military effort was a way of seeking changes in the Sandinista government's position. Rivera said many times that he could expect more understanding and successful response from the Sandinistas than from any other regime, especially one formed by a Contra victory.

Thus, the excessively focused United States goal itself created divisions within the Indian movement. This division was exacerbated as the behavior of these two leaders became more contrastive and the United States reaction to them sought to punish Rivera's wavering while it tried to ignore the atrocities regularly attributed to Fagoth and his troops.

When Sandinista government policy changed, it seemed to further differentiate the positions of the Indian leadership. The hard line (Fagoth) was very close to that of the U.S. That is, Fagoth understood U.S. goals and could translate them into an intelligible idiom for his people. Rivera, on the other hand, was always an object of distrust for the United States since his allegiance to the Contra project was suspect. As a result, any talk of negotiating with the Sandinistas was considered treasonous for Fagoth's people. Rivera, on the other hand, maintained contact with the Sandinista authorities trying to arrange proper conditions to continue dialogue.

Ethnic Identities

The Atlantic Coast of Nicaragua contains more than half of Nicaraguan national territory with approximately ten percent of its population. It has historically been a "wild west", i.e. a region of cultural exoticism, little understood and the object of stereotype. Its indigenous population base, the Miskitu, Sumu, and Rama peoples are linguistically part of the Macro-Chibchan and Chibchan groups. The Atlantic coast has been the locus of settlement for migrating groups over the centuries. They include the Garífuna, an Afro-American Caribbean population who arrived in Central America in 1797; the Creoles, an English-speaking Afro-American population of more recent origin from the British Caribbean; and the Mestizos, Nicaraguan peasants who have migrated from the Pacific part of the country, driven by the encroachments of cattle producers. These six ethnic groups (Hale and Gordon, 1987:7-27), have each adapted in different degree and for varying lengths of time to the Atlantic Coast. Hence, their sense of ethnic identity, particularly its emergence and change in view of recent dramatic and disturbing events, may be different in each case. In the following section, I treat each group independently to assess the impact of the five factors cited above on the formation of ethnic identity.

Miskitu. The Miskitu are the most numerous of the three indigenous groups on the Atlantic Coast, estimated to number about 67,000 (Hale and Gordon 1987:18). Although vastly outnumbered by the Mestizo population estimated at 182,377 (Hale and Gordon 1987:25), the Miskitus have taken the leadership in representing coastal populations in opposition to the Sandinista state. Especially through MISURASATA, the coastal issue has come to mean indigenous people struggling to achieve recognition from the nation-state. Given the world attention to the Sandinista revolution, this aspect of it, indigenous rights, captured the interest of numerous Indian groups in the United States, Canada, and Europe. This greatly expanded forum afforded the MISURASATA leadership the opportunity to frame the terms of the debate, not only to attack Managua's policies, but to shape the definition of the actors themselves, i.e. the indigenous coastal groups. This moment of heightened attention with its need to fashion quick tactical measures in confronting the government as well as responses to government actions, had an impact in the shaping of ethnic identity itself.

As MISURASATA became widely known, coastal Indians were referred to as "original inhabitants" in much the same way that North American Indians are often called the "original Americans" (cf. *Akwesasne Notes,* various issues). This characterization often ignored the history of coastal people's interaction with the Caribbean, especially with the British naval force. The issue of the Miskitu king was given less attention than the characterization of the Miskitu people as a pristine democracy, since this would have emphasized the formative nature of colonial pressures. Such characterizations are problematic in a discussion of ethnic identity since they are made by leaders for a foreign audience. However, rather than discarding them as mere polemic, I feel they should be included as one element in the formation of identity. Time will help settle this.

But even in the present moment, documents exist and are being made that must assume importance for this question. MISURASATA's early policy pronouncements emphasized the point that only members of indigenous groups ("nations", in their usage) are qualified to define group membership. While this point is directed to the state, it raises important questions for anthropology itself. A recently published book represents an attempt to define the Miskitu people (Fagoth n.d.). Once again, this work is meant to serve specific political ends; i.e. to define autonomy as a natural outgrowth of this "communitarian" people. Roughly half of the text deals with Miskitu traditions and culture. Rather than discredit it, its double service, i.e. its conjunctural, tactical nature and its documentary status, merely gives it a point in common with "scientific" anthropological studies.

A good example of the influence of the world network of indigenous groups is the declaration of principles of the World Council of Indigenous People. This document represents perhaps the maximalist statement of indigenous rights at present (CMPI 1984). The bundle of rights and prerogatives of indigenous "nations" according to this document amounts to something similar to those held by states in the present world. The leadership of this organization worked closely with MISURASATA in international forums (UN Commission Against Discrimination), and advised Brooklyn Rivera during the period when he was engaged in discussions with the Nicaraguan government (Diskin *et al.* 1986:15-16.) In addition, MISURASATA has had the support of the Indian Law Resource Center, a Washington-based group that has served as a lobby for MISURASATA. The consistency and increasing sophistication of Indian demands and maneuvers in international forums as well as in direct negotiations now taking place are a reflection of these organizational links (Hale 1987b:111 and fn 26).

The ideological statements made by the Indian leadership in international settings have their counterpart in expressions at the community level and in daily life. People in villages have experienced a militarization of their lives, especially during the period 1981-85. At the present, there is still a military presence in some coastal communities although people have much more freedom of movement and rarely experience the effects of combat. The complaints one now hears are often phrased in terms of an idyllic past where no one interfered with the people. By focusing on the bothersome presence of the state, the notion is propagated that in the recent past, total freedom reigned[8] (cf. Hale 1987b:113-15).

The system of ethnic stratification and the prevalence of wage labor (Hale 1987a), so widespread that it was known by all coastal people, becomes translated into a nostalgia for the company commissary and the North American goods available to those few whose salaries permitted them to buy there. During the Somoza period the ethnic stratification changed, firmly implanting the Mestizos as the dominant group and relegating Miskitus and other Indians to the bottom with no possibilities for social mobility. The nostalgia for things from the United States shows a distinction in the public mind between the *Somocista* state and the North American transnational presence (Hale 1987a:47-9). Ethnic and class stratification are important factors in shaping ethnic identity. Further, they appear to be in direct competition with the more immediate conjunctural events concerning the coast. The approach I favor in this paper is to credit both kinds of factors with influence in changing the expression of ethnic identity.

In addition to these socio-economic elements (i.e. occupational and class stratification, and racial distinctions among Indians, Mestizos, and Creoles), is the recent painful refugee experience. The twenty thousand or so Miskitus who went to Honduras from late 1981, were defined by international law and international agencies as victims of conflict. Those who lived in camps operated by the UNHCR had complaints not unlike those who were relocated inside Nicaragua. That is, they were unhappy with the housing, complained about food shortages, and were distressed about the lack of arable land. Of course, some Miskitu who fled quickly became part of a fighting force that returned to Nicaragua and engaged in combat. The refugee experience thrust many Miskitus into a highly politicized environment. Miskitus at all levels reflected upon and discussed issues of international law, human rights, and the military situation. Refugees in Honduras communicated with their home communities through a variety of means and were aware of changes in the situation in Nicaragua. Some of the earlier refugee arrivals, who were settled in situations that afforded possibilities for cultivation, seemed to be preparing for permanent residence. But the majority hoped for a change that would permit them to return home.

At first, every battle or military engagement with the Sandinista army reinforced the view that the Sandinistas were in the wrong. For example, in May 1985, when the government announced that relocated people were free to return home, there was much complaining about the slow pace and the low level of support offered for the move. When the bridge at Sisin was destroyed, hindering the movement of people to their river communities, it was widely blamed on the Sandinistas although the bridge was in insurgent hands as the result of an agreement entered into by the government and the Indian combatants (Hale 1987a: fn. 37). Earlier, in May 1985, shortly after an agreement was signed between the government and an important insurgent, Eduardo Pantin, he died under mysterious circumstances. Many Miskitus seemed to believe it was an example of Sandinista duplicity. This view was also promulgated by the foreign supporters of the Indian military groups, such as the Indian Law Resource Center. However, by early 1986, when a massive flight to Honduras from some Río Coco villages took place, the interpretation of this event seemed to change. Although the usual groups that lobbied for the Indian fighters stressed that the villages on the Río Coco where the refugees came from were attacked by the Sandinista army, events suggested that it was the Indian fighters who manipulated villagers to produce a stampede of refugees precisely at a time when the fighting was diminishing due to a series of negotiated truces with local commanders. Foreign observers on the Honduran side noted the staged quality of this "exodus" (*Americas Watch* 1986:1-2). Most important, the new refugees began to ask for repatriation almost as soon as they arrived in Honduras. A wave of repatriation began at that time that has grown larger until the present moment. Now, with cooperation from the Honduran and Nicaraguan governments, and with supervision by the UNHCR, the camps in Honduras are fast emptying and the military opposition to the government has greatly declined.[9] The autonomy statute is a well-planned effort to respond to and reduce the tensions between Indians and government in Nicaragua. It too will be one element in defining ethnicity for the Miskitu population. It guarantees cultural freedoms (such as official status for the Miskitu language and freedom of relgion), land tenure, and the use of community funds derived from natural resource use. It openly recognizes that Nicaragua is a multi-cultural society whose constituent cultural and ethnic elements must receive certain protections above those prerogatives enjoyed through citizenship (Gurdian 1987). Through the autonomy law and the mechanisms it creates, the Miskitu people may come to see themselves simultaneously as members of an indigenous group and a national society, as well as participants in a class system.

Indian relations with the government have been largely in Miskitu hands. Although Rivera, the principal negotiator, has spoken about the Sumu and the Rama, his preference for a name for an autonomous Atlantic Coast is *Yapti Tasba* (Mother Land) a Miskitu phrase.

Sumu. The prominence of the Miskitus and their assumption of the leadership of all the indigenous groups of the Atlantic Coast, is the most important contemporary element in the shaping of Sumu identity. Historically, the Sumu population was transformed into a small enclave dominated by the Miskitus. At present, all Sumus speak Miskitu, although many still speak Sumu too, and most Sumus adhere to the Moravian religion. In a sad and curious manner, the violence and upheaval of the past years have helped the Sumu be perceived as distinct from the Miskitu. SUKAWALA has been revived and through projects supported by CIDCA (Centro de Investigación y Documentación de la Costa Atlántica), research has been conducted on Sumu language and culture. MISURASATA and other Indian organizations also speak on behalf of the Sumu and as a result there is wider knowledge of the multi-cultural nature of the coast.

Those Sumu refugees in Honduras tend to live together and have organized to repatriate to their villages in Nicaragua. The major Sumu military leader has suffered a reduction of influence with the deescalation of combat, and especially with the withdrawal of United States military support in Honduras.

Events since 1981 have destroyed Sumu isolation and permitted a greater public voice. Much will depend on how the Sumu participate in the opportunities that lie ahead. For example, in the regional assemblies provided for in the autonomy law, Sumu representatives have an opportunity to affect economic and political events within their region. With their rights guaranteed through the autonomy law in cultural, resource, and land tenure matters, the Sumu, long the silent partners of coastal Indians, may strengthen their position within the Atlantic Coast and undoubtedly alter their own sense of identity.

Rama. The Rama are a very small population, estimated in 1981 to number about 600 persons (Hale and Gordon 1987:8-11), of whom only about two dozen still speak Rama. It is their size that makes their future as a distinct people problematic. While always mentioned, both by the Indian organizations as well as the Sandinistas, the realities of Rama identity are poorly understood. Efforts are afoot to revive the Rama language and to introduce it in a bilingual, bicultural, educational context especially through the work of Colette Craig, a linguist at the University of Oregon. But the results are impossible to predict at this moment. All the Rama people are located in the southern part of the coast, so their cultural setting will be dominated by Creoles and Mestizos, rather than Miskitus. Their future will tell us a good deal about very small linguistic groups and the dynamics of the survival of cultures.

Creole. The Creole population, concentrated in the city of Bluefields, shares many cultural characteristics with other Caribbean Afro-American groups, but within Nicaraguan and coastal society, it has achieved a distinct identity (Gordon 1987:140-44). In part because of this identity (i.e. Creoles maintained ties of affinity with Great Britain, the United States and Jamaica), in part because the Sandinista revolution succeeded without substantial Creole input, the revolution was not received with the enthusiasm it met in the Pacific part of the country. Creole-Mestizo relations were perceived by Creoles to define themselves as the dominant group. Therefore, Creoles were not too willing to accept the Mestizo Sandinistas as the hegemonic force. Further, survey data show that Creoles attributed racist attitudes to the Sandinistas in the early years of the revolution (Gordon 1987:164, appendix 5:1, question 7).

The Creole population conceptualized its discontent with the Sandinista revolution in economic terms. That is, it pointed to the absence of foreign (mostly North American) companies and the goods they were associated with. Many people I spoke to in Bluefields expressed their complaints through a list of previously obtainable items such as yellow cheese, evaporated milk, and corn flakes. Gordon's analysis points out the indivisibility of the economic aspect from the general ethnic identity of the Creole population. That is, the Creole sense of elite status on the Coast is defined by access to certain types of employment as well as a certain pattern of consumerism, both of which underwent changes as a result of the revolution (Gordon 1987:157-8).

Looking toward the future, the Creole community is faced with the need to adapt to radically different circumstances in which their ethnic identity will undergo changes. Many young Creoles have left, using the network of ties that has always dispersed this community (careers as merchant seamen, the existence of relatives in the United States). This adaptation, focusing on maintaining a certain level of economic standards, will lead to a dispersion and probably a loss of ethnic identity. In the United States, these Creoles will be another Caribbean English-speaking group. That is what Ray Hooker, one of the most prominent Creole leaders, means when he says that Creole ethnicity is in jeopardy (personal conversation and various speeches delivered by Mr. Hooker).

If, on the other hand, the Creole community emphasizes the tendency to participate in the ongoing evolution of coastal society, through membership in the autonomy commission as well as through the elected regional assembly, Creole ethnicity will undergo another kind of change. Possibly, under this scenario, Creole ethnic identity will be sharpened in a clearer multi-ethnic environment. If, in the short run, Creoles can defer their desires for pre-revolutionary pattern of consumption, Creole identity may be strengthened through the cultural aspects of the autonomy law and the obvious acceptance of Creole culture throughout Nicaragua.

In the medium term, however, concrete results of coastal autonomy must be visible. These include greater participation in national agencies and ministries, and increased access, already contemplated by the autonomy law, with trading partners in the Caribbean. Since 1985, the government has become keenly aware of the significance of the Creoles and policy has favored these steps. Once again, it will be the next five or ten years that will decide not only the ethnic identity of this community, but its continued existence.

Garífuna. The other Afro-Caribbean population is the Garífuna or Black Carib. This group began as a fusion of African slaves and Carib Indians on the island of Saint Vincent in the Lesser Antilles. They were deported from St. Vincent in 1797 after their defeat by the British in the Carib War (Gonzalez 1988). The Garífuna arrived in Nicaragua through a labor migration during the late nineteenth century (Hale and Gordon 1987:21-4). Known as Caribs in Nicaragua, they seem now to be assimilating culturally to the Creole ethnicity, although even today they are distinguished by various cultural practices, and a certain community "tone" characterized by warm hospitality. The Nicaraguan Garífuna communities (all in the Pearl Lagoon area) no longer speak Garífuna.

It appears that the Sandinista revolution offered an opportunity to the Garífuna to define themselves apart from the Creoles. While little is known about Garífuna attitudes toward Creoles and Mestizos, all observers agree that, unlike the Creoles, the Garífuna did not view themselves as a privileged population. Unlike the Creole, they are a rural population, engaged in subsistence activities. Therefore, they experienced no reduction of status with the revolution. Perhaps they saw it as an opportunity to more openly identify with Garífuna culture and gain public acceptance of this identity. In recent years, they have made contact with Honduran Garífunas, who have come to perform dances and other cultural events. There is considerable interest in formalizing these ties to recover their language as well as other cultural aspects.

One significant characteristic the Garífuna share with the Rama is their relatively small size. The estimated 1,500 Garífuna (Hale and Gordon 1987:23) are scattered through several communities. Once again, through the autonomy law, they will have rights to bilingual, bicultural education, although this will not be easy to arrange and it will not be so much bilingual education as instruction in the Garífuna language if the community maintains its interest. Their own interest in becoming more Garífuna would seem to be the determining factor in the development of their ethnic identity.

Mestizos. Precisely because Mestizos are not normally thought of as an ethnic group, their status on the Atlantic Coast is a fascinating phenomenon. Although the demography contradicts this, Coastal-Sandinista tensions were pictured in ethnic terms with the Atlantic Coast considered Indian country. Yet, Mestizos, largely migrants to the Coast during the past thirty-five years, represent the largest coastal population, accounting for about 65% of all costeños, or about 180,000 people (Hale and Gordon 1987:25). Because of the size of this group and, most importantly, because the entire debate concerning the Atlantic Coast has become *ethnicized,* the ethnic nature of this population must be analyzed along with the other groups discussed above. This must be done even though the Mestizo coastal population has been rather silent during this whole period of conflict. Although somewhat beyond the scope of this paper, a consideration of the Mestizo community within the context of the Atlantic Coast, forces a discussion of the relative significance of the notions of ethnicity and class. The intensity of ethnic-based conflict and the nature of specifically ethnic demands made upon the government in the early 1980s (cf. Vilas 1987, Hale 1987a) required the government to respond to a global situation that was not covered by usual class analysis nor was it resolvable in the ethnic terms proposed by the disputants.

On the one hand, a description of the coastal population as an exploited class missed the point of the complaints voiced by MISURASATA. On the other, the ethnic framework imposed by MISURASATA led to a demand for land that implied that only Miskitus, or at least Indians, populated the Atlantic Coast (Vilas 1987:82). The MISURASATA argument that three-quarters of the surface area of the Atlantic Coast belonged to the indigenous "nations" meant that the relative weight of each ethnic group demand (Miskitu, Sumu, Rama, Creole, Garífuna) would have to be decided by MISURASATA if its point of view won the day.

Even if MISURASATA did not prevail (as it did not) the problem of responding to historic injustices remained. The solution that has emerged is the autonomy law. Under its provisions, the weight given to ethnic demands, i.e. those claims concerning land ownership by ethnic groups (as opposed to communities), with its implication of dispossessing non-group members from the land, can be put into effect through the exercise of a democratic political process by means of the regional assemblies created by the law. In like fashion, pressure and interest groups can be formed according to group interests, not necessarily ethnic in nature.

The existence of this law affords the Mestizo population two choices. Individual Mestizos can, through political debate and electoral contention, engage in alliances across ethnic lines to achieve class-based goals. Or, the Mestizo community can begin a process of ethnic identification, elaborate its content in a particular costeño fashion (something like the emergence of Creole ethnicity) and use its majority to pursue projects in the assembly. Remembering that one overarching identity is that of Costeño, especially in opposition to that of "Español" (as Pacific Nicaraguans are called) may lead one to predict that coalitions of different sorts will be created to defend interests at different levels. In short, the presence of a deliberative instrument, such as the assembly, may generate a system where public affairs may be conducted with regard to ethnic, class-based, and regional interests. That would be a significant accomplishment.

Conclusion

The outcome of this state-ethnic dialogue may depend on the array of power seen in the allies of the negotiating parties. The Atlantic Coast notion of autonomy owes much to the opposition of the U.S. to the Sandinista government. Although its sponsorship of Indian causes seems to this writer quite cynical (Diskin 1987), (witness U.S. treatment of its own Indians), its military threat to Nicaragua meant that the Nicaraguan government had to try to negotiate so that the Atlantic Coast not explode into another war front. The U.S. threat may have accelerated the learning process whereby the Sandinistas have come to understand what a multi-ethnic society is and to create a legislative package that reflects it.

While it is impossible to predict what the resultant impact will be on ethnic identity, the elements that will shape it are all in place. With the imminent implementation of the autonomy law, i.e. the structuring of elections for regional assemblies, and the political campaign for assembly positions, the stage seems set for some groups to emphasize their ethnic particularity. In so doing, they will be defining themselves, perhaps altering their own self-conception. The autonomy statute, cease-fire, repatriation of refugees, and now the existence of a unified Central American solution (the Arias plan), each provide significant contextual factors to aid this process. The result of such a process could be a blend of cultural uniqueness and participation in a multi-cultural nation-state. That would be an interesting model to contemplate for the rest of Latin America.

Finally, whatever the consequences for ethnic identity, these eight years of conflict have established Indians and ethnic groups as active participants in their own analyses. If the essence of ethnicity is its tactical importance within a context of conflict, the peoples of the Atlantic Coast have learned this lesson well. In the future, their own account of themselves will be an increasingly significant factor, one that will stimulate corresponding changes in anthropological practice.

NOTES

1. This paper is not a definitional exercise. Here "ethnicity" or "ethnic identity" is taken to mean the answer one gets when asking a member of a group to define the group. Unstated, but crucial for this work, is the fact that the context all these groups are presently in, is one of conflict or tension with the state. That tension provides the motivation for the constant definition of group identity. Many other aspects of this phenomenon are left out here. For a recent treatment of this subject see De Vos and Romanucci-Ross 1982.

2. Advocacy groups include those composed of indigenous people such as the Shuar Federation of Ecuador and MISURASATA of Nicaragua as well as organizations of non-indigenous people such as IWGIA and Cultural Survival. While relations are occasionally strained because of this indigenous-non-indigenous distinction, in general there is a productive collaboration between the two kinds.

3. For a good account of the founding moment and subsequent early functioning of MISURASATA, cf. Jenkins Molieri 1986 (pp. 197-212). His account is rich in detail with names of many participants and is an explicitly Sandinista point of view.

4. Cf. Dunbar Ortiz 1984a, especially parts I, II, pp.27-123.

5. The period of the forced removals has the been the subject of charges and countercharges concerning the real intentions of the Sandinistas and the Indian military organization. The government accused MISURASATA of planning, together with United States military and intelligence support a "Red Christmas" attack on the Río Coco in December 1981. MISURASATA charged that the removals were part of a Sandinista plan conceived long before the military situation intensified. For two accounts of the human rights implications cf. Americas Watch 1984, 1985 and the OAS, Inter-American Commission on Human Rights, 1984.

6. Brooklyn Rivera left Nicaragua for Honduras in 1981 but he quickly left there too because of disagreements with Fagoth. Rivera told me that Fagoth had hired people to kill him and therefore he had to flee to Costa Rica.

7. See Helms 1971 for the most complete Miskitu ethnography; also Nietschmann 1979.

8. In 1985, in conversation with Miskitus who were to return to Asang on the Río Coco, I was told that the community was so well-knit that there was no need for money. One person told me that the cacao grown there was simply distributed to any and all neighbors who wanted it. Such statements, while indicating generosity between neighbors, were in opposition to the description

by Helms (1971) of the same community, where she stressed the role of the economic intermediary and the cash significance of cacao.

9. Brooklyn Rivera returned to Nicaragua in January 1988 and held a successful first round of negotiations with the government. Presumably, the negotiations between Rivera and the government will include a definitive cease-fire as well as some alterations in the newly ratified autonomy law.

3

SYMBOLIC IMPERATIVES FOR A DEMOCRATIC PEACE IN GUATEMALA[1]

Alexander Moore

On December 8, 1985, Marco Vinicio Cerezo Arevalo, a Christian Democrat, won a run-off election to become the first civilian president of Guatemala since Julio Cesar Mendez Montenegro in the last years of the 1960s. Like Mendez, Cerezo has faced tremendous problems. Keeping the peace in the wake of protracted social conflict and a new habit of civil violence is one of them. Identification of mechanisms of reconciliation and forgiveness, of ritual redress, and of rededication of erstwhile adversaries to new common goals are useful anthropological perspectives to bring to Guatemala's effort to reconstruct civilian rule and reconstitute democracy. Indeed, I shall argue that peace-making is the essence of the task of establishing a viable, long-term democracy.

The return of constitutional democracy to Guatemala in 1985 represented the victory of one of several political ideologies, yet its ascendancy is by no means assured. Left and right ideologies still compete for Guatemalan allegiances. The two previous chiefs of state were military dictators who mobilized the state in a war against leftist "subversion." What amounted to an open civil war raged from 1979 to early 1984. Leftist guerrilla groups espoused a Latin Americanized Leninist ideology. Their violent opponents on the right, including "death squads" and such terrorist groups as the Secret Anticommunist Army and the *Mano Blanca*, may be suspected of holding fascist views.

A clearly enunciated rightist ideology -- corporatism -- was only proposed in the last days of the rule of the military chief-of-state, Efrain Rios Montt (1982-83). This singular ruler, in concert with his son's father-in-law, a protestant pastor, set forth what he called an "equicratic" solution. The rhetoric was corporatist. Equicratism would do away with cross-cutting mechanisms of political interest aggregation, that is, political parties; elections would be held only for local offices; special, co-opted "vertical" bodies, that is, syndicates and guilds, would be licensed. These bodies would be represented on the Council of State, a consultative body Rios Montt had already formed.[2] Rios Montt was overthrown and replaced by another military caudillo who, nevertheless, prepared the way for the historic democratic elections of 1985.

Of course, critics may fairly argue that the practice of democracy in Guatemala has been historically more a formality than a reality. Since 1872, Guatemala's many successive constitutions have all prescribed the division of powers, citizen guarantees, and elections. Yet, these forms have been consistently abused by leader after leader, most recently in the electoral frauds that reportedly accompanied the elections of 1974, 1978, and 1982.[3] This paper will explore the possibilities for on-going civil peace in a country that has long been rent by conflict spawned by both class and ethnic differences, and in which the various interest groups are only now beginning to succumb to a sense of national, in addition to ethnic, identity. Civil peace does not mean a life free from conflict. The latter is natural to human social life and its absence can only indicate repression, or a moment of frenzied commonality, *communitas*, in some -- usually revolutionary -- liminal period during a collective rite of passage or transition to a new way of life.

Refereed conflict, however, is the essence of democracy. Conclaves, parleys, councils, and parliaments all exist to deliberate issues, referee opponents, and make informed decisions on matters of public import. Parliamentary procedures, as they are practiced in the West, are a way to deflect conflict from the battlefield into a legislative arena (Moore 1984:30). Civil peace can only be secured by the channeling of conflict, and by the guarantees of personal rights and dignities to all citizens within a constitutional settlement.

That principle -- that peace means refereed conflict -- is far from being achieved in Guatemala. Cerezo took office only after the conclusion of an extensive and bloody civil war. He had to deal with the remnants of that conflict and with the ongoing expressions of a lingering habit of violence. "Death as a way of life" (a phrase used by June Nash (1967) to describe a highland Maya community in Chiapas) has, unfortunately, become the Guatemalan way. In order to avoid the terror, large numbers of innocent persons, as well as others who had actively opposed the oppressive military regimes, fled the country -- many merely crossing into Mexico or Belize, but others going on to the United States. Most of these were members of the various Amerindian groups who inhabited the highlands, continued to speak their native tongues, retained many of their ancestral values and behavior patterns, and were seen by many non-Indian Guatemalans as a hindrance to the developmental process, while at the same time they were viewed as an indispensable captive cheap labor source by the landed gentry. In order to eke out a minimal standard of living, many Indians migrated each year to the south coast to harvest crops such as coffee, cotton and cardamom.

Thus, in the absence of a democratic settlement, a *de facto* peace is, as it was in Franco's Spain, the "peace of a game preserve." That is, after civil conflict, exhaustion and a wary cease fire prevail. An authoritarian settlement, whether of the left or the right, preserves the peace. But erstwhile opponents, many of them in exile or in detention centers, are by no means reconciled to that state of affairs. Such a settlement exists as much by coercion as by consent.

Long-term peace, then, requires a constructive political process, in which conflicts are freely expressed and openly resolved by non-violent means. The problem is twofold: reconciliation -- and forgiveness -- on the one hand;

openness in political debate and decision-making on the other. Such a reconciled and open society is neither immobilized nor rancorous, nor does it cling to privileges, hatreds, and institutional blockages.

Conflict Theory: Social Drama and Ritual Redress

Social anthropology has its own phase model of competitive conflict processes -- Victor Turner's social drama (1957), since refined by Marc Swartz and Arthur Tuden (Swartz *et al.* 1966). In this phase model "ritual redress" may come into play at two points in the unfolding of conflict -- midway to prevent escalation into violence; or after violence to provide for reconciliation of erstwhile opponents. Let me set forth these phases. First is the *mobilization* of political capital, in which one leader builds up resources and allies in preparation for a move against the opponent. Moves are often kept secret. Next comes the *showdown* in which one party precipitates a crisis in which opposing resources are thrown into relief. The two contenders then face each other in *crisis*. Violence or a full scale *fight* may occur in the crisis. Or there may appear *countervailing tendencies*, such as the mediation of third parties, and the "deployment of redressive mechanisms." The end of the game is "the restoration of the *peace*" (Moore 1984:30).

Social Dramas in Guatemalan History

Since achieving its independence from Spain in 1821, Guatemala has played out many social dramas, including the revolution (and Reform) of 1872, the social revolution of 1945, and the anticommunist "liberation" of 1954. Each of these conflicts has concluded with the victors calling for symbolic consensus to their right to victory. Thus, Guatemalan definitions of political legitimacy have changed. All such definitions have some basis in nationalism. In addition, there have been continuing appeals to revolution, and to the charismatic right of several historical presidential figures to rule by force of personality.

In colonial and neo-colonial times the state's legitimacy was based on the claims of Church and Crown (later Nation) to divine sanction. Implicit in the claims was the right of conquest inherent in the actions of a manly and -- originally -- Christian conqueror. This right of conquest was first that of the Spanish conquistadors, but it was also that of Rafael Carrera, the conservative peasant *caudillo* -- war-leader, strong-man -- who led guerrillas to a reactionary victory against elite creole liberal reformers in the 1840s.[4] Several other caudillos and would-be caudillos have claimed this personal right of conquest, the most recent being Castillo Armas, after his "liberation" of the country from the liberal reformist (some said communist) Arbenz in 1954.

In 1872 another revolutionary caudillo, Justo Rufino Barrios, claimed legitimacy both from personal revolutionary charisma, and from transcendent values that were explicitly anti-clerical. His Utopian appeal was to nationalism, progress, free markets, and the goal of developing a free-thinking, anti-clerical electorate/citizenry ideally schooled in the national language and symbols.[5]

Since then, long-term historical processes of political development in Guatemala have been consistent. The secular state has expanded slowly, developing ministries, bureaus, and agencies in predictable areas. Within each generation the state interacts more directly and more frequently with its citizens. Historically it did this first through the imposition of land titles and land registries as part of the Reform of the 1870s. Every plot of land and every citizen-owner were registered. A variety of fees, taxes, and conscriptions then followed. Each citizen tax-payer and voter was issued a national identity card. The state also took over schooling, which had been run -- where it existed -- by the church on a voluntary basis.[6] Then, with the 1945 revolution came the meaningful extension of the franchise to the entire population, and the beginnings of incorporation of the peasant masses into the political process through elections. Officially, then, since 1872 the Guatemalan state has been a constitutional democracy: liberal, democratic, secular and often anti-clerical.

The actors in these political dramas have been first and foremost a nationalist elite, crystallized productively around the heroic figure of Justo Rufino Barrios and his revolution of 1872. Barrios started to rationalize and develop the organs of government, yet today the only one of these to be thoroughly rationalized is the military. It developed slowly over three generations, not emerging as a fully professional force until the late 1950s. The military establishment considers itself the peculiar heir of Barrios, his revolution, and of the subsequent 1945 revolution. More than the civil service, the military officer corps embodies the nationalist elite.

The secular-progressive, anti-clerical, reformist state started by Barrios was also intimately related to the landed aristocracy, whose interests the state furthered in developing coffee as an export crop. The 19th century land and labor reforms swept away feudal restrictions on Indian land and labor. Indian "idle" land reserves were opened for sale, often forced, to outsiders. Indians were drafted into cheap labor gangs on new estates. By these measures many men of low to middling origin, associated with government, were able to found fortunes in landed estates in the late 19th century. Since the time of the Spanish conquest, government service has been one avenue to wealth and eventually, after at least a generation, admission to the ranks of the prestigious aristocracy.

The landed elite tend to live in Guatemala City. They own large estates, called *fincas*, which they manage by visits of greater or lesser frequency and duration. These were historically cattle haciendas, inefficient and vast; then coffee plantations, smaller and more efficient; and, since 1954, semi-mechanized cotton plantations, often on land leased from cattle estates, and run with seasonal labor migrating from densely populated peasant villages.

Thus, the primary elites of Guatemala consist of a landed aristocracy and an associated group of newly rich bidding for upper class status. On the next rung are the military officers; and lastly come their fellow nationalists, the civil servants and associated professionals: architects, lawyers, engineers, physicians, agronomists, schoolteachers, and others. These latter form an amorphous "intelligentsia," to borrow an apt term from eastern Europe. Since 1945, non-elite political contenders have also included urban labor and the peasant masses, variously organized in competing leftist groups, often led by intellectuals.

In recent conflicts in Guatemala certain crises stand out. First, the revolution of 1944-45 and the peaceful election of Arevalo, the intellectual, stand as mythic events accepted as a charter for political action, more or less, by all current contenders (including the leftist guerrillas). Opponents are charged with betraying this revolution. Second, is the "liberation" or "counterrevolution" of 1954, the violent overthrow of the Arbenz regime by Castillo Armas, backed by the United States. That event saw the exile of much of the left, many of whom returned under General Ydigoras Fuentes, who succeeded Castillo after the latter was assassinated in 1957.

Actual leftist insurgency, however, dates not from 1954, its mythic justification, but from November 13, 1960, when a group of younger military officers led an abortive coup against Ydigoras. That coup petered out, and a remnant of the officers took up prolonged guerrilla insurgency. These rebels all perished in the 1960s,[7] but their heirs-in-arms, organized into four distinct guerrilla groups, reappeared in the 1970s. These second generation insurgents have learned from the failure of Regis Debray's revised Leninism. That is, they replaced Debray's doctrine of the isolated rural insurgent *foco* with the notion of prolonged struggle from a mass peasant base.

The first Guatemalan guerrillas, as I have said, were dissident military officers, who were soon joined by romantic student rebels. The second-generation core of Guatemalan guerrillas is almost certainly composed of university youths. These vary in social composition from downwardly mobile scions of aristocratic families, through the middle class, to -- probably the great majority -- *petit bourgeois* or lower middle class youths, whose parents are for the most part merchants, clerks, and petty officials with minimal education.

Finally, the peasantry, divided ethnically between Ladinos (Spanish-speaking Mestizos), predominantly in the dry and infertile eastern part of the country, and Mayan-speaking Indians, in the fertile western highlands, have been increasingly brought into the political arena since the electoral reforms of the 1945 revolution. Not until recently, however, was an attempt made by the guerrillas to enlist them in the armed struggle.

A key substantive and symbolic issue in Guatemalan politics is land reform. Barrios's 1872 reform launched the new coffee elite, many of European or U.S. origin. Arbenz' 1952 peasant-oriented reform is now interpreted "mythically" by opposing sides in Guatemala. The extreme right -- especially members of Castillo Armas' MLN (National Liberation Movement), -- view that reform's implementation by members of the PGT, (Guatemalan Communist Party) as proof of subversion intended to deliver the nation into the hands of the Comintern. The left, especially the PGT, and all the guerrilla groups, view the reform's cancellation under Castillo Armas as a betrayal of the 1945 revolution and a sellout to the United Fruit Company and its patron, the United States. Because of the symbolic weight placed on the issue, a rational land reform policy is extremely difficult to devise in Guatemala today. Cerezo's Christian Democratic platform espouses a "technocratic" land reform, which uses taxation of idle land rather than expropriation as its principal instrument. As a result, this policy is likely to have the effect of stripping the issue of its symbolism.

Second generation Guatemalan guerrillas, like social anthropologists, have their own phase theory for conflict. First is implantation of a solid base among the peasants, spread with armed propaganda. Second is generalized rural warfare from a social, political, and military base. Finally there is the establishment of liberated zones and frontal combat with government troops (expounded by George Black 1984:80).

What actually happened in Guatemala, however, was premature entry into the second phase of generalized war. In consequence the full weight of army counterinsurgency came down upon the countryside. This itself occurred in three phases: the efforts of the Lucas Garcia regime (1978-1982), the campaign by Rios Montt who ousted the former president in March, 1982; and the mop-up efforts under Mejia Victores (1983-1985) who ousted Rios Montt.

There can be no doubt that military violence -- sheer bloodletting, the killing of noncombatants, as well as state sponsored terrorism -- was disproportionate to the violence it was combating. Moreover, warfare against the guerrillas in the late 1970s coincided with an increase in labor discord, strikes, and their violent repression by Lucas Garcia. Atrocities and human rights abuses by the three regimes are well documented.[8] Each regime rejected the possibility of negotiating with the rebels, opting instead for a military solution.

By 1983 that option had apparently worked. Proof of its success was the ouster of Rios Montt. Like many a leader who owes much of his strength to the need to unite forces against an enemy, he found his support divided once the external threat seemed to be diminished. Moreover, Rios Montt's vision of a reformist, honest, and corporatist state with himself as its anointed guardian was too much for the old guard. They overthrew him.

In Guatemala rewriting the constitution is a ritual act undertaken to show that the previous regime was symbolically bankrupt and had profaned its own constitution, which therefore must be replaced. Thus, the Mejia Victores regime sought to consolidate its victory by convoking elections for a constituent assembly to rewrite the constitution. This is political ritual and drama. Guatemalan constitutions have been rewritten in 1944-45, 1954, 1965, and most recently in 1985. After 1945 each successive document has differed little from its predecessor. And in fact, the revolutionary 1945 charter differed little structurally from that of the 1870s.

Vinicio Cerezo took power as the first president to be elected under a new constitution, and as the first *civilian* president since 1970. In the first elections in recent memory not to be marred by widespread accusations of fraud, Cerezo emerged as a popular social democrat with a clear electoral majority. He started, symbolically, with a clean slate. Moreover, by endorsing the new constitution the military as an institution is once again repudiating the last two governments that operated under the previous constitution, those of Kjell Laugerud (1974-1978) and Lucas Garcia. Rios Montt's coup had repudiated these regimes on the grounds of fraudulence, corruption, and ineffectiveness in the war against guerrillas. In Cerezo's election the military's previous habit, started by Arana in 1974, of anointing the Minister of Defense as the president's chosen successor, has also been repudiated. It is important for the continued success of democracy that this habit not be resurrected.[9]

However, the last democratically elected civilian president, Mendez Montenegro (1966-1970), was unable to achieve peace or a widely supported program of social and economic development. Broadly speaking, his regime was immobilized. In spite of high rates of economic growth, an electorate weary of prolonged urban and rural civil war, returned war leader Carlos Arana Osorio to the presidency in 1970. Mendez Montenegro's regime, humane and progressive as it was, is not the model one would wish for Cerezo. Immobilism, the experience of Mendez Montenegro shows us, is not conducive to peace. True "social control" is a by-product of ongoing activity and group effort (Homans 1950:281-312). At present, the problems facing the civilian president, in essence, consist of focusing the nation on tasks of reconstruction and development whose direction must be guided by open debate, while at the same time providing for reconciliation of erstwhile opponents.

Local Immobilism Under Mendez Montenegro: 1968

My field work in Guatemala culminated during the presidency of Mendez Montenegro. Between 1960 and 1968, I engaged in four ethnographic field trips to a community pseudonymously called Atchalan. My "ethnographic present" there ended in 1968, save for occasional visits and a brief field trip to Guatemala in the summer of 1984. Local politics in Atchalan in 1968 were distinctly stalemated and immobilized. An uneasy settlement had come in the aftermath of traumatic and disillusioning violence, that of the so-called "liberation" of 1954. The violence of that episode is quite minor when compared to that of the late 1970s and early 1980s. In Atchalan, fortunately, no one lost a life in either upheaval.

In Atchalan reconciliation was effected after 1957 by a grudging political truce -- compartmentalization of political tasks, which was accompanied by a veritable explosion of traditional ritual (Moore 1966). With the wisdom of hindsight I now recognize that its amazing ritual explosion in the 1960s must have had to do with "ritual redress" to the recent political conflicts.

After another decade Atchalan's dominant symbolisms were to become less coherent, and to prove inadequate to the task of political integration and consensus. Yet they were splendid, baroque, florescent, expensive, and absorbing. By looking at them now we may at least raise the question, what symbolisms *are* adequate for a task of democratic reconciliation and dynamic nation-building? Ethnography can teach us some lessons.

Between 1945 and 1954 -- in the aftermath of the 1944 revolution -- Atchalan's politics had been quite dramatic; first with the rise of a charismatic agrarianist boss, Cesar Reyes, and his peasant following; second, with their success in effecting a land-reform that benefited the group's inner circle; and, third with their ouster in the local elections of 1953. This small, local political arena was then radically deflected from its dynamic course by the counterrevolution of 1954.

In the immediate wake of the 1954 counterrevolution, political activity virtually ceased in Atchalan. Cesar Reyes, an Indian, had been the head of the local chapter of the PRG (Partido Revolucionario Guatemalteco) and the *comite agrario* in 1954. He had presided over the local land reform, and with high placed followers was its principal beneficiary. Jailed for four months after Castillo Armas' "liberation" of 1954, he had been released after professing conversion to protestantism and securing the intervention of two young North American missionaries on his behalf. For the next few years Reyes put his considerable organizational skills at the service of the local protestant chapel. (This was not his first stint as a religious leader. In the 1940s he had been the steward of a traditional *cofradia* or saint's brotherhood.)

Under President General Ydigoras the political arena opened up again. Reyes returned to electoral politics in 1960 by placing a nephew at the head of his slate for town office. They won. Reyes' political clientele, however, was not primarily protestant; it was simply landless. With their support, Reyes held the electoral arena unchallenged for over a dozen years. He was in control of the town offices and a sizable corps of youth constables. Indeed, Atchalan elected Reyes to office as mayor by a landslide vote in 1966, in the same election that put Mendez Montenegro into the presidency. There is some irony in this, given Reyes's persecution under Castillo Armas.

Reyes was far less powerful than he seemed. Formal office does not necessarily disclose the full position of power holders. In fact, much of the locus of political activity had shifted in Atchalan from the *juzgado* (municipal courthouse) to the church, where the town's *principales* (Indian elders) presided over a resurgent fiesta system of *cargos* (ritual burdens conceived of as obligations incumbent upon all adult Indian men and their families.) The principales were in command of the secular committee that administered both the church building and the sacred town common. These woodlands had been expropriated by the agrarianists in 1952, turned into farm plots, then returned to the commune to be reforested after the "liberation" in 1957.

The principales next won a number of victories in the para-political arena of ritual competitions. Thus, they gained control of a newly important *hermandad*, or brotherhood, which sponsored popular and -- if left uncontrolled -- potentially personally profitable Holy Week celebrations. This the principales coopted into the cargo structure, staffing it and rotating the new "burden" every few years like any other.

The principales, ritual traditionalists, further coopted a group of newly orthodox Catholics, the Third Order of St. Francis, by inducing them to take on the cargo of San Francisco. This Order had originally been very much opposed to fiestas and to alcohol. After one attempt at sponsoring the fiesta without drink, they gave up. The next year, 1965, they celebrated it properly by allowing alcohol. This was an extraordinary victory on behalf of traditional ritual. Throughout highland Guatemala the newly orthodox Indian Catholics, or catechists, often form a faction violently at odds with the "traditionalists" and their cults of the saints.[10]

Finally, the principales even induced one faction of kinsmen among Reyes' agrarianists to sponsor a high ranking cargo. The principales were then in full control of the suddenly burgeoning ritual life of the local Indian community. They had brought potential dissidents -- the festive entrepreneurs and potential profiteers of Holy Week, newly orthodox Catholics, and agrarianists -- into the cargo system, which was exploding in new fiestas and more elaborate old ones. Ostensibly all were agreed on common symbols.

In turn, Reyes dedicated himself to material works, his equivalent to the spiritual works his aged rivals were elaborating. Reyes the protestant did not partake of those symbols. Land reform was forbidden. Locally, the principales were against it, not to mention the coffee planters. Engineering replaced reform as the primary area for secular political activity. New projects included a large modern schoolhouse on the plaza. Reyes then constructed a commodious market place for Indian women on the *Calle Real*. Since these women had been displaced from the plaza by the schoolhouse. Subsequent administrations, also controlled by Reyes, were to extend the potable water system and to cobble portions of the town's dirt streets. Not an impressive list, but it was *the* activity of local statecraft.

Today, the local immobilized settlement has continued immobile but has lost its coherence. Reyes eventually lost control of his agrarianist group, which fell into two kin-based factions after ousting him from leadership. Local politics has fractionated even further into a welter of parties, whose performance in office is as inconclusive as Reyes' was. Still, Atchalan has not been touched by the recent insurgency.

In the 1970s the principales, too, lost control of ritual life, which has fractionated into a welter of uncontrolled brotherhoods and their protestant counterparts, evangelical congregations, each under a local native pastor. That local explosion of traditional ritual was cathartic, no doubt. For twenty years it sopped up the tensions engendered by economic and demographic growth and by political transformations. But even then that ritual had lost its traditional coherence.[11]

The cargo system essentially was a set of alternating ritual obligations, meshed to rotate between civil and religious office as the Indian man cycled through the minimal obligations his community demanded. Politics was subsidiary to the ritual order, and ritual dramatized the political life as civil life subordinate to spiritual concerns. Even in their ephemeral ascendancy of 1968 the principales could dramatize no such thing. The most dramatic career, that of Reyes, had *used up* ritual office, and gone beyond it. He had found other sources for his charisma; although he had been a ritual leader in both the traditional Christo-pagan hierarchy and later in the Protestant one. In the political arena itself, the sense of drama, of contest, of performance, of meaningful alternative, was lost in local elections. Reyes had the field almost to himself and to his proteges.

Compartmentalization, stalemate, and an explosion of baroque quasi-Christian ritual is not a solution I would recommend for either local or national level politics in Guatemala in the 1980s.

Some Exemplary National Symbols and Their Rituals

If we consider North American history, the conclusion of the Civil War was a moment requiring redressive ritual action. On the Northern side, the cult of Lincoln, expressed in Memorial Day, was certainly an attempt to find common national symbols. As analyzed by Warner for Yankee City, Lincoln and Memorial Day served to unite social classes and ethnicities as well as to reconcile Northeast with South and West (Warner 1961).

No one has thus far attempted a similar analysis of Lincoln's value as a symbol of reconciliation for the South. Unfortunately, although Robert E. Lee did become the southern hero and a model of honor in defeat, the region did not really take to other reconciling symbols. Jim Crow and segregation was the consolation prize former confederate patriots exacted from defeat and reconstruction. What they could not win from the North, they took out on the black southerner. Displacement theory in psychology accounts for this behavior among the only segment of the English speaking world to be defeated and conquered since 1066. It also accounts for the enthusiastic jingoist response of the South to foreign wars since 1865 (as well as the enthusiastic North American Indian participation in those wars against a common enemy).

Still, the example of Memorial Day is instructive. It is celebrated in the cemetery and veterans' hall and honors the war dead, on both sides, and in effect, all dead. The dominant themes are those of human equality, social mobility, the frontier, and sacrifice. In the figure of Lincoln were reconciled the themes of the common man and the superior man, the ideals of the East in a man from the frontier were met, and the South imagined him as a man who would have forgiven them in defeat. All saw him as one sacrificed for unity. Says Warner:

> Lincoln, the superior man, above all men, yet equal to each, is a mystery beyond the logic of individual calculators. He belongs to the culture and to the social logic of the people for whom contradiction is unimportant and for whom the ultimate tests of truth are in the social structure in which, and for which, they live. Through the passing generations of our Christian culture the Man of the Prairies, formed in the mold of the God-man of Galilee and apotheosized into the man-god of the American people, each year less profane and more sacred, moves securely toward identification with deity and ultimate godhead. In him Americans realize themselves (Warner 1962:23).

Thanksgiving Day, with its family feasting, was adopted by the United States (i.e. the North) in 1863. Later, that *did* take hold in the South. Although ostensibly it is a feast of Pilgrims and North American identity, its adoption in 1863 at the peak of the Civil War, and its unquestioning heartfelt acceptance in the South today, indicate that it was perhaps unconsciously an instrument of national symbolic reconciliation and consensus. It was then, a redressive mechanism.

Turning to Mexico, there are a number of political rituals that re-enact nationalist myths and dramatize consensus. It is precisely because of the deeply rooted nature of such political rituals in Mexico, that the authoritarian regime of the PRI and its quasi-monarchical but rotational presidency are so widely regarded as legitimate. This legitimacy has allowed the regime to survive contemporary shocks that almost certainly no other Latin American regime could have withstood.

Take, for example, Mexican Independence Day, September 16. Victor Turner has an essay entitled "Hidalgo: History as Social Drama" (1974:98-165) in which he examines the power of the origin myth of the Mexican Independence. In Hidalgo Mexicans have a liminal figure, a creole priest who reverses the Spanish Conquest with a reconquest of Mexico by Indians and Mestizos, says Turner. I should add that he is also a sacrificial figure: Christ-like, he died that the nation might be reborn. In that, he resembles the apotheosized Lincoln.

Evon Z. Vogt and Suzanne Abel (1977) have analyzed Mexican Independence Day ritual: the *grito de Hidalgo*. On the eve of Independence Day the President, and every territorial executive -- of states and *municipios* -- give the ceremonial cry from the balcony of each one's particular "palace." The grito is putatively Hidalgo's call to arms after proclaiming Mexico's independence. It is repeated throughout Mexico at roughly the same time and unifies all Mexicans in symbolic space and time. Moreover, I might add, each Mexican official leader, by giving the grito, ceremonially takes on the role of Hidalgo by speaking his words. It is a drama in which the mythical Father-of-the-Country lives on in all national officiary who impersonate the apotheosized figure.

Vogt and Abel have also analyzed the revelation of the *tapado* or official candidate for the presidency in Mexico. *Tapadismo* ritual reveals the man who has been chosen, but theretofore hidden (tapado), as the next President. Thereby the institutional charisma of the office is transmitted to the candidate, who immediately thereafter must conduct a thorough presidential campaign in every state and many municipalities of Mexico, just as if the outcome of the election were in any doubt. The mystification surrounding the selection of the future president, say the authors, is in order to identify him with the personalism of the office and with "the continuity of Mexico's historical and mystical identity" (p.181).

Carlos Rangel has analyzed tapadismo more cogently. By naming one *any man (un hombre cualquiera)* to the presidency Mexicans are, almost in lottery fashion, bestowing the office of "Sun-President" upon the citizenry and, while preserving its power, answering the most critical problem in their history, presidential succession. Tapadismo thus dramatizes the battle cry of the 1910 Mexican revolution, *no sucesion*. Presidents may not succeed themselves. Each Mexican president is all powerful, for six years only (Rangel 1977:204-207).

Finally, Vogt and Abel have looked at the voting of Mayan Indians in national elections in Zinacantan, Mexico (1977:173-188). There, elections for the tapado and his full slate named by the PRI, the national political party, are conducted ritually. In Vogt and Abel's analysis, the Indians offer their votes to the PRI precisely as they make offerings to their deities in repayment for their agricultural well being. Thus do Indians participate on their own terms in the

Mexican political system, which is united in history-as-myth, symbols and ritual surrounding the events mentioned, and many others as well.

A Democratic Guatemala: Reconciliation and Group Tasks

Vinicio Cerezo strives to establish a program of economic development and social justice on the basis of recommendations made by a number of study groups within his party.[12] He has a notion of timing, of phased measures. The military must be brought to police itself, he assured me in an interview in August of 1984. Rather than expropriate large landowners, his program seeks to put high taxes on idle land, aiming thereby to induce landowners to either cultivate it or sell it. The state is the largest landowner, and recolonization projects in empty areas must also be a priority. Ideally Cerezo would establish a democratic Guatemala in which all political ideologies, from right to left, may be debated openly. To do so, he shall have to go step by step and gather support as he goes. For example, leftist groups must be induced to give úp arms and come back into the electoral arena. But they reasonably would not do so without the assurance of personal safety from right-wing attack.

Cerezo shall very much need common symbols in order to orchestrate the consensus he desires. Indeed, it is perhaps precisely because myths, symbols, and rituals that might mediate among erstwhile adversaries in Guatemala have not yet evolved that the republic is in such a sorry state today. What is needed are what Barbara Myerhoff calls *definitional ceremonies* (1978:185-186). These are the symbolic representations used to forge consensus precisely after moments of conflict. Definitional ceremonies are spontaneous and make use of some symbols already present in the culture and of others quite new and specific to the situation. Such ceremonies transcend ideology, in that they draw on the stuff of traditional culture. They mix the primordial with the modern and the ideological. Thereby they can be used to unite both right and left. Unfortunately, they are used all too often by demagogues to manipulate crowds. Dictators find them useful. It is no accident that the militant atheists of the socialist bloc preside over some of the most ritualized states in history.

Primordial symbols are those that are immediately recognized as signifying the identity of a people. They include nationalism, cults of charismatic leaders, cults of particular localities in local rites of intensification, that is, of seasonal rites, and deep seated themes of the culture at hand. Thus, each spring on Memorial Day the cult of Lincoln invokes the figure of an apotheosized charismatic leader, drawing on Christian themes of sacrifice, while at the same time venerating the locality -- Yankee City -- and the local dead.

To be made to stand before a court of justice is to be presented with the most powerful symbol of the constitutional state. Let us take up the problem of punishment of wrongdoing during the ongoing violence Guatemala has suffered. The courageous stand of Alfonsin in Argentina against the crimes of the "dirty war" perpetrated by the Argentine military indicates the nature of the problem. Yet Alfonsin confronted a military disgraced and divided by defeat in a foreign war, and Cerezo confronts one triumphant in a civil war.

The problem is also to induce the military and police as institutions, at least in some measure, to bring themselves to account. Alfonsin, for example, gave the Argentine military that option; only when military courts refused the task did he invoke a civil tribunal. The Guatemalan military and police force, in alliance with private groups, have engaged in state terrorism and in atrocities in combat. Individuals responsible must be brought to account. It is typical of Cerezo's belief in a measured, phased approach, that he moved first against the secret police, having a military detachment arrest all 500 of them.

The problem of retribution, of punishments and of reparations adjudicated through the judicial process, is beyond the scope of this paper. Suffice it to say that democracy in Guatemala can only succeed if accountability before the law is enforced. The problem is a delicate one: too extensive a campaign becomes, not a matter of law enforcement, but rather, a witch-hunt aimed at repressing and expelling whole sectors of the population -- a new civil war. That is not what I had in mind, but rather, exemplary punishment of key criminal elements. It is important, moreover, that neither side in the recent armed conflict be branded, in toto, as criminal. To do so would only fan the flames of hatred and help perpetrate local blood feuds.

Returning to the theme of primordial symbols, the figure of the president himself in any Latin country is endowed with tremendous official charisma. Cerezo, in great contrast to Mendez Montenegro, is personally charismatic as well, and was expected to exploit the office to great effect. A Latin president regularly makes tours, inaugurates projects, and visits local fiestas. It is reasonable for any president to seek to identify himself with popular heroes, especially when the heroes he chooses illuminate his program. Cerezo has told me that Romulo Betancourt of Venezuela -- who inaugurated the current epoch of democratic rule there -- is one of his personal heroes. He also greatly admires the civilian ex-president of Guatemala, Juan Jose Arevalo. Of all the Guatemalan presidents, Arevalo is the most apt to serve as culture hero and charter figure for the current administration. Heroes can be honored symbolically by a rich array of rituals at the disposal of a modern chief of state.

Guatemala has made precious little of its national storehouse of myth and symbols, including heroes. The *proceres*, forebears of Independence such as Galvez and Morazan were, after all, losers in the failure of Central American union. However, Galvez, the valiant liberal who struggled to reform Guatemala in the 1830s, could perhaps serve as a reconstructed, sacrificial hero. Rafael Carrera, the common man who became caudillo of Guatemala through guerrilla warfare, was officially branded a barbarian in the historiography of the liberals who overthrew the regime he established in 1871. In fact, however, Carrera was a champion of the peasantry. Still, it would be hard to raise a democratic cult to a personalistic and uneducated dictator, no matter how populist and tolerant of Indian culture is policies might have been.

Among Guatemalan cultural figures Miguel Angel Asturias, Nobel Prize winner for literature, also provides the stuff for a national culture hero. Certainly his novel *El Senor Presidente*, a surrealistic account of the Estrada Cabrera tyranny, is a powerful myth about the devil within. The novel is already required reading of all educated Guatemalans; its frequent performance as theatre could only be a positive addition to their political culture. (There is at least one dramatization, by playwright Hugo Carrillo.)

Political symbology needs not only heroes to emulate, but demons to exorcise. Demonology is at the heart of the symbolic task. What is needed is exorcism of the devils at home shared by all Guatemalans, not the whipping up of one segment of the population against another by identifying the other with foreign demons. The right in Guatemala decries "godless communists" with sectarian fervor. The left decries "the lackeys of U.S. imperialism." Guatemalans must identify and exorcise their own devils.

I suggest that the most appropriate figure is the tyrant Estrada Cabrera. The novel *El Senor Presidente* dramatizes abuses during his twenty-year tyranny that are chillingly familiar. By putting on this work as theatre, Guatemalans would be pointing to the devil within, and could scapegoat an historical figure, rather than contemporaries. Estrada Cabrera, surely one of the most monstrous figures in Latin American history, represents evils in the common culture that must be extirpated. The custom of dramatic performances on ritual days is deeply rooted; *El Senor Presidente* would be a timely nationalistic performance for the Day of the Dead.[13]

As for successful rituals for a Guatemalan democracy, we can be assured they shall appear or that democracy is doomed. I suggest they shall appear at both the community and national levels at two points -- at local *fiestas titulares* and at national secular holidays. The first has great local potency. In contrast, the national holidays have little symbolic weight in Guatemala, precisely because the Hidalgos, the Lincolns, are missing.[14] However, much shall depend on the dramaturgical sense of Cerezo himself. Presidents can call forth celebrations on almost any pretext in the modern world.[15]

Local fiestas already have large secular components. Although a democratic government in Guatemala may stress general Christian themes, unfortunately Christianity itself is now a source of conflict. Traditional Christo-pagans have been arrayed against catechists or newly orthodox Christians. In the summer of 1984 I verified that in some communities, at least, conflicts in the insurgency revolved around this prior source of tension. In addition, Evangelical Protestantism is on the move in Guatemala, and is gaining far more ground among the Indian peasants than I would ever have supposed during my field work in the 1960s. The use of feast days already identified with communities and regions is probably wise; but it would be unwise to celebrate these days as sectarian holidays.

There should be days set aside to commemorate the victims of the recent conflict. Certainly the 300 Christian Democrats (Cerezo's party) lost to the death squads should be honored. All victims might be honored on All Souls Day, the widely practiced Day of the Dead. Special foods are served on this day making it reminiscent of our Thanksgiving as a family feast, but one that honors the family dead. Among the Indians this extends to the more remote ancestors as well. The potential exists to convert this feast, with its truly primordial symbols and its tradition of dramatic performances into a unifying national feast honoring the *national* dead.

Thanksgiving in the United States is instructive here. It is a folk and family holiday that Lincoln made a national day only by dint of much agitation from the female editor of Godey's Ladies Book, a woman's magazine.[16] Of our national holidays it is the one which for individual citizens is the most primordial, the one Americans abroad strive to celebrate. Folk holidays such as these may arise spontaneously in Guatemala, and ought to be celebrated.

In sum, to be effective, democratic rituals shall have to tap deep themes in the culture of Guatemalans and combine them with ideological ones. The task demands intelligence and skill in conception, dramaturgy, and performance. Guatemalans are well inured, alas, to insincere and absurd manipulations of their national symbols. Estrada Cabrera's travesty of Guatemala City's fiesta titular in his "fiestas de Minerva" are a case in point. In these surreal celebrations the city pantomimed classical civilization at temples to Minerva on the day of the Virgin of the Assumption, saintly patroness of the city. Here, the day itself was rooted in popular culture, the symbols grafted onto it were absurd ideological evocations of anti-clerical liberalism.

In the end, of course, rituals cannot take the place of vigorous and creative statecraft. They can only aid and abet that statecraft. Instead of "bread and circuses" for the next government of Guatemala, then, I recommend "work and festivals." Such festivals must touch on common values, on respect for all Guatemalans, on dignity for all citizens, and should ideally commemorate all the fallen, including those who have "disappeared," the *desaparecidos* in the recent violence. That is a tough symbolic bill. Luck and imagination are required. Guatemalans never lacked for the latter. Let us heartily wish them luck.[17]

Appendix:

Some Notes on Symbols, Ritual, Democracy and Power

Rituals are a human universal and predate the appearance of organized religion. Rituals may be imbued with magical power, but their function -- to allay anxiety and prepare the individual and the group to act -- of itself gives the ritualist, the ritual leader and specialist, power over others. The origin of the state, cities, and civilization is in all cases linked with the rise to power of ritual specialists who controlled the calendar, planting and harvesting, with or without irrigation works, and the collective ceremonial life with its feasting and redistribution of wealth.

Democracy is by definition based on consent. However, the third world experience, in the wake of Ataturk in Turkey, is replete with attempts to coerce people into democray. "Guided democracies" tend to oscillate between periods of authoritaranism and perods of openness.

Power is never simply the control of external resources, of the environment in which one actor, finding himself confined by the material resources of another, is bound to obey the will of the first. This view of power is incomplete. Sophisticated political science realizes that consent plays a part in even the most coercive polities.

S. F. Bailey divides political systems into teams of followers around leaders. Each leader must, in an exchange model, pay off his followers. Followers, in turn, comprise both hysterical converts and true believers. The latter are fanatics who are willing to forego any material payoff, for the present at least, in the quest to fulfill a mission, the leader's program. Their rewards may be deferred, ultimately forever, to a utopian future, or they may be primarily symbolic.

This distinction between the fanatic and the mercenary fits with what we know about revitalization movements, nativistic cults, and prophetic processes in general. It is a distinction that can be applied to the partisans of reform as well as of revolution. Belief, mediated by symbols in ritual performance, is a strong part of garnering allegiance to any leadership.

NOTES

1. This paper is based on one read at the annual meeting of the American Anthropological Association, Washington, D.C., December 8, 1985, in a symposium entitled "Anthropological Perspective on Peace in Guatemala and Peru," Paul L. Doughty, organizer, sponsored by the I.U.A.E.S. Commission on Peace. A lengthier version was given at the invitation of Nancie Gonzalez and Edward Azar at the Center for International Development and Conflict Management at the University of Maryland in March, 1986. It formed part of a one-day seminar on the topic, "The Symbolic Contexts of War." This final paper is a product of our discussions there and includes revisions made to bring it more into line with the other contributions in this volume.

The paper draws on many conversations with Vikram Jayanti, and I thank him for patiently listening and responding. I am indebted to Richard N. Adams, Charlotte Arnauld, and James A. Morrissey for comments, in spite of friendly disagreements, and to Ian Gonzalez for comments and editorial criticism. Field work in Guatemala in July and August, 1984, was supported by a Haynes Foundation Grant for Faculty Research at the University of Southern California. Vinicio Cerezo kindly granted me a long interview then, in company with journalist Ambrose Evans-Pritchard. I thank them both.

2. Equicraticism constituted itself as a political party in the elections for a Constituent Assembly in 1984, and was roundly rejected by the voters. The state it conjures reflects the neo-corporatist state Torrijos established in Panama in the 1970s. See Moore 1984:40f.

3. These frauds represented the attempts of each incumbent to deliver the presidency to his own client, or appointed successor. Mexico has institutionalized such a succession through presidential patronage, but Guatemala has not, since it has a multi-party electoral system, and the appointment of the successor to the president within his own political party does not guarantee his succession, as it does in Mexico with its single party politics, dominated by the PRI.

4. Carrera is described vividly by explorer John L. Stephens, who as U.S. envoy to Central America in 1839-40, vainly sought a Central American government. He interviewed Carrera during the latter's successful campaign to

wrest Guatemala from a unified Central America (Stephens 1949 [1841]:195-198).

5. Barrios's revolution was typical of the liberal reforms throughout 19th century Latin America. For a survey and assessment of these reforms see Burns 1980.

6. My own study (1973) looks at schooling in the context of traditional ways of coming of age and getting through life in Guatemala. For an analysis of the extension and penetration of the nation-state into the countryside and the peasantry see pp.122- 124.

7. The rural insurgency of the 1960s was concentrated in the Ladino east of Guatemala, and in spite of widespread loss of life, attracted little international comment compared to the recent insurgency, which was concentrated in the western highlands among an Indian, rather than a Ladino peasantry. The guerrillas rejected an amnesty offer from Mendez Montenegro at the start of his administration; in consequence, he gave the army under Defense Minister Arana *carte blanche* to pursue the rebels. Rebel leaders at that time were former junior military officers who had lead an abortive coup in 1960. Perhaps as traitors to their corps they received greater hatred from their former colleagues than would others. Sectarians hate heretics much more than they hate non-believers.

8. See especially the Americas Watch reports (1983 and 1984) and those by Amnesty International (1981, 1982). Cultural Survival has published one account (Clay 1983), followed by a chilling eyewitness document of the massacre of an Indian village by government troops (Clay, ed. 1983). Denunciation and documentation combine in the published proceedings of the Permanent People's Tribunal in Madrid (Jonas *et al.*1984).

9. Caesar D. Sereseres calls this habit of the 1970s the *esquema politico*. This was a law and order authoritarian settlement; it wanted a democratic facade, but an orderly political succession without any "unpredictable and unmanageable processes" (1984:24- 28). Modeled quite consciously on the PRI's government of Mexico, it was unable to build a dominant political machine, coopt the popular classes or evolve popular ritual and symbology. The model of the PRI was articulated in the rhetoric of the PID, the party of these presidents, in its initial statement and program by Peralta Azurdia, military Chief-of-State from 1963 to 1966. The imitation turned out to be inept.

10. The catechists as I knew them and as they have been described by Ricardo Falla (1975, 1978) are a puritanical group of rationalizing entrepreneurs. Their conversion experience is often self-generated, in response to dreams that specifically call on them to reject alcohol, the authority of the elders, and the expense of the traditional fiestas. In Atchalan they are forming an endogamous group, just as Falla has described for Ilotenango. There they are also segregating themselves by hamlet, forming "confessional communities."

11. Moreover, the same explosion of baroque ritual came from the local Ladino elite of tradesmen, who were *not* under the control of the *principales*. They, each January, paraded themselves in a procession of trucks, the source of their wealth, in the "fiesta de la Virgen [de la Concepcion]."

12. Broadly speaking, Cerezo would agree with this assessment of some members of a study group on United States-Guatemalan relations:

Guatemalan political stability...will remain uncertain in the absence of:
(1) a fundamental redistribution of economic resources... (2) the unhindered formation of peasant and worker association to increase the political and market powers of the underprivileged; and (3) the establishment of a political system in which power alternates on the basis of a fair electoral process (Roett, ed., 1985:15).

What Cerezo would add to this is the observation that such measures cannot be made at once, and overnight.

13. Vinicio Cerezo already is using demonology in his rhetoric. The front page headline of the *Los Angeles Times* dated December 10, 1985, reads "'Guatemala Devil' Dead, President-Elect Pledges." The account tells that "the streets of the capital roared with bonfires and firecrackers for the 'Burning of the Devil,' a ritual to exorcise Satan from the path of the Virgin Mary...Cerezo spoke fervently:...'The devil in Guatemala is the past, the inflexible...the one who raises ghosts against freedom and democratic participation. Today we burn the devil, and tomorrow we inaugurate a new era in Guatemala."

14. Guatemala lamely celebrates a number of national holidays, the most important of which is the 15th of September, Independence Day. In my experience it also has celebrated the Revolution of 1871 and the 3rd of July, the day of Castillo Armas's "liberation." Both of these have been holidays marked by quite un-inspiring ceremony. The 15th of September is marked by boring parades of schoolchildren throughout the republic, and by military parades in the capital.

15. During the first ten years of Castro's revolution in Cuba, mass rallies, *manifestaciones*, were a source of popular support and a means of education. I believe a democrat can learn from them.

16. Anthropologist Ralph Linton, in company with his wife Adelin, wrote a little book about Thanksgiving, for a popular audience (1949). It stresses the tradition of harvest festivals in England, and narrates its proclamation as a national holiday by Lincoln 250 years after the mythic event, but misses its role as a symbol of reconciliation and unity.

17. This paper was written in optimism in 1985. By 1988 it seemed that Cerezo measured the success of his democracy against three goals only: Presiding over open and democratic elections for his successor, providing a climate of free political expression, and keeping the economy at least stable (Los Angeles Times, Feb. 19, 1988 p.1). These goals fall short of a lasting reconciliation, but they point in the right direction.

4

INTERNAL AND EXTERNAL IDENTITY AMONG KANJOBAL MAYAN REFUGEES IN FLORIDA[1]

Allan F. Burns

The uncertain chances for asylum of Guatemalan Mayan refugees joins the United States to neighboring countries such as Mexico, and Belize, as well as to Central America. Guatemalan Mayan refugees are a part of a striking sequence of involuntary migrations that has affected these countries in the past ten years. There are an estimated two million refugees from the conflicts of all of Central America (Manz 1988:7); close to a quarter of a million of these are from Guatemala. While the more visible confrontations in Nicaragua and El Salvador attract much more media attention, Guatemala remains a country that produces a major flow of refugees from Central America (Ferris 1987).

In contrast to other refugee cases in the world, refugees from Guatemala call into question traditional and legal ways of understanding forced migration. The United Nations definition limits "asylum" to the first country encountered. Refugees from Guatemala did not migrate *to* another country of "first asylum" so much as they fled *from* a country of devastating violence. Most Mayan refugees from the Guatemalan highlands first went "next door" to Mexico, where they were, nevertheless, subjected to the raids of Guatemalan government troops, who crossed the border into Chiapas for this purpose in the early 1980s. These raids showed that "first asylum" was not to be found in Mexico (Valencia 1984). Since asylum there had proved to be a cruel hoax, many sought real asylum by becoming undocumented aliens in the United States.

In the case under consideration here, entire hamlets and communities of a relatively small but ethnographically significant group of Guatemalan Maya known as the Kanjobal fled to refuge both in Mexico and the U.S. Beginning in late 1982, over a thousand of these Kanjobal Maya settled in the small unincorporated farming community of Indiantown, Florida. This small community, already host to other migrant populations, was chosen because work was available and legal services of asylum petition were provided for them.

For the Kanjobal, their identity has changed as they have sought refuge in this multi-ethnic town and is being tempered through interethnic communication and conflict within the community. In addition, their identity has evolved in the view of others in the community. Their early image, as presented in newspapers and local discussion, was one of sad and unusual victims of an undeclared war between leftist guerrillas and a military government in their homeland. There was sympathy for the great culture shock they encountered in the United States. Recently that image has shifted to one of the Kanjobal refugees as migrant workers with little to offer the community aside from their work. These changes in identity occurred in a context of shifting political structures both here and in Central America. In this paper, the areas of residence, work, leadership, religion, and communication are examined to illustrate how this identity has changed through the Kanjobal experience as unofficial refugees in the U.S.

Kanjobal Maya: Guatemalan Context

The Kanjobal Maya make up one of 24 distinct Mayan language and culture groups of Guatemala. Their homelands are in the Cuchumatan mountains of the northwestern highlands of Guatemala, close to the border between the Mexican state of Chiapas and the Guatemalan department of Huehuetenango.[2] They lived in what was already a region of refuge (Aguirre Beltran 1967) as a result of colonial and modern pressures on choice lands in the area. As Lovell (1985) pointed out in his history of the area, the Kanjobal were pushed higher and higher into altitudes where subsistence agriculture had to be supplemented with a pattern of migration to work on the coast.

The Kanjobal Maya lived in dispersed settlements surrounding the municipal center of San Miguel Acatan. Most hamlets contained one or two extended families of up to 20 people. Historically, the Kanjobal were quick to move to find seasonal work on the coastal cotton plantations or in coffee growing areas in order to survive as an agricultural community on some of the highest and least productive land in Guatemala. In San Miguel, shops, markets, and services were also part of the Kanjobal economy. Because land in the highlands was scarce and agriculture poor, the Kanjobal were very interested in innovative ways of improving their incomes. Interest in agricultural cooperatives, new crops, and education was high before extensive violence swept the area in the early 1980s.

The Kanjobal were caught in an area of considerable guerrilla activity during the 1980s. The Guerrilla Army of the Poor passed through the area in its retreat during the early years of the decade; on the way, they conscripted many young Kanjobal boys and men. Soon after, the Guatemalan army followed and continued to devastate the population. One fourteen year old refugee noted,

> They would come and they would ask 'where are the men or the boys, then they would take them. (What would they do to them?) They would take them or threaten them or kill them (Field notes, 4/22/85).

In the face of such conflict, many Kanjobal were sympathetic to the message of change that the guerrilla movement embodied. Government reprisals during the years 1980 through 1985 were vicious. As a result, Kanjobal people fled as families and as entire communities, migrating to places like Indiantown, Florida. In this expression of the "adventurous" spirit of their identity, one refugee described the Kanjobal as willing to leave their homes with little knowledge of Spanish, and no knowledge of English, for the United States.[3]

The Guatemalan government has changed dramatically in the past several years. Vinicio Cerezo was elected as a civilian president from the Christian Democratic party in 1985, which replaced the military leadership responsible for programs of village destruction. Because of this shift from a military to a civilian government, many people believed that the lives of Guatemalan refugees would henceforth be safe. However, returning refugees have not been able to resume their former lives. They have found their lands confiscated, extreme restrictions on personal freedoms, forced concentration of people in "model" villages, and much continuing resentment against them.

The Kanjobal Maya now find themselves in a situation with little chance of resolution. They are in exile, a group of people who have been forced into a diaspora to places far from their own lands. Those who chanced a return to Guatemala did not fare well. If not picked up by the military, they migrated to Guatemala City, where they live a miserable experience in the informal economic sector. More importantly, the Kanjobal are different from many of the refugees in that they have migrated in large family and community groups.

Children, Families, and Communities as Refugees

Boothby (1986) and others have pointed out that political violence in this part of the world involves children in much greater numbers than in other areas. Children are prominent among the combatants in the conflicts of Central America. Regular army and insurgency troops conscript children who are old enough to manage weapons (Ressler et al. 1988), and in some cases young children are sent to join movements such as the "contras" in Nicaragua so as to earn money for their poverty-stricken families. Children are also disportionately victims in much of the violence in the region, especially in Guatemala (Americas Watch 1984). Guatemalan army figures list some 400 villages that were destroyed in the early part of the decade (Boothby 1986:28). The reinforcement of ethnic identity in the United States for those who have fled Guatemala is an important issue in their survival. Guatemalan Mayan refugees need an identity apart from other undocumented aliens so that deportation can be forestalled when these refugees are brought before immigration officials. One issue relates to their right to speak their own language. As Kanjobal Mayan speakers, they must be provided with an interpreter during deportation hearings, for example. At a cultural level, identity of the Mayan refugees is important as a base for self-confidence and success when faced with the rigors of living in a radically different environment. Changes in Kanjobal identity occur in a context of shifting political structures both here and in Central America. Here the Kanjobal must adapt to the Immigration and Control Act of 1986, which has been subject to different interpretations since it was enacted. Political asylum, while popular among civil liberty lawyers at the local level, has not been a viable means of maintaining legal status in the U.S. The U.S. position toward

Guatemala is not clear, especially in an area like South Florida where the large politically conservative Hispanic population limits discussion of foreign policy among politicians.

Mayan People in Multiethnic Florida

The Kanjobal began arriving in Indiantown, Florida in late 1982, when a Mexican-American crew boss brought several refugees from Arizona to Florida. As with many refugees, the only jobs available to them were as migrant laborers. Soon, family members were contacted on the west coast of the U.S. and in Guatemala. Indiantown offered a "safe haven" from both the violence of Guatemala and the *anomie* of the large American cities of Los Angeles and Phoenix.

The immediate reason for leaving Guatemala for most of these refugees was fear of persecution. One refugee told me that he and his family left Guatemala when there was no place left to flee:

> We were living in that town when my *compadre* was killed. He and three others were killed one night. They shot him and left him on the street. We heard it. He was dying all night and his wife was crying. No one could go out and help him because they were sure they would be killed. His wife was crying all night. The next morning we went out and he was dead. A bullet came in here (points to his stomach), and came out here (points to his back); another one went in here (points to his head) and came out here (points to other side of head) and another one went in here (points to his forehead) and came out here (points to back of his head) -- *cruzado* (criss-crossed)!...Well, later we went back to our own town, the same thing happened there! We had to leave because there was no where else to go so we came here (field notes, 9/26/86).

There are many more refugees in the communities and camps in Mexico than in the U.S. Problems of Mayan refugees in Mexico are numerous, including raids by Guatemalan military units, lack of resources for growing crops, lack of resources for health assistance, and lack of economic opportunities. Manz (1988:1) notes that there are over 46,000 Guatemalan refugees in the official United Nation camps in Mexico. Another 134,000 are thought to be living outside of official camps in Mexico (Manz 1988:173).

On the one hand, this makes the small number of Kanjobal Mayan refugees in Indiantown seem less important than the numbers in the camps. But on the other hand, an understanding of the refugees in Indiantown portrays the effects of the strategy of refugee survival outside of camps: moving to communities where safe haven and work can be found away from the restrictions of camps. Figures for the number of Guatemalan refugees in the U.S. do not exist, although a sense of the possible number can be understood by noting the number of Guatemalans apprehended by immigration authorities. Between 1980 and 1985, this number was over 26,000 (Manz 1988:186). A conservative estimate of the total number of refugees based on this figure might be a third more, or close to 35,000. By far the largest number are found in the Los Angeles area, but small agricultural communities or neighborhoods like Indiantown, Florida are common refugee sites across the U.S.

Indiantown is a small community where face to face contact and a social service network that is effective in forestalling deportation make survival more feasible. Family connections and the vague hope of safe haven were important in people's decisions to come to Florida. One sixteen year old young man recalled his decision to come to Indiantown as follows:

> One morning I woke up and knew that I could not stay in Mexico by myself any longer. I knew there was a place in the United States called Indiantown, in a place called Florida, where an uncle and aunt of mine had gone when they escaped from Guatemala with their children. I did not know if they were still there, but since I could not go back to my home, I decided to go to Indiantown and try to find them (Ashabranner and Conklin 1986:41).

Once in Indiantown, Kanjobal Mayan refugees had to adapt to a multi-ethnic migrant community. In Guatemala distinctions between Kanjobal people and Jacaltec people were important in the department of Huehuetenango, as were distinctions between Mayan and non-Mayan people or Ladinos (Davis 1970). Even when Kanjobal people went to the coastal plantations of Guatemala to do seasonal work, they stayed with friends and neighbors in work groups, and so had little experience with multiethnic communities. In the years since late 1982 when the first Kanjobal Maya arrived in Indiantown and today, the social world of the Kanjobal has widened to include groups found in U.S. migrant work: American Blacks, Whites, Haitians and other people from the Caribbean, Mexicans and Mexican Americans, as well as other Central Americans. In addition, social workers and social service volunteers have also become an important part of daily life in Indiantown. Church workers and volunteers, legal assistance lawyers and aides, hospital and clinical workers, as well as journalists, social scientists, and union organizers are now common actors in the social fields of the Kanjobal.

Identity and Culture

The Kanjobal have found ways of surviving and at the same time have been innovative in their approach to the problems of living in a new land radically different from what they knew in Guatemala. I will outline some of the ways that their identity as Kanjobal people has been expressed in Indiantown by focusing on five areas where interethnic conflict has been present in their lives. These include residence, work, leadership, religion, and communication. Identity, as De Vos and Romanucci-Ross (1982) advanced the concept, indicates both a "shield" that protects people from outside threats and dangers and an "emblem" that provides self awareness and confidence for individuals and groups.

This dual nature of identity as an external and internal symbol is particularly important in the case of the Kanjobal refugees, as they were a relatively unknown group in terms of their background, culture, and refugee status when they began to arrive in Indiantown. They have gone through changes in their external identity from welcomed strangers to tolerated farmworkers. From their own point of view, they have changed from refugees shocked by their recent experiences to a diverse community of survivors; once Guatemalan Mayans, they have become now American Mayans who take their place alongside other migrant groups working in the fields and groves all over the United States.

Indiantown is the hub of the Florida Kanjobal community today. It is the center to which Kanjobal people return from seasonal agricultural and construction work that they find in the north. The town itself contains about 4,000 residents whose numbers can easily double during the harvest months of October through April. The Kanjobal Maya who have settled there in the past four years are a minority, who number between 2,000 and 3,000, but one whose ethnicity is salient and apparent, both to outsiders and themselves. The five areas that were noted earlier - residence, work, leadership, religion, and communication -- have all contributed to making the reinforcement of Kanjobal ethnic identity a viable strategy for survival in their community of refuge in Florida .

Residence

In the first few years of migration to Indiantown, residence was localized in a few areas known in the community as "camps." The Kanjobal refugees found available housing in an apartment building known as "blue camp" *(campo azul)* and in "yellow camp" *(campo amarillo)* infamously known locally as "the roach palace." and in a series of shacks known as "white camp" *(campo blanco)*. These buildings had rooms large enough to house more than one family. High rents (up to $300.00 a month for two bedroom units) made sharing quarters with relatives, friends, and sometimes strangers, a necessity. As more and more Kanjobal refugees arrived, rooms were taken wherever they could be found. When a group of Kanjobal people were asked by a social agency worker what they had here that they did not have in Guatemala, one answered with great sarcasm, "In Guatemala we do not have 'blue camp!"

In the past four years, residence has become dispersed from Indiantown throughout the region of south Florida, in a way replicating the dispersed *aldeas* or hamlets around a municipal center such as San Miguel in the highlands in Guatemala. Within south Florida, smaller Kanjobal groups found in communities such as Boynton Beach, Immockalee, or West Palm Beach are known as addresses for people from particular *aldeas* such as Coya' or San Rafael. West Palm Beach has many residents from the municipal center of the Kanjobal area of Guatemala, San Miguel Acatan. Even within Indiantown, the lack of housing and the need for Kanjobal people to take whatever housing is available has meant that they have ended up dispersed throughout the general community of the poor.

Indiantown, then, functions as a center, even a ceremonial center, for Kanjobal refugees. Their use of the community as an identifying locale is a residence pattern that the Kanjobal people have retained from their past. Crowded housing conditions with many unrelated people living in one apartment is an adaptation to the realities of poverty in the U.S. Kanjobal women report that they are learning to cook Mexican food, for example, as migrant workers from Mexico share houses with Kanjobal families.

Work

Work is an area where identity is just now beginning to emerge. As with any new group, low paid, difficult jobs such as fieldwork or construction were among the first jobs that Kanjobal people were able to get. Conflict occurred in the first years in the citrus orchards where taller, more experienced migrant workers quickly outworked the Kanjobal. Jobs harvesting sugar cane are difficult for the Kanjobal to obtain because the labor recruitment strategies largely favor immigrants from the Caribbean. In addition, the latter make the working climate uncomfortable for outsiders, who then leave the fields. Thus, this kind of work was unavailable to the newly-arrived Kanjobal. Although the majority of families have resorted to farm and migrant work, a new pattern of work identity is emerging in the community. Some refugees have found jobs in commercial nurseries and in golf-course construction, where their careful attention to agricultural detail has earned them an excellent reputation as employees. One refugee reported that he recently moved to Fort Myers on the other side of the state to work in a commercial nursery. Since he began working there, the nursery owner has hired several other Kanjobal people because of the good work they do in this employment sector.

A fledgling textile cooperative has begun in Indiantown, the idea of a Catholic nun experienced in textile cooperatives in South America. In the 1970s several cooperatives were developed in the area of San Miguel, although most were agricultural, and not artisanal. The Indiantown cooperative uses Guatemalan weavings as an accessory to women's dresses and skirts, and so capitalizes on traditional Mayan designs and fabrics. Although San Miguel was not known for its textiles, the men traditionally made shoulder bags for their own use. That fact, plus the promise of providing year-round work and a healthy work environment has generated a good bit of interest in the Indiantown cooperative on the part of the Kanjobal. The difficulties of breaking into merchandising have kept the cooperative small, with only fifteen to thirty employees.

Leadership

Leadership patterns are another aspect of Kanjobal identity. No equivalent of the political leadership structure of a civil religious hierarchy so common in Guatemala (Nash 1958) has emerged. When questioned about this, one refugee noted simply that in Indiantown the Kanjobal are guests; they have to ask permission for everything they do, whereas in Guatemala they are the principal officials of the towns.

One area where leadership can be seen emerging is in the organization of meetings and the process of consensus building during the planning of the annual patronal fiesta of San Miguel over the past three years. The festival is sponsored as an event of the Catholic Church in Indiantown. Each year Kanjobal people have taken a larger role in the organization of the fiesta. The "committee of the fiesta" has grown in authority so that the activities have become more and more like those in Kanjobal. A plethora of smaller committees for entertainment, sports, and the election of queens (of which there are three) have been added. Leadership within the committees is exercised through consensus decisions, and the patronal festival has enjoyed greater succcess each year.

Meetings are characterized by participation of both men and women, with a characteristically Mayan sociolinguistic structure of decision making. A topic is first brought out by one of the visible leaders or committee directors. Then a free-ranging discussion ensues with many people talking at once with no attention given to any one person. After five or ten minutes of such polyphonic conversation, people quiet down and someone sums up the decision of the group. Outsiders, such as church workers or non-Maya visitors, find the process difficult, as the turn-taking based on Western ideas of hierarchy and rules of order is not present.

The festival corresponds to the time when the Kanjobal return from migrant work in northern states. Those who have access to transportation and are unencumbered by small children travel north each summer when the vegetable crops of south Florida have been harvested. The "north" for them includes states from Oregon to New York, where summer vegetables and fruits need to be picked. The summer, then, is a time when the Kanjobal are dispersed into small groups of one or two families for several months.

The fiesta of San Miguel, in addition to recalling their home village in Guatemala, is now a signal to return to the area of Indiantown. It has become an important event in the public lives of the people. For many the festival is an occasion when they can quietly socialize with each other, not doing anything more than standing around in small groups and quietly visiting. It is also a time to put on a public show for Kanjobal and non-Kanjobal alike which stresses the identity of Kanjobal people. Traditional clothing is worn, children are taught to dance to *marimba* music, and the queens of the fiesta work hard to prepare speeches in three languages: Kanjobal, Spanish, and English. Both men and women are masters of ceremonies during the events.

This past year included a surprise innovation. At the end of the second day of the fiesta a group of masked and costumed men came out and danced to traditional *marimba* music. Masked performances, such as the dance of the conquest, or in this case, the dance of the elders, are important features of patronal festivals in Guatemala. Masks for the Indiantown performance were purchased from a discount store rather than being made of paper mache, as in San Miguel, but the dance demonstrated a self confidence in Kanjobal identity that had not occurred in previous years. One refugee brought out a video camcorder to record the event. It is apparent that the symbols of their Guatemalan past continue to be important to the Kanjobal in their new setting, and that a kind of revitalization is underway.

Religion

In religious activity, the new Kanjobal identity challenges the layman's stereotypes about the Catholicism of Guatemalan peasants. While Catholicism remains an important part of the lives of many Kanjobal, even to the extent of using the grounds of the Church for the annual patronal festival, the Kanjobal are not all Catholic. This parallels changes in religious allegiances in Guatemala, where Protestantism has made significant inroads among Indians, as well as among Ladinos.

In a survey of 89 families that Maria Miralles (1986) carried out in Indiantown, only 36% of the families reported being Catholic. The others were split among Seventh Day Adventists and other Protestant groups (37%) and a surprisingly large number (27%) who replied that they did not follow any religion. This last group may include those who practice traditional *costumbre* or Mayan religion, as well as those who may have learned to deny their religious affiliation when such knowledge was the basis for being singled out for violence.

The Catholic Church in Indiantown has been an important ally to the Kanjobal in their quest for political and social asylum in south Florida. An activist priest from the parish was known throughout the migrant streams of the state as an advocate and defendant of undocumented aliens. Migrant workers remember religious services in the church early in the decade that included practicing what to do during immigration sweeps.

In terms of identity, religious heterogeneity characterizes the Kanjobal Maya in Florida. Religion, then, must be seen as an independent variable in the ethnic equation. According to residency applications and what community residents say, as the Kanjobal people have spread into other areas of the state, Adventists are more likely to be found in West Palm Beach, while Catholics remain in Indiantown. This suggests that conversions "run" in families and communities.

Communication

Kanjobal communication strategies have been another way to express identity in south Florida. Playing the marimba has been one of the most evident forms of Kanjobal communication. The marimba is used in Kanjobal family ceremonies such as baptisms and birthdays, and is also used for community wide celebrations such as the patronal fiesta. The marimba has also become a positive marker of identity beyond the community. The Kanjobal marimba players were invited to the U.S. Folk Festival in Washington, D.C. in 1985 as an example of an endangered folk tradition. There they played before enthusiastic audiences during the week of the fourth of July. They have played throughout Florida and the Southeast since then, and have received a grant from the state of Florida to teach Kanjobal teenagers the marimba musical tradition.

The Kanjobal language continues to flourish, even as people in Indiantown learn Spanish from their Mexican co-workers and housemates and English in schools and other institutions. Last year the pre-school teacher of the town noted that out of 18 new Kanjobal children in her class, 13 spoke only Kanjobal. In the annual patronal festival that I mentioned earlier, the queens of the fiesta each gave a speech, first in Kanjobal, second in Spanish, and third in English. There are no formal attempts in the community to maintain Kanjobal through media or education, which makes Kanjobal language retention even more remarkable. The Kanjobal people are faced with shopping in English, learning about work in Spanish, English, and sometimes Kanjobal, watching television in English, seeking help from English-speaking police, lawyers, and social service workers, and hearing English around them in the community. But Kanjobal continues to be the principal means of communication even under such a strong push toward new languages. Cassette tapes sent back and forth from Guatemala with news from both the U.S. and the homeland contribute to indigenous language strength. Also, Kanjobal political asylum seekers have insisted that their cases be heard in Kanjobal so as to be sure that the stories of their political persecution were properly told.

External Identity and the Community

Kanjobal identity is also an external feature of their life in south Florida. I will turn now to an exploration of how others have seen the Kanjobal in the community. The image of the Kanjobal has shifted from one of victims undergoing culture shock to one of sometimes dangerous migrant farmworkers. This shift has occurred as more younger, single men have arrived in the community without families to constrain their leisure behavior. Weekend drinking has become the most common recreation for them, again reflecting a long-standing Guatemalan pattern for men. In addition, the sheer numbers of refugees, as well as other migrants working in the area, have stretched the carrying capacity of the community to its limits. Housing, transportation, health care, waste disposal, and the educational facilities have all become overwhelmed by the tremendous increase of immigrants to this unincorporated community.

The emergent Kanjobal ethnic identity is partly due to the circumstances of their arrival, their appearance in the community provoking an outpouring of sympathy and concern. There were whole families whose blistered feet and anemic state told of a flight from terror. The fact that they were modern-day Mayan people also forged their identity in the U.S. Few people in the area of Indiantown knew that the Mayan civilization still existed. Those who did and knew the state of Guatemalan violence, saw these first refugees as people from the movie "El Norte."

The Catholic church in Indiantown became an advocate for farmworker rights and migrant workers in general prior to the coming of the Kanjobal Mayans. The appearance of the Kanjobales was fortunate for the efforts of the church. The Kanjobal Maya were very visible because of the uniqueness of their heritage and were easily represented as victims of Central American politics and as exploited workers here in the U.S.

Outside of the community of Indiantown, the identity of the Kanjobal Maya during the first several months of their arrival was not known. At a flea market in a nearby town, many people surveyed did not know that their customers were Kanjobal Mayan refugees from Guatemala. One manager who was interviewed replied that she thought the Kanjobal people were from the Far East, perhaps the Philippines since they didn't speak Spanish and looked different from the Mexican and Central American farmworkers who often came to the market on weekends.

Today, only a few years later, the Kanjobal are known as Guatemalan -- not Mayan -- undocumented aliens. A recent series of letters to the local newspaper documents this shift. On one occasion, a carload of young Kanjobal men drove through a local resident's yard, destroying the lawn and flowers. The resident wrote to the local paper to express her outrage:

> Most of those people do not know what laws are, let alone abide by them. Where are they a credit to our community? When they are pushing us aside at the post office to mail their $500 + money orders to Guatemala?...or living a dozen people to one house?... *BEWARE*: The Guatemalan Tornado is on the road again. Next time it might be your yard, your house, or worse, your child...Thanks again for letting me express my anger and frustration resulting from the damages incurred at my residence caused by a drunk Guatemalan. (Indiantown *NEWS*, June 24, 1987).

Note that the resident makes several comments that reflect a dramatic shift in labeling from the earlier report. The people are Guatemalans in this letter, not Mayans. Second, they are unaware of laws, they are "outside" of normal society. Third, they are depicted as affecting the balance of payments and deficit by sending U.S. money away. Fourth, they are described as socially uncontrolled because of the way they live and drink. Another writer to the newspaper complained the following week, "I can see [that] the influx of Guatemalans and Mexicans has dropped the value of property over fifty percent..." (Indiantown *News*, June 30, 1987). In this the Kanjobal people were grouped with other Hispanics in the community, a circumstance which led to a counter-response:

> The editorial column is starting to become a column of hatred. It is now being directed to racism, especially on Hispanics and Guatemalans...If it weren't for all these migrant people picking crops you would not have all the fruit and vegetables at the supermarkets. You American people sure wouldn't get your buns out in the hot sun and labor in the fields all day. Wake up, criticizers, and stop judging races. We pay taxes the same as you... (Indiantown *News*, July 6, 1987).

The newspaper quickly stepped in with an editorial and asked its readers to refrain from continuing the outpouring of both anger and pride about the Kanjobal refugees in the community. Many residents regretted the bigoted image that the letters gave the community. After a few weeks the Kanjobal themselves began to joke about their new reputation: They began referring to certain drivers as "Guatemalan tornados".

When Oliver LaFarge worked in the Kanjobal area of Guatemala in the 1920s, he noted that the Kanjobal drank heavily. He said:

> ...one would hesitate to remove the bottle from them until the entire pattern of their lives is changed. They are...eternally chafing under the yoke of conquest, and never for a moment forgetting that they are a conquered people. In occasional drunkenness...they find a much needed release (LaFarge, 1947:100).

If local residents or social workers are asked what they consider to be the principal problem with the Kanjobal people today, they will usually say drunkenness. The parish priest, for example, equated beer drinking with prostitution during his homily delivered during the patronal festival mass. He exhorted people to reach for a can of Coca-Cola instead of beer when they are tempted to drink. Kanjobal people themselves see the deplorable effects of drinking on their families, work, and status in south Florida. But as LaFarge noted, they are under the yoke of conquest. That is a feature of their identity that has persisted here in the U.S., seasoned over five hundred years of experience. Those Kanjobales who are members of the Seventh Day Adventist and other Protestant churches do not drink. These people attend events along with the rest of the community, but are becoming more and more separate from the others because of their weekly trips to West Palm Beach to attend services.

Summary and Conclusion

Kanjobal identity today is being tempered through interethnic communication and conflict in the small community of Indiantown. A precarious existence continues in Indiantown while the Kanjobal Mayans wait for a time when they can return to Guatemala. In the meantime, the Kanjobal refugees of Florida are in the process of creating a new identity, both internal and external, through the areas of experience discussed here. That identity is now based on life in a small U.S. migrant town, and so partakes of the issues and conflicts that other migrant workers face. This past year the local middle school of the community put together a booklet of poems, stories, and even a play written by students. One Kanjobal student condensed his experiences into a short story that summarizes the emergence of identity described in this study.

> I lived in a town that's called San Miguel. Everything was fine. Then my dad worked in California picking apples. I lived with my grandpa and grandma and my brother and sister in Guatemala. They had a big farm. There you can pick corn and beans. There were no phones in the houses. I went to kindergarten when I was seven in San Miguel. My aunt had a big store. We always had a lot to eat. We helped pick the vegetables. I had to work with my grandpa. Then I didn't get to go back to school. Sometimes we sold corn in the town. I was nine years old when the government soldiers came into San Miguel. They had guns

and they lived there a long time. They think that the villagers started the war. The soldiers killed a lot of villagers. The guerrillas wanted to kill the soldiers of the government. I was afraid of both of them because when they came to San Miguel, they wanted to kill my grandpa. They were thinking that my grandpa was the boss of the guerrillas, and they thought my grandpa started the war with them. They, the guerrillas, wanted to kill the government soldiers because they wouldn't pay for the crops that much, only 50 cents a day. In American money, it's only 10 cents. They would come into people's houses at night and kill the men. My grandpa had to go somewhere else to sleep every night so they would not find him. We were sad because my grandpa wasn't there every night. The men were safe during the day because they were at work until six o'clock at night. Everyone went inside. My dad came to a town called Huehuetenango. Then he mailed a letter to grandpa that he was coming to get us. Grandpa took us to my dad. We paid for a car to take us. Then we went to eat some food and we went to a hotel and got some sleep. About eight o'clock in the morning, my dad rented a car in Mexico, and we got a guy that crossed us to this side of the U.S. Then we went in a truck. He had papers for the U.S. First we made a plan. We hid in a big box in the truck. When we got to Arizona, we hid in the trees. In the morning we walked with the man who helped us. We paid him about $150 dollars in American money. We walked 15 hours to a city. We met another man in a van. he took us to the airport. We paid $170. My dad bought tickets to West Palm Beach. My stepmother met us in West Palm Beach. We paid a friend to get us at the airport. I was happy to get here. It was Sunday, Mother's day, May 10, 1984. Nobody will kill me here. We came to Indiantown. My dad got a job cutting cabbage. It was hard because we didn't know what people were saying. We had to learn English to come to school. The Americans were good to us. They liked us because there were just a few of us, not like now. I went to Warfield, but they sent me to Indiantown Middle School because I was 11 years old. I wouldn't want to go back to Guatemala. We have more things here and more money, and the food here tastes better (Perez 1987).

The Kanjobal Maya of Indiantown Florida are a refugee group different from many others. Their identity has been shaped by their own heritage: they are not Spanish speakers, but Mayan speakers whose politics and culture are quite different from those of other Central American peoples. The destruction of entire villages and the militarization of the countryside of Guatemala has forced them to flee in family and community groups. Mexico has offered little haven as military forces from Guatemala have operated with impunity in the country. Now in places in the United States such as Indiantown Florida, the Kanjobal confront a multiethnic community which is sometimes helpful and other times suspicious of their status. Some areas of daily life in the community, including residence, work, leadership, religion and communication exhibit patterns of Kanjobal identity in a configuration of action and cultural style.

While these forms of identity are expanding in complexity, the rigors of migrant work, lack of opportunities for the Kanjobal to work together as a community, and the lessening prospects for a return to Guatemala have changed Kanjobal identity in eyes of others in the community.

Scudder and Colson (1982) discussed stages in forced migration as a sequence of activities including recruitment, transition, development, and incorporation. In the case of the Kanjobal Maya, few of these stages have been passed. The Kanjobal have been in a period of transition since arriving in Indiantown in 1982. New refugees and families of those already in the community have precluded a shift to incorporation in the town except as migrant workers. In this case, Indiantown has provided the Kanjobal with relatively safe haven, but it has not provided them with an economically or socially satisfying context within which to thrive. The Kanjobal came to Indiantown as unusual people from a culture thought to have vanished. They are now seen as just another group of migrant workers, exhibiting behavior that is sometimes offensive and threatening to many in the community.

NOTES

1. Research in Indiantown has been carried out with the generous hospitality of the Holy Cross Service Center and support from *El Centro* and many individuals in the community. Fieldwork began in 1984 and has continued since through short trips several times a year by myself, and long term work of three to six months by a field team consisting of Maria Miralles, Joan Flocks, Alfredo Gonzalez, Sherri Dorman, and Greg MacDonald. This work owes its insights to these researchers. Jeronimo Camposeco, Antonio Silvestre, and Pedro Francisco have been especially important as assistants, friends, and colleagues in Indiantown who have given me the chance to understand the Kanjobal refugee community through their experiences. Frank O'Laughlin, Joan Gannon and Kathy Komarek have been hardworking allies in the work. Participants in the symposium organized by Nancie Gonzalez at the 89th annual meetings of the American Anthropological Association on ethnic conflict and identity helped in the conceptualization of the issue, as did colleagues at the University of Florida Center for Latin American Studies and Department of Anthropology. Even with such good counsel, all interpretations and conclusions in this article are my own.

2. The Kanjobal and their linguistic and geographic neighbors, the Jacaltec Maya, were studied extensively in the 1920's by LaFarge (1947), more recently by Davis (1970), and through a historic perspective by Lovell (1985).

3. At an immigration hearing in 1987, a U.S. immigration judge found it hard to believe that a Kanjobal woman would flee Guatemala, cross Mexico, illegally cross into the U.S. and make her way to Florida without a knowledge of English and only a rudimentary knowledge of Spanish (Camposeco 1987).

5

ETHNICITY AND IDENTITY AMONG MIGRANT GUESTWORKERS IN WEST BERLIN

Ruth Mandel

This article discusses specific ethnographic examples of the migrant experience in West Germany. In doing so it attempts to locate identity and situate ethnicity in the specific context of the culture of migrants. The ethnographic setting described here spans several countries and centuries. Most immediately, the focus is on the contemporary situation of labor migrants in the Federal Republic of Germany. This context will be shown to set in motion the emergence of separate identities which, previous to the migration, were either unexpressed or differently valorized. Of the many possible instances of identity negotiation and revalorization within this migration, I discuss a number of examples illustrative of differing populations; I deal with minority populations already defined as such before the migration -- such as Kurds and the Muslim Alevi minority -- as well as emergent identities specifically as a result of the migration, such as the category of *Almancîlar* (see below).[1] In addition, on a more general level, the interactions of German to non-German or Turk, and of Turk to Greek is brought into the analysis.

It is now a quarter century since the first Turkish guestworkers, or *Gastarbeiter*, as they are most commonly known, were recruited and imported to the Federal Republic. Their presence has caused a major upheaval in West German society, and the ramifications are being felt as well in the cities and the countryside of Turkey. It was intended that the imported workers would assuage West Germany's labor shortage, and fill the lacuna which partially had been created by the freezing of East-West relations brought on by the Cold War, which halted the large East German labor pool upon which the post-war West German boom economy had become dependent.

Currently approximately four million guestworkers and their families reside in the Federal Republic of Germany. Turks account for the largest guestworker population, two million of the four, also making them one of the largest foreign migrant populations in Western Europe. They were recruited by West German industry via the Foreign Labor Office in the 1960s, following a bilateral agreement, signed in 1961, between the Federal Republic of Germany and Turkey allowing for the importation of labor. The bilateral treaty was similar in kind and intent to other treaties drawn up in the same period between the Federal Republic and Italy (1955), Yugoslavia (1968), Greece (1960), Spain (1960), and Portugal (1964).

The guestworker program was intended to be a temporary economic buffer; the imported workers were meant to stay only as long as they were needed to serve West Germany's famous "economic miracle." After weathering economic recessions in 1967 and 1973, West Germany closed its doors to foreign labor and ceased the recruitment programs. Thus began the "foreigner problem," and with it the growth and establishment of what appear to be permanent minority "ethnic" communities in a country that continues to vigorously define itself as a "non-immigration country." The fact that Turks make up half of the foreign migrant population has led to a situation where "Turk" is often used synonymously with "foreigner;" thus the "Turkish problem" implicitly is another name for the "foreigner problem."

The status of these minority communities is far from settled, and they pose a problem both externally, for German society, as well as internally, as emergent factions   split off and dissociate themselves from the larger communities. In addition, for the social scientist the situation presents a complex set of problems, as the internal dynamics of the many groups defy simplistic "ethnic" designation or description. Moreover, the multifaceted identities of the migrants must be understood in a dialectical relation to the German host society and its problematization of the foreign migrants.

Attitudes within the host society are bitterly divided as to the future of the foreign population. The public debate is discussed in terms of (at the two extremes) assimilation (what is called in German "integration") versus expulsion of foreigners. The German attitudes, however complex and even contradictory they might be, find their way into the legal system in the comprehensive set of Foreigner Laws. Though some of the legislation concerning the foreign guestworkers varies from region to region, certain commonalities in emphasis can be identified. Expectedly, both informal attitudes about the resident foreign population as well as formal legislation affect the responses of the migrant communities in terms of issues such as repatriation, investment patterns, children's education, and so on. At the heart of the migrants' concerns is the future of their offspring, the so-called second generation. An interesting result of this has been the divergence of responses of different migrant groups. This article introduces some of these different groups and discusses them in terms of their varied responses.

Many migrant guestworkers feel themselves balancing on a precarious and shaky fence. They often understand this to be the dangerous frontier of Western culture, which implies the delimitation of their own culture. It is not an overstatement to say that the obverse of this is shared by those Germans of the political/social center-to-right persuasion, who feel threatened by a Turkish presence, which they see as encroaching on to the limits of their Western/German culture (see for example, the *Heidelberg Manifesto*).

Gastarbeiter and Ausländer: Emergent Ethnic Groups at the Price of Homogenization

Embedded within any discussion of ethnicity is the question of identity -- which is anything but static.[2] A central dynamic encompassed by an analysis of identity is the complementarity of the notions of self and other. At issue are the ways self and other articulate, historically and in the migratory situation, with shifting hierarchies of `others.' For example, the category of "Turk" threatens to fall apart at the seams, as it is newly employed in a novel, generalized fashion, and sometimes applied to all guestworkers. We are then left with the categories of *Gastarbeiter*, guestworker, and *Ausländer*, foreigner. But do guestworkers as a solidary unit comprise an ethnic group?

In West Germany one hears the terms "*Gastarbeiterkultur*" (guestworker culture) and "*Ausländerkultur*" (foreigner culture); even more specific categories such as "*Gastarbeiterkrankenheit*" (guestworker diseases) and "*Gastarbeiterliteratur*" (guestworker literature) are used in some contexts. Though these terms clearly represent trends toward objectification and homogenization of foreigners, the crucial question must be asked: *whose* trend? Is it indeed intrinsic, emerging from the various foreign populations, or is it extrinsic, an imposed homogenization from outside and above?

One poignant illustration of this is a poster advertising a foreigner festival, called "Begegnungen" -- encounters. The poster chops into eight squares a human body, and each square is dressed in a different "costume." To a knowing eye, the obviously Greek, Turkish, and Yugoslav fragments are readily identifiable; an unknowing eye might interpret it as 'generic foreigner.' As the glance travels down the body, the lower squares jar the perception, as they reveal provocatively non-customary costumes, Western dress: cuffed blue jeans, sneakers; a high heeled shoe and shapely leg. Several readings are possible: it can be seen as an equalizing or relativizing statement, but one observer noted to me that it appeared to her as a progression -- that the poster was meant to be read from top to bottom, perhaps ironically, but as the recommended raiments for a social evolutionary model of development, progress, and ultimately, assimilation.

Another way the homogenization takes place is in the realm of public discourse. For example, the Christian Democratic Interior Minister, Zimmermann, has been noted for his linguistic assimilation of the word "Ausländer" (foreigner) to the more derogatory word "Turk" -- the lowest social/linguistic denominator. This interchangeability of the two words provides a convenient shortcut for those who would prefer not to deal with individuals, distinctive groups, sub-groups, nationalities, or cultures. It serves those who would seek to further objectify the "other," as it relegates the "Ausländer/Turk" to a peripheral place, to the marginal social category of the outsider. These examples and those to follow try to address the questions just posed, about the source of the homogenization of the foreign guestworkers.

Intra-Ausländer Divisions

Just as clear divisions between segments of the German population can be identified, with the "integrationists" opposed to those supporting a "Turks go home" policy, parallels within the foreign community are found as well. First, reproducing the Germans' perception, the many nationalities place themselves within a hierarchically ordered scheme. Christian European guestworkers clearly rank at the top. Italians, Greeks and Yugoslavs comprise this group. Spaniards and Portuguese, though less numerous, also would be ranked here. Italians would probably be at the top of the pecking order. The more distant and different from German society -- in terms of social, cultural and physical proximity -- the further down a group finds itself. That the Turks occupy the lowest rung is indicated linguistically. As mentioned above, the word "Turk" has often come to be synonymous with "Ausländer," foreigner.

Among the various migrant groups, internal differentiation is also apparent. For example, urban Turks from Western Turkey often feel little if any kinship with their poorer rural compatriots. Worse yet, from their perspective, are the Kurds from Eastern Anatolia, whom they regard as little better than wild, primitive, barbarians. The self-designated "westernized" urban Turks sense no end of shame and resentment towards their "backwards, embarrassing" compatriots, who, they say, give *all* Turks, "even the well integrated, modern ones" a bad name. They also blame them for the considerable prejudice, stereotyping, and xenophobia most Turkish guestworkers claim to experience.

Turks in Turkey are well aware of the anti-Turkish prejudice and xenophobia in Germany, as the media gives extensive coverage to the situation of the Turkish workers abroad. Urban Turks will often invoke a popular folk theory, of one- vs. two-step migration. They often rationalize the 'unadaptability' of the rural villagers:

> These Anatolian villagers come to Munich never having seen
> even Istanbul! They go straight from the village to Europe;
> they should learn how to get along in a city in Turkey before
> they go to Europe. This way the Germans think that all Turks
> are backwards and uncivilized.

Alamanyalî: Ethnic or Other?

Repatriation and temporary return migration to Turkey pose an interesting case for reflecting on how we want to conceive of the relation between identity and ethnicity. It involves the creation of the *Alamanyalî* (or *Almancîlar* or *Almanyalî*), the 'German-like' or 'German-ish.' It is a play on the word *alman*, German; it is a very precise and deliberate twist (see Mandel, n.d.). Typically, the returnee or repatriot has endured the best years his/her life as an unwelcome stranger in *gurbet*, exile, the foreign land. Annual summer vacations to Turkey have served as much to reinforce ties to the homeland, as they have to accustom their compatriots back home to this new sort of Turk -- the Turk with a German affect. The resentment toward the "rich Germanized cousin" has built up over many years, just as it has taken many years for the idealization of the pristine, wholesome Anatolian village to crystallize in the mind's eye of the guestworkers away from home.

The work year in Germany is oriented around the idealization of the five weeks spent in Turkey last summer, and the five weeks to come, next summer. The migrants hope that the degradation and alienation they experience as foreign workers and third class citizens in Germany will be rectified by the summer journey home, where they will be accepted and respected. But instead, they are met with the mocking appellation of "*Alamanyalî*."

Migration consists of a large number of people moving from a state of unmarkedness in Turkey prior to the initial out-migration, to a marked category of *Gastarbeiter* abroad, and finally as repatriots to yet another transformation, that of *Alamanyalî*. This reproduction of markedness, the central irony of the migrant predicament, begs the question, of whether or not all such processes and situations of differentiation and affiliation are indeed properly or usefully thought of and understood as "ethnic" ones. But the question "is *Almanyalî* an ethnic group?" is more than merely rhetorical. For the category *Almanyalî* is composed of people who, though living in the land of their birth, speaking their native tongue[3] with their original compatriots and kin, and practicing the same religion, have undergone a fundamental change; they now think of themselves as different and are labelled as such. In other words, the category of *Almanyalî* fulfills many of the objective criteria set out by some ethnicity theories -- particularly if viewed ahistorically. When framed by its own history, however, a different picture emerges.[4]

Kurdish Questions

The experience abroad can be an extremely positive one for many Kurds, who, for the first time, find themselves free to express themselves as Kurds, and in Kurdish.[5] Kurdish political and cultural organizations and parties have proliferated in Western Europe at a rapid pace. This is in sharp contrast to the situation of Kurds in eastern Turkey; there the area is still governed by martial law and involved in civil, guerilla warfare.[6] In Turkey Kurds are subjected to severe, repressive assimilationist policies. These include deportation to non-Kurdish regions, widespread imprisonment and torture for any suspicion of sentiments or expression of Kurdish self-determination, and the ban on speaking, reading, or writing in their native tongue. In Turkey formal, offical censorship is practiced, and an informal tabu is upheld, against discussing anything Kurdish related. In Turkey monolingual Kurdish children routinely experience severe corporal punishment when they enter first grade with no knowledge of Turkish. Official government census takers have reported that they were instructed to register monolingual Kurdish speakers as Turks speaking Turkish.

Even in the foreign, German context, Kurds from Turkey sometimes complain that Turks resent them for speaking Kurdish, and dismiss their claims to a separate identity. Ironically, in the diaspora situation Kurdish children also suffer from their inability to speak Kurdish. In bilingual schools they are included under the Turkish rubric when they are assigned to foreigner classes. Yet when the teachers see that they are unable to communicate in either Turkish or German, the children are presumed to be retarded and placed in special classes or schools for this "problem." Thus, the Kurdish identity, an illegal, officially non-existent ethnicity in Turkey, in some contexts becomes assimilated into a more generalized ethnic Turkish category in the German migrant diaspora.

The Kurdish regions of eastern Turkey have long been marked by their feudal and tribal ogranization.[7] Not surprisingly, the structure of some of past relations are transposed abroad, as clan and tribe affiliations might determine who joins which association. Thus, the dozens of Kurdish organizations, parties, and associations that have blossomed in Western Europe may assume a wide range of manifest guises. At one count twelve different Kurdish groups coexisted in West Berlin alone. However, this coexistence is not always peaceful, just as in former times, rival bands organized by religio-political leaders were known to stage raids. Paris, in particular, has been the site of recent violence -- including murders -- between opposing Kurdish political parties and factions. In addition, some leftist political parties, outlawed in Turkey, vie for Kurdish support abroad by their stances on Kurdish autonomy.

One group of Kurdish speaking migrants in Western Europe are the Alevis. In the subsequent section I discuss Alevis at greater length; briefly, they are a heterodox Shi'ite minority despised by the Sunni majority.[8] Alevis cross-cut traditional "ethnic" categories, and are found among semi-nomadic Turkish speakers in Western Anatolia as well as within Kurdish areas in the east. In their homeland, Kurdish Sunnis and Alevis rarely associate with each other, nor do they intermarry. On the other hand, the migrant diaspora provides a more neutral social and political context where some affiliations do take place. Among the second generation migrants, romantic links between Alevi and Sunni youth occasionally are the cause of social turmoil and melodramatic tragedy. Kurdish speaking Alevi and Sunni activists abroad sometimes have joined together with common political goals; other times Alevis report that their Sunni colleagues do not accept or respect them as equals. Many Kurdish speaking Alevis strongly oppose the idea of a Kurdistan, believing that should such a state ever come into being, the Alevis would be persecuted even more than they are currently by the Turkish State.

Many of the young, politically active Kurds (and Turks) have obtained or are in the process of trying to obtain refugee status. However, a very small and shrinking number of applicants ever receives asylum, which makes their situation tenuous indeed. Unable to ever return to Turkey (barring an general amnesty) these young people live in a liminal state, on the margins of society. During the mandatory two year waiting period prior to a decision about their asylum status, they may not legally work, so many resort to "Schwartzarbeit" -- illegal (black) jobs. Many of them are constantly on moving, avoiding immigration officials, using false names, residing illegally and unregistered with the foreigner police, and sometimes entering into "white" or "paper marriages" by paying German women to marry them in order to obtain a residence permit.

Despite the large number of refugees (Kurdish and Turkish), their plight has not been widely known among Germans. In 1985 a dramatic made-for-television movie was aired, and showed the predicament of one such young man. The evocative film was quite effective in raising public consciousness. The film was loosely based on the story of Cemal Kemal Altun, a young Turkish political refugee from the junta who, after having spent thirteen months in a West Berlin prison, had his petition for refugee status denied by a West Berlin court, which ordered for his immediate extradition to Ankara. Believing that deportation would result in torture in a Turkish jail and most likely death, Cemal took his own life by jumping out a sixth floor window of the administrative court building.

The Turkish-Kurdish and intra-Kurdish rivalries are not the only ones prevalent in the migrant community. The following section discusses the role of different Islamic identities and the ways they articulate and are expressed in the migration context.

Islam and Identity

Emergent identities in the foreign migrant community also come to the fore in the context of Muslim aspects of identity. Both inter-and intra-sectarian conflicts arise in the diaspora situation. A wide range of Muslim religious groups co-exist in the migrant community, but the deepest chasm is the one dividing the Alevi and Sunni communities. This separation has grown still deeper, as Alevis and Sunnis have responded in radically opposed ways to the West Germany diaspora context.

Many Turks in West Germany were observant Muslims already in Turkey, prior to the migration. However, for others it is the foreign, Christian, German, context that provides the initial catalyst for active involvement in religious organizations and worship. One interpretation of this increased identification with Muslim symbols and organizations might see the popularity of Islamic groups and identifications as a form of resistance against prevailing norms of an alien society, a society commonly perceived of as dangerous, infidel, and immoral. The migrants' distance from Turkey and feeling of marginality not only vis-á-vis Turkey but also vis-á-vis mainstream German society, provide the context for explicitly religious expressions and concerns that might not be relevant where they are part of a society's mainstream.

Questions of legality, power, and authority also enter into the picture, if we consider that a great deal of the organizational, preaching, and educational modes currently widespread in West Germany clearly would be illegal in Turkey. While for some Turkish Sunnis in West Germany the distance from Turkey ensures freedom from legal constraints, Turkish Alevis also find in the diaspora an environment conducive to expressing their Alevi identity, free from what they perceive as the pressures of a Sunni-dominant, repressive order in Turkey. Thus, embedded in the process of the dual peripheralization or marginalization -- both from Turkish and German societies -- of migrant Turkish Alevis and Sunnis, are the seeds from which may be observed the blooming of alternative expressions of Islamic identities.

Alevis suffer from an unambiguously negative reputation and image among Sunnis. At the same time, however, Alevis take pride in their difference, displaying strong convictions and commitment to a value system which they perceive as antithetical to that of the Sunnis'. It is this value system and the behavior and code for conduct it implies that the Sunnis point to when they make their damning accusations. Yet Alevis scoff at the accusations, upholding their separate orientation. In particular, the points of contention revolve around issues concerned with women, morality, and religious observance. In many cases this has explicitly political implications. For example, the label "Alevi" in many contexts is synonymous with the term "leftist," or "revolutionary." This association is as true for Alevis as it is for Sunnis and those on the right of the political spectrum; only the valorization changes.

In a similar way, beliefs about Alevi women converge to an extent, yet are assigned opposing values. Sunnis speak of promiscuity of Alevi women, often citing specific traits and practices. As "proof" they point to the fact that Alevis include women in their rituals, which Sunnis claim are nothing but incestuous orgies. By the same token, the Alevis proudly boast of how "democratic, progressive and tolerant" they are, and they sharply criticize Sunni purdah-like practices, calling them degenerate and reactionary. Furthermore, they answer Sunni charges claiming that Alevis are bad Muslims with counter charges, accusing the ostensibly pious Sunnis with hypocrisy:

> The Sunnis think that hitting their heads against the ground five times a day [in prayer] is enough to make them good Muslims; but they are hypocrites, because then they turn around and lie and cheat. We believe that it is the quality inside, of the heart and soul, that counts -- that must be clean and pure, that's what's important, not the externals, such as praying in the mosque for all to see...

The Alevi alternative value and worship system is seen as threatening to many Sunnis, to whom the Alevis represent a dangerous, secret cabal, replete with mysterious beliefs and rites. To Sunnis, Alevis are seen as renegade, bad Muslims, even infidels. The distinction is most often expressed on religious and moral grounds. The articulation of differentiation is more complex among the Alevis, however. Alevis sometimes refer to Sunnis as "Muslims," a puzzling designation to say the least, since most Alevis see themselves as the true, legitimate Muslims who have followed the correct path, traceable to their martyred central figure, Ali.

The migration context renders the relations between Sunnis and Alevis still more complex as their relationship becomes triangulated when the two groups' differentiated relations with the host society are elaborated. In a certain sense, while Sunni identity abroad can be understood as an intensification of its latent and manifest expressions in Turkey, Alevi identity undergoes a movement away from Sunni oppositional referents and even toward replacing them with German.

Indeed, Alevis in the diaspora have successfully reversed their hierarchically subordinate position to the Sunni Turks. They point to what they see as their more "democratic, tolerant, and progressive" world view. While steadfast in their identity as Alevis, they identify with and admire many aspects of West German society that the Sunnis interpret as threatening. Ultimately, they find that the act of dissociation from Sunnis abroad renders them superior, not inferior, in the eyes of the mainstream German society. This novel rearrangement of past relations and valorizations offers new horizons for expressing identity, and in the eyes of some, political freedoms. Thus, by adopting symbols and practices thought of as German, Alevis have managed to distance themselves from Sunnis in an unprecedented manner, and to allow themselves new social fields within which they may express themselves. The resulting paradox: what for one group is counter-hegemonic, replicates another group's hegemony.

While Alevis abroad are doubly liminal, with respect to both Germans and Sunni Turks, their relative position vis-á-vis Sunnis has undergone a transposition. In West Germany, the reference point of Sunni dominance becomes less and less relevant. Alevis, who had defined themselves primarily in opposition to Sunnis, and always in reference to them, have in some respects gradually replaced the latter with Germans in the process of identity construction. While some Alevis in Germany have taken advantage of the freedom to adopt a more inward, communal orientation unfettered by past political and social constraints, some have opted for an ecumenical stance, and still others choose to dissociate from anything they perceive as religious.

Some groups of Alevis, however, have organized themselves into proto-nationalist associations, modeled on Kurdish separatists parties and organizations. They speak of the struggle for an independent "Alevistan" (nation of Alevis; on the order of Kurdistan, which, not surprisingly, is nearly identical topographically). The critical word this group uses is *millet*; the rough gloss is nation or religio-ethnic group, depending on the context. Thus, there is anything but consensus within the Alevi community -- if indeed it can be spoken of as "a community" -- as to the terms of self-representation. Depending on one's perspective the Alevis are alternatively "renegades," "infidels," "Muslims," "a religious sect," "an ethnic group," or "a nation denied its statehood."

Redefining Others: Greeks and Turks

Life in the Federal Republic of Germany can be seen as a social scientific laboratory for Greek-Turkish interaction. It is not the first time Turks or Greeks have come into contact with an "other;" on the contrary, prior to their relatively recent incarnation as guestworkers, they served this role for one another for centuries (more so the Turks for the Greeks than vice-versa; see Herzfeld 1982, 1987. Elsewhere I have dealt with the complexity of Greek attitudes towards Turkey, Turks, and Greek identity in its close historical, social, and cultural connections with Turks; Mandel 1988).

How are the Greeks -- and Turks -- received in Germany? To many Germans, the Turks are the most distant and 'other' of the "ethnic" ensemble that constitutes the category *Gastarbeiter*. First, the Turks far outnumber any of the other nationalities represented. Second, they are the furthest away in terms of cultural and social criteria: they are Muslim (non-Christian), Asian (non-European), they speak a non-Indo-European tongue, and they are the inheritors of what is perceived by the west as a violent, militaristic, wild tradition, with images of the conquering Turko-Mongol hordes, a threat to western civilization.

By contrast, the Germans trace their intellectual heritage to Greece (albeit the Greece of 2500 years ago). Germany produced schools of classical Greek philology, and Goethe was much enamored with Greece, idealized it and translated modern (nineteenth century) Greek folk songs. Furthermore, Greece has been a favorite vacation spot for Germans for many years, growing numbers of whom own property there and return annually. The vacation potential of Turkey, on the other hand, only recently has been discovered by adventuresome German tourists; thus, the familiarity of Greece is far greater than that of Turkey to many Germans. Also, Greek music and food are well-known and appreciated in West Germany. Moreover, Greece has been a member of the European Community since January, 1981, the economic links symbolizing a sense of inclusion into Europe that Turkey lacks.

Greeks often come face to face with Turks for their first time in West Germany. Though some Greeks come to the Federal Republic and leave with prejudices intact, others find that what they have been led to believe all their lives about their "natural Turkish enemy" simply does not correspond to the new reality. In Greece the most salient "other" has nearly always been the Turk, to the extent that Greekness is often conceived of in direct opposition to imagined and feared Turkishness (see above). But in West Germany the labels, treatment, and concept of *Ausländer* and "Turk" are frequently used synonymously and interchangeably, and it is therefore surprising and confusing, if not highly upsetting, for Greeks to be mistaken for and called "Turks." The situation elicits novel reactions and responses, from a critical rethinking and re-evaluation of the traditional nationalist, acutely anti-Turkish animosity, to the Greeks' wholesale appropriation of the dominant culture's values and attitudes about Turks (cf. Herzfeld 1987:107).

One informant's response illustrates this situation:

> With my Turkish friends I don't have to explain things -- they simply understand, we have the same mentality, the same way of thinking; whereas with Germans I'm obliged to explain everything. They have problems understanding my thoughts, feelings, ideas.

Another young Greek man in Munich explained it this way:

> A Greek prefers to do *parea* (keep company, hang out with) with a Turk rather than a German because the Turk is `Greek style' -- the German isn't...he's blonde, a different type altogether. The Turk has a moustache, a dirty face, he's dark skinned, with messy thick hair, like us -- *idhia fatsa, idhia ratsa* (same face, same race). Before I came to Germany I used to hate Turks. I learned here, in Germany, that we are the same.

Thus, the different histories and differentiated attitudes of Germans towards Greeks and Turks occasionally account for unequal treatment. However, on the other hand the German trend toward homogenization and *lack* of differentiation between groups of foreigners can lead to greater affiliation of groups previously dissociating from one another.

Changing Definitions of Turkishness and Inclusivity

Two trends of new formulations of identity can be identified in the diaspora context. First, on the most inclusive of levels, a process of redefinition of Turkishness is experienced by the migrants. The fact that the salient other in Germany is different than it was in Turkey leaves open the option for new forms of solidarity among formerly unaffiliated and unaffiliating groups of Turks. In a nation where regionalism and local identity still carry important currency, despite sixty years of stalwart efforts on the part of the founders and shapers of the Turkish Republic to replace this with a superimposed national identity, these new modes of affiliation do not come easily, and prejudices common in Turkey are still heard and acted upon in the diaspora. Formerly salient criteria for distinction and discrimination, operative in Turkey, pale in *gurbet* (exile) where those who at one time thought themselves superior now face daily the inescapable fact of their own inferiority in the eyes and laws of mainstream German society. The reactions to this, neither generalizable nor uniform, are often determined by the specific social context or field of action. Conscious dissociation from the perceived lowest group is sometimes the response, accompanied by attempted adoption of traits, behaviors thought to be German. On the other hand, a different reaction might be a more diffuse solidarity with groups formerly thought to be unacceptable.

The following example, highlights in greater relief some of the possible ambiguities of definitions and categories of ethnicity. In a business district of West Berlin is a restaurant called "Akropolis." Though equipped with the requisite accoutrements of Berlin's other Greek restaurants (blue and white decor, touristic posters of Aegean islands, Greek-style lettering, a Germanized-Greek menu, Greek wines and spirits, tapes of Theodorakis music, etc.) there remained a crucial difference from the other Greek restaurants. The owner and several of the waiters presented themselves publicly as "Yiannis" or "Yiorgos," but when addressing each other it is as "Mehmet" and "Yusuf," and though in low tones, they spoke in Turkish. A bit of probing revealed that the owner and waiters were from a village in Western Thrace, the north-eastern-most region of Greece, bordering Bulgaria and Turkey. (A large Turkish-speaking Muslim minority lives here,[9] a continual thorn in the side of the Greek government.)[10]

Though the members of this minority group carry Greek passports and are Greek citizens, they generally identify themselves as "Turks, from Western Thrace" never as Greeks. This is a direct hold-over from the Ottoman Empire, where for centuries people were legally separated, categorized, taxed, conscripted, and often granted limited autonomy, according to their *millet*, a system based primarily on religion. Today the Turks of Western Thrace have close connections with the modern Turkish Republic. Many have moved to Turkey voluntarily, send their children to university, buy property there, regularly visit, and so on.

The ethnography of restaurant-going in Berlin reveals that Turkish restaurants, almost without exception, are patronized nearly exclusively by Turks. (Only a handful of strategically designed and located Turkish restaurants cater to Germans [of the counter cultural "alternative," or stylish "schickeria" populations] as well.) Greek (and Yugoslav) restaurants, on the other hand, do excellent business with German patrons. Clearly, "Yiannis/Mehmet" was hoping that he and his restaurant would 'pass' for Greek -- at least vis-á-vis German restaurant goers. This is an interesting twist to the questions of the presentation of self, construction of identity, and the permeability of ethnic boundaries, especially since, as mentioned above, Greeks and Turks have often served as the salient other for each other. Herzfeld writes "...Greeks faced with a choice of nouns will still often use the "Turkish" alternative to signify deprecation. Otherness in the self is a categorical confusion, "matter out of place" (1987:15).[11] The above example certainly represents a categorical confusion, of matter out of place; one would be hard pressed indeed to assign an ethnic appellation to the "Akropolis" restaurant or to its owners. It is an example of what Herzfeld calls "domestic alterity" (p.42), which perhaps reflects a single, idiosyncratic case, but possibly indicates as well that the foreign context offers a wider range of possibilities for expression of alternative identities, not easily captured by ethnic labels.

Conclusion

Identity, an elusive terrain, proves difficult to chart regardless of the mode of surveying employed. The difficulty derives in part from the nature of the domain itself -- constantly in flux, and thus variously delimited and contingently defined. Axiomatic to a definition of identity is an understanding that it is essentially malleable, a dynamic, flexible construct, grounded within the confines of historical, ideological, social, and political-economic structures. It suggests the setting and re-setting of boundaries, and, in the case addressed here, identity has been shown to be a contested domain, implying agency on the part of the actors involved.

Parts of this chapter have attempted to situate a symbolic approach to culture within a historical and political domain; cultural signs and symbols are, after all, potent mediators of changing power relations. The contest or struggle for control of the sign is an excellent example; the personally contested nature of the identity of the Turkish/Greek restaurateur demonstrates such a struggle.

Thus, in the same way that a culture implies a shared meaningful, symbolic system, the system at one and the same time might operate as an exclusionary one. The Turkish/ Greek was acutely aware of the benefits of an externally perceived ethnicity. Due to an historical and topographic accident of birth, he could exercise the choice to represent himself as the unmarked ethnic rather than the marked, thus assuring himself of a more lucrative outcome. His purview was of sufficiently wide range to allow him to reconstitute his reality from the multiple possibilities open to him in the foreign context.

A case of this sort also questions the nature of cultural boundaries, their permeability, and the subsequent relevance for the notion of ethnic identity and boundary. It suggests a rethinking of theories of ethnicity. Most often studies of ethnicity inquire into problems of identity in heterogeneous settings. However, their concerns have too often been with the organizing of objective criteria into ethnic categories, a pursuit which offers little by way of representing internal group dynamics and subjective constructions of identity. My concern here has not been with the definitional problem per se: the task of fitting Group X or Group Y into a Procrustean ethnic bed seems futile at best. Instead, I have been interested first, in modes of self-representation and the representation of the other; and next, in the underlying dynamics of such representation in the migration context of changing socio-political systems and power relations.

I have tried to show how the migration discussed here opens the door to radically different possibilities for expressions of inter-group relations. This was demonstrated with the Kurdish minority. These new expressions also imply redefinitions of relations of inequality and domination between groups. And, as exemplified in the case of the Sunni and Alevi Turks, such a situation paves the way for new social movements as well as novel arrangements and movements in social mobility. Also it was shown how, within a changed and changing social, political, and physical field, the setting and re-setting of social boundaries takes place. Finally, the relevance of agency must be stressed, as the processes underlying boundary setting involve the often self-conscious acceptance or rejection of symbolic practices, objects, space, attitudes, and an accompanying revalorization thereof -- for Germans as well as the resident foreigners.

NOTES

1. The letter -î- represents the undotted I/i in Turkish, pronounced like the i in the English word "fur." The letters Ç/ç are pronounced as "-ch-" in English, as in the word "chose." S,/s, are pronounced as is "-sh-" in English, for example, in the word "show." C/c in Turkish is similar to the English letter J/j.

2. The analytic category 'ethnicity' has been and continues to be used in a myriad of contexts referring to as many different ideas and phenomena. Often it is assumed to be an objective given -- of a natural kind with an obvious essence. In many cases conventional notions of ethnicity have tended to distort the complexities of identity constructs. One problem I see in the confusing body of ethnicity theory is the mistaking of a folk theory for an analytic one. Too often social scientists have accepted and appropriated the native boundaries and categorizations, elevating them to assumed givens and analytic constructs, rather than questioning the ideological bases for such groupings. Following from and extending Handler and Linnekin's discussion of tradition, I would argue that ethnicity represents less an "artifactual assemblage" (1984:274) of objective traits or attributes -- the laundry list approach -- than a thought process of intentioned actors seeking to establish and justify social boundaries. The salient boundaries may be intrinsically delimited; drawn, in other words by those who choose to create and express themselves as a collective solidary group. Or, the boundedness may be extrinsically determined, for example, for purposes of subordination and domination. Thus it refers to a fundamental ordering of differences, of discerning a meaningful "us" from "them."

3. Many *Alamanyalî*, particularly those of the second generation, use some code-switching between German and Turkish.

4. For a more extensive discussion and analysis of return migration, see Mandel, n.d.

5. Despite their demographic significance -- the Kurds of Turkey are estimated to comprise perhaps twenty percent of the nation's population, or ten million -- they officially do not exist. The official definition of "Kurd" is "a mountain Turk who speaks poor Turkish." One of Turkey's more famous human rights cases involves Ismail Besikci, a (non-Kurdish) sociologist who published studies on the social structure of Kurdish villages, became an outspoken Kurdish-rights advocate, and has spent many years in prison and undergone severe torture. Amnesty International has been active in his case. (For more on Kurds, see van Bruinessen 1978; Chaliand 1980.)

6. The term "Eastern Turkey" or "Eastern Anatolia" is often used euphemistically to refer to Kurdish provinces, or Kurdistan.

7. See van Bruinessen, 1978.

8. The majority of Turks adhere to the Hanefi legal code, one of the four branches of Sunni Islam; small pockets of followers of Shafi Islam -- another branch of Sunnism -- exist in Turkey, as well. A large minority of Turks are Alevis, members of one of many of small (and not so small) groups that would fit under the loosest of Shi'ite purviews, sharing a mystical, sufi belief system. They are widely hated, mistrusted and informally discriminated against in Turkey, where they probably make up about twenty percent of the total population of fifty million. Due to centuries of persecution, they practice *taqiya*, dissimulation. The Sunnis are in the majority of the officially secular Turkish Republic (see Birge 1937; Gökalp 1980; Melikoff 1982; Rahman 1979).

9. The Muslims of Western Thrace, along with the Greek Orthodox of Istanbul were the only two groups exempted from the massive exchange of populations (stipulated by treaty in Lausanne, Switzerland, January 30, 1923), when approximately one million three-hundred thousand Orthodox Christians (Greeks) from Turkey were forcibly relocated in Greece, and some four hundred thousand Muslims (Turks) moved to Turkey (Stavrianos 1958:590).

10. This population is a political hot potato in Turko-Greek relations. Turkish is their native language (many are probably bilingual) and Islam their religion, but their passports are Greek. Frequent charges of discrimination, harassment, etc. are regularly levied against the Greek government -- just as the Turkish government is often accused of mistreating its Christian (Greek, Armenian, Assyrian) minorities.

11. Particularly since the war in Cyprus [1974] and the subsequent partition of the island, antagonism between the two nations has been consistently high. On the other hand, there have been occasional overtures between high profile Greek and Turkish individuals which have had surprisingly positive public reception in both countries. I think in particular of the collaborative effort of musicians and singers Zülfü Livaneli and Maria Farantouri whose album set a record for the highest sales of any long playing album in Greece. (It was banned in Turkey, so only fans with good underground connections heard it there.) Unprecedented high level secret meetings in Switzerland took place between

Prime Ministers Papandreou and Özal early in 1988. They met again, in Athens, in June 1988. As a result a number of Greek-Turkish cultural exchanges have taken place, and tourism between the two countries has increased.

6

THE CHRISTIAN PALESTINIANS OF HONDURAS: AN UNEASY ACCOMMODATION

Nancie L. Gonzalez

Since the last decades of the nineteenth century, Arab migrants have settled in every nation of the New World; their numbers, prominence and provenience vary, but in general, their forebears came from the Levant, especially from what are now Syria, the Lebanon, Israel, the West Bank and Jordan. The largest numbers are said to be in Brazil, Argentina, the United States, Canada, Chile and Mexico in that order. One expert has commented that in the Caribbean they are "more widely dispersed than any other minority." All of the Central American republics have identifiable and considerable Arab populations, although their exact numbers are unknown. Most are Christian, and in Honduras they are primarily Palestinian. Nowhere else in Central America have these Arab migrants and their descendants achieved such local prominence as in San Pedro Sula, Honduras' major industrial city, where they dominate the business community in both commerce and industry. Yet, they are less than fully accepted by the larger Honduran society. This seems likely to be related to the endurance of their ethnic identification, which in turn is related to their initial migration strategies, the nature of their settlement in Honduras, and the protracted conflict in their original homeland. It is this group and its unusual circumstances with which this paper will deal.[1]

Historical Background of the Migration

With few exceptions, the Palestinians of Honduras came from the town of Bethlehem or one of its two adjoining villages, Beit Jala and Beit Sahur. This population cluster, which herein will be treated as a single unit, is only about twelve miles from Jerusalem, yet it exhibits a marked sense of separateness from other Palestinian communities.[2] Until the last few years, the majority of its inhabitants have been Christian -- mainly Greek Catholic, Greek Orthodox or Roman Catholic -- and many claim descent from European Crusaders. This was true even after Christians became a minority in the holy land as a whole (see below). In the diaspora they remember with great nostalgia their community's beauty, its olive groves, vineyards, orchards of almond and fig trees, and they romanticize the distinctive peasant costume worn by many women until the 1930s. Until the nineteenth century, Bethlehem was primarily an agricultural village, famed regionally for the wine they manufactured from local grapes (Volney 1787:322).

Today's emigrants are, as Christians, proud as well as of their community's worldwide fame as the birthplace of Jesus Christ. Because of the latter, tourism has long been important to the local economy, and many families still earn their livelihood by manufacturing and/or selling religious and other souvenirs of olivewood, mother-of-pearl from the Sea of Galilee, and the so-called Stone of Moses, a shiny, blackish-grey, bituminous limestone which was worked into bowls, cups and inkpots (Scholch 1982:39).[3] Male Bethlehemites, as well as the men of Beit Jala and Beit Sahur, were widely known for their skill in cutting stone for construction purposes, while the women produced fine embroidery (Stillman 1979:30-32). In the 1890s, almost half of the 792 artisans, traders and entrepreneurs of Bethlehem specialized in trades related to construction. It was men from these towns who largely built the "new" Jerusalem after the Crimean War (Scholch 1982:29).

Historians indicate that Christianity had become the dominant religion in the Roman province of Palestine by the time of Constantine the Great (A.D. 337), and a century later the only non-Christians were various scattered and localized Jewish communities and a small community of Samaritans (Runciman 1968:3). However, Arab Muslims conquered Palestine in 634 A.D. and set up the *dhimmi* system in which each religious group was treated as a separate "nation." This began a tradition that has persisted throughout the Middle East ever since, generally known as the millet system today. By the eleventh century, Palestine was still largely Christian, although hopelessly splintered into many different sects. It remained so, in spite of repeated conquests by various foreign elements, until 1517, when the Ottoman Sultan Selim I conquered Syria, Palestine and Egypt. Since that time the territory has been continually occupied by foreign powers and there has not been an independent national entity called Palestine, although the name has hung on despite the fact.

Under the rigidly Muslim Ottoman Empire the Christians and the Jews became less-favored, if not oppressed minorities, even in towns and cities where they constituted a numerical majority, such as Jerusalem (Ma'oz 1968:198). The Christians' religious allegiance, as well as their tendency to flaunt their wealth in ostentatious house-building, plus their proud and arrogant manner, often led to Muslim retaliations -- sacking, looting, even murder. In spite of the fact that both groups were seen as outsiders, some think the Jews got along better with the Muslims than did the Christians (Kayyali 1978:16). However, in the area known as Palestine, the special status accorded Christians allowed the development of sociocultural patterns that in the long run gave them certain advantages over local Jews, as well as over other Palestinians who worshipped at the "establishment" mosques. As is so often the case for foreign minority groups, they had an advantage in money-lending and trading, and eventually throughout the area much of the commerce was in their hands. The frequent outbreaks against the Christians caused them to seek support from Europeans from whom they learned western political techniques (Migdal 1980:219). Indeed, from the time of the crusades many Christians aligned themselves with the European merchants who largely financed and participated in those expeditions (Epp 1970:94). When Egypt took over Sinai, Palestine, Lebanon and Syria between 1839-41, the British supported the Turkish Ottomans. This established what became a sustained European influence in the area -- one that consistently favored Christians over the other confessional groups (Blumberg 1980:19). Finally, new laws allowing land ownership by non-Turks in the Ottoman Empire were passed in 1858 and 1867. Under these, the commercial bourgeoisie, consisting primarily of local Christians and Jews, as well as Europeans, were able to acquire large plots of land as a result of peasant indebtedness (Scholch 1982:22). Thus, Christians managed to consolidate a favorable position as educated, worldly, propertied persons, in spite of their second-class civil and religious status.

For all these reasons, they were also increasingly city-dwellers, where, according to all records, they "set the tone" by the end of the nineteenth century. Their schools were better than those of the Muslims, largely due to Christian European assistance; although they were not permitted by the Ottomans to establish mission churches, they did build schools and hospitals. Most Christian children learned either French or English or both as part of their general education. By the time of the Palestine Mandate, when England ruled over the area (1918-1948), the Christians were widely considered to be more "western" than other Palestinians in general, due not only to their religious preference, but also to linguistic and dress patterns, which by then clearly distinguished them from Muslims. Notably, for example, Christian Palestinian women wore no veils and many dressed in the latest Paris fashions or locally-produced copies thereof.[4]

In 1948, when partition of the area occurred by vote of the United Nations in order to create Israel, Christians made up 22% of the Arab population, four fifths of whom were urban dwellers (Tshimoni 1981:18-19, 23). In defiance of the close UN vote, violent conflict broke out, and at the end of the so-called 1948 War of Israeli Independence, the Palestine Arab population in the cities had been decimated (Tsimhoni 1976:20).

Christian infant mortality and crude birth rates were significantly lower than those of Muslims and Druzes in 1978 (Tsimhoni 1976:176), a pattern which probably began some time earlier due to the European assistance mentioned above. During the British Mandate and occupation (1920-1948), Christian infant mortality dropped by 51% (Peretz 1958:54). Thus, both the numbers and percentage of Christians in Israel and on the West Bank have been decreasing for some time. In 1920 there were 78,000 Christians, mostly town dwellers, in Palestine (Rosenfeld 1978:375); by 1931 this figure had diminished to between 40 and 50 thousand (Runciman 1968:16). I have not seen estimates of figures for today, but by all the evidence, there are no more than half that number.

What happened to the once Christian majority over time, since they seem to have prospered and might have been expected to increase in numbers? Migration seems to have been the primary mechanism by which the demographic balance was altered, although some, of course, were forcibly converted to Islam, most notably under the Mamelukes of Egypt in the thirteenth century, when whole villages were put to the sword if they refused the new religion. The percentage of Christians declined precipitously with the immigration of Muslim Arabs during the Ottoman period, and of Jews during the nineteenth and twentieth centuries. But it was over the past century that the Christians also began to emigrate. A church record in Bethlehem indicates that a local son died somewhere in South America in 1797 -- the earliest indication of emigration to the New World from that town.[5] Unfortunately, such entries provide only peepholes on reality, and actual numbers and patterns of behavior may forever remain inscrutable. Yet, according to Scholch (1982:39) at least from the 1870s, and very likely before, enterprising merchants from Bethlehem undertook long commercial trips to Europe and America to sell the products of their town and to find imports to retail on their return.

Although emigration of Lebanese, Syrians and Palestinians from the Ottoman Empire to the Americas has been documented as early as the 1870s (Naff 1983, Migdal 1980:59) it is not until the turn of the century that we find evidence of a trickle of Palestinians arriving in Honduras. By 1914, when Palestinian youths were being recruited by the Turks to fight on behalf of Germany and the Ottoman Empire in World War I, the trickle became a stream, as young men fled the draft.

Even though the British Mandate period was not particularly onerous for Palestinian Christians, the general poverty in the area following World War I was generally disheartening. Mogannam (1937:222) documented the fact that in the 1930s there was a serious problem of unemployment among Arabs. He noted, "The increased use of cement, reinforced concrete and silicate bricks, all manufactured by Jews, is replacing dressed stone for constructional purposes, and so displacing a large number of stone dressers and stone-masons, nearly all of whom are Arabs. The Arab quarrymen are also being displaced."

It appears that most of the earliest emigrants of that time left in order to bolster family incomes, firmly believing they would one day return to reside in Palestine. But soon the handwriting on the wall in regard to Zionism became clearer, and more and more of those who left elected to stay abroad. Since 1948 the ranks of emigrants have swelled with each succeeding crisis. Activists have been forced to leave by the Israeli authorities; sixty-two men were reported as having been deported from Bethlehem between 1967 and 1978 (Lesch 1979:103). Most who leave now do so because they can no longer tolerate the daily humiliations of living under Israeli domination. They tend to go where they already have established relatives, so as the earlier arrivals become successful, this stimulates further immigration to those locations. Indeed, in Honduras businessmen still sometimes send for young cousins, nieces, nephews -- mainly to work as underpaid administrators in the shops and factories. But leaving Israel or the occupied West Bank today is risky. Those who own property of any sort, including residences, are likely to have them confiscated, even if their intent is to stay abroad only for a few months. Still, the exiled Palestinians I have encountered in Honduras, even fairly recent arrivals, are not by any means poverty stricken by local standards. Almost no Christians are in the Palestinian refugee camps of Jordan and Lebanon, although many are to be found in business in Amman and Beirut (Peretz 1958:71) Egypt also became home to thousands of these Christians, and many others are in France, England or other European countries (Hadowi 1967:177). Their condition varies, but is generally better than that of their Muslim compatriots.

The Honduran Experience

Many informants say that the first immigrants often had no idea where they were headed, and many were appalled by the primitiveness of the Honduran north coast, which presented standards of living far below what most were used to in their homeland, regardless of their social status.[6] Men who arrived single soon returned home to seek, or sent for Palestinian brides, although some cohabited with local Honduran women, and a very few married the latter. Many began as itinerant merchants, selling whatever wares they could in the countryside, often reaching their inland clients by canoe on the rivers, but also by railroad, which in Honduras gave good service on the coastal plain where the fruit industry had become well-established by 1900.

The early banana and tobacco trade in Honduras stimulated general commerce, and the Palestinian immigrants located themselves strategically in places where growers brought their fruit or tobacco for sale to the companies that engaged in export. Unlike some of their compatriots who went to Jamaica in the 1890s (Ammar 1970:4), they themselves did not grow or purchase bananas, but in the mountainous reaches of Santa Rosa, they sometimes acted as middlemen in the purchase and sale of tobacco.[7]

Through frugal living and judicious business practices, many of these itinerant merchants prospered enough to settle down after a year or two in a small town or village where they set up a general store. With continued success, they often moved to a larger town such as El Progreso (today, 100,000) or San Pedro Sula (today, 350,000). Frequently they brought over a younger brother or cousin and set him up in a neighboring town, often having him work only for his keep until the young man finally rebelled and started out on his own. The phenomenal success enjoyed by some of these early immigrants caused many Hondurans to believe that they had made pacts with the devil -- they simply could not believe that the Arabs had been able to manage so well in a foreign environment.[8]

Of course, individuals differed, and not everyone became an instant millionaire, as Honduran mythology would have it. Some struggled on alone, never married, and died in obscurity, their illegitimate children by Honduran women not even perpetuating their names. Others gave up and returned to Palestine. Still others moved on to South America -- especially to Chile or Colombia -- or to Mexico, Monterrey being a favorite destination. But for every one who left, several others arrived. Because marriage ages for women were very low at the turn of the century (13-15 years), the population grew rapidly through natural increase as well. Accurate figures are impossible to obtain for the period, but mortality appears to have been relatively low. Although they were as susceptible to yellow fever as other non-blacks, as Mediterraneans, they may have had some genetic resistance to malaria.[9] In addition, their relative affluence and native dietary patterns probably resulted in their being better nourished than many other Hondurans, which helped them resist infectious diseases.

Upon arrival, they spoke Arabic and often either French or English, but no Spanish. The former languages, especially English, were in considerable use on the north coast of Honduras at that time, giving them a distinct advantage over other merchants. The United Fruit Company imported workers from the English-speaking Caribbean islands in the early 1900s to work on the docks and plantations, while many of the white collar and professional workers were from the United States. The eighteenth century hegemony of England along the coast from Nicaragua to Belize had also left its linguistic stamp among the native Hondurans.

The existence of a non-peasant, laboring population with cash to spend made this part of the Central American coastline extremely attractive to small merchants -- especially to those whose own traditions and internal social organization gave them a competitive advantage over natives of the area. Their stocks were brought in largely from the United States, and consisted of yard goods, buttons and bows, needles and thread, dishes, pots and pans, medicines, foodstuffs, and general hardware. Itinerant Palestinian merchants were able to buy on credit from their compatriots' stores. They also could take orders in the countryside and buy only what they were sure would sell. In turn, the small store owners could buy on credit from the larger wholesalers and importers, who were often their relatives. The latter, in turn, early established their credit in the United States, in both banks and with suppliers.

But at the same time, they were careful never to fall too far into debt. It was a passion among them to save money, often living so frugally as to earn the contempt of non-Arab Hondurans. They gained a reputation for being skin-flints. A still current joke tells of the Palestinian who was drowning in the sea off one of the docks. A Garifuna boy called out that he would save him for five *lempiras*. The Palestinian called back, "How about three"? A similar, but more vicious sentiment is expressed in the apocryphal story about the Palestinian who forced his family members to sleep on the counters in the store, each night using different bedding from stock that they would later sell, thus also avoiding the necessity to do laundry. But in spite of such allegations, today some of the most modern, well-stocked department stores in the country are owned and managed by Palestinians.

From buying and selling they turned in two directions -- importing and manufacturing. Platt (1972:179) notes that, "Almost daily steamer communication was maintained with New Orleans and Mobile in connection with the banana trade (in Honduras) and by the middle of the decade 1900-1910 the United States had gained a near monopoly of the Honduran market for imported dry goods, principally cheap grey and white shirting, prints, printed ducks and drills, and hosiery." The primary importers on the north coast of Honduras at that time were Palestinians, and some very early began to make trousers and shirts of imported goods for local sale. Today the ready-made clothing industry is highly advanced in San Pedro Sula, where items ranging from women's lingerie to men's work shirts and blue jeans are made in large factories for local sale and export, often under franchise by well-known American companies. Much of the cotton cloth used for the local market is also manufactured from Honduran cotton by Palestinian entrepreneurs.

The last twenty years have seen a proliferation of Palestinian businesses and industries in San Pedro Sula. In addition to textiles and clothing, these immigrants and their descendants dominate the hardware and furniture industries of the country. A generation ago one of the most venerable of the older immigrants opened what was touted by the Chamber of Commerce at the time as the most modern car dealership in all of Central America, selling Fords. Plastics, paints, drugs and chemicals, liquor and alcohol, and cosmetics are among the items made in local Arab factories. In the professions, pharmacy was an early favorite, but today there are many architects and engineers, and a good sprinkling of physicians. So far law has not attracted them; nor are they numerous in the scholarly world. In the 1950s many reorganized, abandoning the family-owned company in favor of corporations of share-holders; increasingly for some of the wealthier these were in collaboration with non-Arabs -- both Honduran and foreign, often Jews. Some obtained large governmental or international loans during the borrowing heyday of the 1970s -- a few nearly going bankrupt as a result of their over-extension. As I shall demonstrate in greater detail elsewhere, the average amount of reported capital invested by Palestinian business people in San Pedro Sula is significantly larger than that for non-Palestinians.

On the other hand, the majority of Arab businesses in San Pedro Sula today are still small, owned and managed by the same person, often with only family members as help. Newcomers with only small amounts of capital tend to start small "mom and pop" stores, and recently, bakeries. The demand for *pita* bread, as well as the French baguette and other European bread forms is strong both within and outside of the Arab community. From the earliest immigration, wives worked in the stores, often managing them entirely alone while their husbands were on the road. Today it is not uncommon for the wife to own and manage her own business in addition to whatever her husband is doing. Frequently they have small boutiques where they sell women's and/or children's clothing, bridal outfits, gifts, perfumes and cosmetics, and the like. Several women run catering businesses out of their homes, specializing in Arab foods, now eaten by everyone on occasion. Some Hondurans are unaware of the fact that *marmahon*, a special pasta-like wheat dish, is not of Spanish origin. Grape leaves are sold in the regular market, and most super-markets, three of the largest of which are Arab-owned, have special sections with Arab foods -- some imported from the Middle East or the United States, others locally manufactured.

Palestinian Identity in Honduras

How does one know when one is dealing with a Palestinian? First of all, by the surname, which is still recognizably Arabic. I was able to uncover only two instances in which a surname had been changed to make it more pronounceable or perhaps to try to assimilate more quickly to Honduran society. First names are also very commonly Arabic, the individual sometimes also being known by the Spanish translation -- as in the case of Hanna (Juan), or Khalil (Carlos).

Secondly, the Palestinians nearly always self-identify as Arabs, Palestinians, or even on occasion as *Turcos*. It should be noted that Palestinians, Lebanese, Syrians, and even Jews are collectively known as *Turcos* throughout the Central and South American countries. Informants explain this today by the standard myth that they all arrived with Turkish passports. Certainly it is the case that the first immigrants arrived during the time of the Ottoman Empire, and some of them may even have carried passports. However, before 1896-97 the Ottoman Empire forbade emigration, and even after that time, when passports were easy to obtain, many left without them to avoid paying the fees or to avoid the trouble of getting the proper documents together (Karpat 1985:188-89). But in addition, most of the stories given me indicate that the people were fleeing from the Turks, some leaving in disguise, or otherwise smuggled onto ships, and one wonders whether they had papers of any kind. Most went to some other country before arriving in Honduras, often securing a passport there so as to pass for something other than a Middle Easterner, since the latter were sometimes excluded as being "undesirable" immigrants. In Guatemala the 1909 immigration law specifically rejected Asians, although in Honduras in 1906 it did not. After 1917, of course, there was no longer any question of Turkish citizenship, and most of the immigrants actually arrived after that time. Between 1948-1967 people from Bethlehem traveled on Jordanian passports. Since the Israeli occupation of the West Bank, they have had no passports at all, only identification papers and Israeli permissions to travel.

The term *Turco* is generally considered a pejorative today, although it is sometimes used affectionately both by members of the in-group and by outsiders of *confianza*. Also, in the countryside and among the less sophisticated urbanites the more polite form, *Arabe*, is likely not to be understood at all, and *Turco* is simply the customary usage. *Palestino* is less commonly heard, although some of the more fanatically "ethnic" say now that they prefer it to *Arabe*. It is my opinion that the term *Turco* was without any particular affect when it first came into usage, probably indeed because Palestine as such did not exist at the turn of the century. It may even be that the first immigrants did not strongly object to the usage, in spite of their own clear sense that they were not really Turkish. After all, they had been nearly 400 years under Turkish rule by that time. Yet, they never reported themselves as Turks to church authorities, using "Palestinian" instead.[10]

Only as the Palestinian group became numerous and their success apparent did the Hondurans become nervous and resentful of them. Then the Turkish jokes and slurs began, and the term *Turco* rejected by them in an effort to cast off the identification, the reputation and the imputed ethnicity, along with the term itself. Non-Arab Honduran informants suggest this began in the 1930s or 1940s. Arab informants claimed not to be able to remember, although they agreed that they were better accepted in the early days.

The desire for status within the Honduran community was not intense during the first generation's sojourn. Bethlehem, Beit Jala or Beit Sahur remained their primary reference point. Trips were made to visit kin, purchase and/or tend property, obtain wives, marry, baptize, and generally reconfirm their Palestinian Christian identity. Since many of the immigrants were Greek Orthodox, they never felt comfortable with the local Roman Catholic services. However, in 1963 did they finally establish an Orthodox Church in San Pedro Sula. Catholic baptismal records are, therefore, spotty, but marriage records, which must indicate the couples' baptisms, show that a large number of people had been taken "home" to Palestine for this ritual, even when born in Honduras Marriages were often performed both in Honduras and again in Bethlehem -- the first for the sake of legality and local reputation; the second for nostalgia, for their significant others in Palestine, and for what they believed to be the good of their souls.[11] One 40 year old woman born in Beit Jala said she really doubted that marriage ceremonies performed in Honduras before the existence of the Orthodox Church were valid. Many of my elderly informants who arrived here in their teens say that they have never really accepted Honduras, that they would go back in a minute if it were not for the present violence and impossible political situation occasioned by the Partition and subsequent events.

There is also a sizeable group of Palestinian-Hondurans, born in Central America, who are annoyed by the whole idea of being classified as Arabs. These people tend to be Roman Catholic (many were already of that religion, and others converted because it seemed more convenient), they live in Honduran style, their children have often intermarried with Honduran families, they know no Arabic, and some have never visited the homeland from which their parents or grandparents came. Ironically, most of these are still obviously of Arab origin in the eyes of most Hondurans -- in part because of their surnames, but even more so by their ostentatious life style, a complete reversal of their parents' custom. In one sense, they have tried to outdo the Hondurans themselves -- perhaps in order to overcome the jokes about sleeping on the store counters. They build enormous, palatial houses in eclectic styles of their own design, and often have beachside or mountain retreats of comparable luxury. They drive late-model luxury cars, make frequent trips to Miami, New Orleans, Houston, or New York to buy clothes, jewelry, furniture, and especially to have medical checkups. Some own and maintain apartments in these northern cities.

A frequent charge against the *Turco* was that he was uninterested in the problems and development of Honduras, and that he would not contribute to worthy local causes. The new elites, struggling to become accepted, have adopted many strategies to overcome this reputation. They are strongly behind the Chamber of Commerce, as well as the Lions, Rotary and other similar community-action groups. The women adopt charities to help orphans, the mentally retarded, children of poor working mothers, and the like. They contribute to their own, as well as other local churches. Finally, although few have actually run for political office, they have found it expedient to assist various candidates in their campaigns, frequently giving the same amount (clandestinely) to each possible winner so as to ensure having an open door, regardless of who wins.

But in spite of it all, they are still looked upon askance by many who consider themselves to be of "purer" Honduran descent. When Arab capital and management became influential in one of the more prominent local banks, a new bank was formed that advertised itself as being "by Hondurans, for Hondurans."

A non-Arab informant told me that this was understood by many Hondurans to mean that one could be safe from prying Arab eyes by doing business there.

At the same time, the wealth that they have accumulated is attractive to Hondurans, many of whom now seek to marry off their daughters or sons into the Arab community. But even when such unions occur, Hondurans retain a sense of distaste. One non-Arab female informant said that a frequent introduction to malicious anti-Arab gossip was, "I shouldn't be saying this, since we now have *Turcos* in the family, but...". A prominent Palestinian business-man from Tegucigalpa once complained to me that he had sent all of his children to the United States for advanced degrees in various fields, yet none of them, in spite of their education and wealth, were "really" accepted by the Honduran elites. He was confounded and saddened by this observation, totally unable to explain the situation.

Yet, largely unobserved and misunderstood by this element, is the larger and less affluent Palestinian population of Honduras, which still identifies itself as Arab, speaks Arabic at home, attends the convivial masses and social events at the Orthodox Church (still the only one in all of Central America), lives well but not ostentatiously, yearns for the Bethlehem area, follows the news about current events on the West Bank, and hates Jews with a vehement passion. Almost without exception, these are Palestinians who were born or educated in the old country. Some came as families or couples, but many of them are Palestinian women who married Honduran-Palestinian men. In spite of the fact that this remains a highly patriarchal community, the presence of a Palestinian wife today puts a man in a somewhat different position than formerly. She is likely to be sought after and will become active in the local Orthodox Church, whose songs and prayers are still largely chanted in Arabic, and whose salon has become the primary social center for this faction. She will also be worried about her immediate family, left behind in the war-torn West Bank. She may wish to bring her parents or other relatives to Honduras. Before February, 1988, there were frequent phone calls, letters, and even visits between Hondurans and their relatives in the Bethlehem area. During my fieldwork this ceased, as communications were cut off by the Israelis in retaliation for the *intifadeh*, or rebellion that began in December, 1987.

A committee was formed during my fieldwork to raise money for the Palestinian victims of the violence on the West Bank. According to an informant on the executive board, it was difficult to find people who would donate large sums to this cause. Those who wanted to, didn't have the capital; those who had the money, had other things in which they were more interested. Nevertheless, this committee used some of its collection to pay for an Orthodox mass in honor of the assassinated Muslim PLO leader, Abu Jihad, in April, 1988. The mass was attended by about 100 people, most from the so-called "fanatic" group of Honduran-Palestinians who brook no compromise with Israel, but follow the hard-line of "the only good Israeli is a dead Israeli; let's push them all into the sea."

What else does the community in Honduras actually *do* in support of the Palestinians on the West Bank? They send money to their own relatives and harbor them if they become refugees. It is said that some influential Arab-

Hondurans secured false passports for the use of PLO terrorists who were later caught in a hijacking in Europe a few years ago. Some of the most fanatic talk as though they would support any Palestinian terrorist activity, but most are more moderate. Indeed, this group is basically conservative in its local politics.

Discussion

The only way I have found to make sense of these apparently confusing and contradictory data is to combine what we know of migration in general, with an historical analysis of the specific situation in the context of the Middle Eastern conflict. The earliest migrants to Honduras seem to have been temporary. As Hamilton (1985:409) has said, temporary migrants do not necessarily view their home society negatively, in comparison to their proposed destinations. Numerous cases suggest that temporary migrants so highly value their home societies that they are willing to work elsewhere for a while in order to increase the meaningfulness of their participation in the home society at a later time. Given this orientation, temporary migrants attempt to preserve their established relations with those at home and only reluctantly build long-lasting relations with the inhabitants of the host society.

The concept of network as used in migration theory is also important in understanding what happened in Honduras. Hamilton again suggests that temporary migration networks start slowly, as the result of the efforts of a few individuals, and build gradually to encompass large numbers of people. Small migrant businessmen all over the world typically have recruited relatives and countrymen as described above; in addition, the continual flow of return migrants provides first hand information which stimulates and facilitates the migration of others. All of this has been true for the Palestinian immigrants to Honduras.

Under certain conditions, however, temporary migration may become what I have called permanent removal (Gonzalez 1961), and what Hamilton calls permanent residence. He points out that the reasons for their decisions to stay are varied; some fail in their plans and are ashamed to return. Some marry local residents, while others come to like the new society better than the old one.

> Whatever the reasons, temporary-turned-permanent residents may continue to support the temporary migrant sequence, by continuing to work, live, and associate within the ethnic enclave and by supporting the patterns established there. Therefore, what began as a sojourner community now continues as an ethnic minority, fueled by new arrivals and stabilized by permanent residents. This is institutionalized temporary migration (Hamilton 1985:417).

How does it all add up in the case of Honduras? My sense is that for all of the reasons mentioned by Hamilton, many of the earliest temporary migrants had become permanent residents, or their children had made such decisions, even before 1948. And for some time after that they continued to support the classic temporary migrant patterns just described. As each new crisis occurred, they became increasingly nervous, especially since the Palestinian cause was not generally supported by Latin Americans (Sharif 1977:122).

The establishment of Israel and the ensuing conflict situation in their homeland has left the Christian Palestinians in a most peculiar position. Unlike the Muslims, they cannot consider their fight with the Jews as a Holy War. Although there is still a feeling that they should hate the Jews for having killed Christ, their very religion teaches forgiveness. Furthermore, in the diaspora they found that they had a good deal in common with immigrant Jews who were also engaged in commerce and industry. But more and more they have come to hate Jews -- both the Israelis and those in the diaspora whom they believe uniformly support the Zionist cause -- for having usurped their land and for having changed the face of what they remember as their ancient cultural domain. A few have lost loved ones, more have lost property, and all have lost their anchor to history and their ethnic identity. It is difficult for them to forget this, and many Hondurans, both Arabs and Jews, told me they had the sense that relations between the two groups were not as friendly as they had been. One Jew told me that he sometimes feared for his life -- even among people he had known all his life.

In Honduras the Palestinians have found a land in which they are able to survive and even prosper financially, but wherein they are scorned and excluded from mainstream society. So long as they considered themselves temporary residents with a homeland to visit and return to, they could tell themselves that they weren't, and didn't really want to be Honduran anyway. But even before the present crisis, that outlook was not meaningful for many of those in the second and third generations, who, even when of pure Palestinian ancestry, still yearn to be Honduran. Undoubtedly the ostentation in residential and dress patterns, which takes considerable wealth to support, is a reflection of their recognition that they are not going to return, and of their hope to impress Hondurans with their worth as fellow citizens.

In a sense, however, they wish to have their cake and eat it too. They are not yet quite willing to follow the road of those who intermarried with Hondurans in previous generations. Many of the latter, even though they still bear Arab surnames, have found their niche in Honduran society, but at the cost of their Arab heritage. One woman told me that the only thing Arab about her was her father's name. She had been raised by a Honduran mother, who she thought had modified her father's extreme patriarchal temperament as well. She recalled having been teased as a "*Turka*" when in grade school, but others suffered similar insults for having protruding teeth or a lisp. In the past, and among many families even today, Palestinian parents try hard to prevent exogamous marriages. Nevertheless, some of the more acculturated are happy to have their children marry Hondurans -- particularly when they choose mates from prestigious families. Many recent business partnerships reflect these new marital arrangements.

But recent immigrants, those who have come since 1948, seem to exhibit somewhat different patterns than those described by Hamilton and others. They would like to be temporary, but many of them realize that their chances of returning to a decent life in Bethlehem are very slim. Many sought Honduran citizenship almost immediately after arrival, since otherwise they had no prospect at all, and they have invested heavily in their homes and their children's education, as well as in their businesses -- small though they may be. But at the same time they, more than those above, have retained their language, religion, and Palestinian identity. I believe that for them the happiest solution (aside from an expulsion of the Jews from Palestine) would be to establish a tiny bit of Palestine in Honduras -- in other words, to create an ethnic enclave in which they can maintain a life not unlike what they left, but without the constant threats to their values, life, property, and dignity that they suffered at home. This group seems nearly oblivious to the slights and low esteem of the Hondurans toward them. Rather, they are socially self-sufficient, meeting Hondurans only in the market-place. Their more acculturated fellows of long-standing residence seem embarrassed by this group, while at the same time feeling a certain amount of sympathy and pity for them.

In conclusion, Palestinian migration to Honduras can be seen to have been originally stimulated by a desire to escape the Ottoman Empire and its resultant political and economic hardships, including the threat of being drafted to fight on behalf of Turkey and Germany in World War I. Since 1948 it has been maintained by the protracted conflict between Israel and the Arabs of the Middle East. The choice of America as a destination was in part determined by ethnic factors, including, but not limited to religion. The American republics, like many other parts of the world, had been visited by Palestinian merchants for at least 100 years. Stories about opportunities there certainly found their way back home, and in the case of Honduras, it cannot have been totally by chance that the Arab migration coincided with the rise of the large fruit companies. Indeed, they may have learned about the banana boom in Honduras from Palestinians who had settled in Jamaica and elsewhere in the Caribbean a short time before.

The ethnicity of the Christian Palestinians in their homeland had clearly already diverged from that of others of their countrymen before the major migratory stream began during the last quarter of the nineteenth century (Rosenfeld 1978:375-76). The facts that they were already Europeanized to a great extent; shared many of the values of the receiving Latin American societies; were, on the whole, as well educated as their hosts with whom they shared many phenotypic traits; and fulfilled a niche in Honduran society not previously exploited by other groups, should have led to their rapid acceptance there. Indeed, at first they seem to have been accepted as a bit strange, but nevertheless friendly and useful neighbors.

However, the Palestinian custom of bringing wives from their homeland, baptizing their children elsewhere, living too frugally at first and later too ostentatiously, and finally, their continuing and to many, inexplicable economic success, eventually led to the development of a prejudice and a set of myths about them that have proven difficult to dispel. All of these behavior patterns might be expected of temporary migrants planning to return to their homelands, but to the Hondurans they spelled arrogance. Indeed, as we might expect of temporary migrants, many of them felt they were coming to a backward, primitive society. Yet the members of that society saw the newcomers as being little different in this regard from themselves -- perhaps even inferior, since they ate strange foods, lived in apparent poverty, spoke a peculiar language, and tended to marry women Hondurans would have considered kin.[12]

Nevertheless, time would probably have healed the rift between the Palestinian immigrants and the Hondurans when the former became permanent residents had it not been for the continuing conflict in the holy land. News of the latter has served as a constant reminder to the migrants of their origins and at the same time it has perpetuated the migration. The resulting continual presence of unacculturated newcomers has underlined the foreign origin of the Arab population to both Hondurans and the Palestinians themselves. Some of the more recent arrivals who might once have assimilated now do not even think of doing so, perhaps out of a sense of guilt for having escaped the hardships and violence to which many of their cousins are still being subjected. Assimilation might be construed as disloyalty.

For the second and third generations, many on the verge of assimilation, the situation is nearly intolerable as well, but for different reasons. This group is ambivalent about the events on the West Bank, even though their fanatic compatriots expect them to be sympathetic. They feel little loyalty to the primarily Muslim Palestinian masses. Again, the question of ethnicity becomes salient. The new Palestinian national consciousness -- now manifest in Israel, on the West Bank, and in the diaspora -- tends to override some of the most important symbols that formerly ordered their society. Religion, with its accompanying behavior patterns, as well as the social organizational elements it implies, remains a significant variable, no matter how ecumenical the people are encouraged to be by those more interested in current politics. Honduran Christian Palestinians have found a home among other Christians. For the most part, they know they are in Honduras to stay, yet they are unable either to turn their backs on the land of their ancestors or to assist in the ongoing struggle there in any meaningful way.

I fear that the immediate future will lead to increased prejudice, perhaps even some open conflict, as the more vocal Palestinians continue to press their views on their homeland, and as their anti-Jewish attitudes and pronouncements become more virulent. The tendency of many to isolate themselves as an ethnic enclave creates more hostility at the same time that it enhances their own sense of well-being.[13] Toward the end of my stay a prominent non-Arab business man voiced the opinion that by clustering together, flaunting their wealth and their foreignness, the Honduran Arabs were inviting hostility. Some have already been the victims of criminal activity underscored by latent revolutionary sentiments among the disadvantaged Honduran masses. If more violence occurs, more of them may yet end up in Miami, New Orleans, or Houston. At least there they are more likely to be perceived as Hondurans -- a somewhat larger group but still a minority among the U.S. Latin American population that itself is largely a product of conflict migration.

NOTES

1. My interest in Central American Arabs began many years ago as a sideline to my work on the north coast of Guatemala and Honduras with Garifuna (see Gonzalez 1988). I began archival research on Palestinians in 1986 and made two exploratory, or pilot trips to Honduras in 1986 and 1987 before undertaking intensive fieldwork in January of 1988 in San Pedro Sula, Honduras. A Fulbright nomination to Bethlehem on the West Bank was canceled in May, 1988 due to the continuing hostilities in the region, but I was instead appointed to Jordan for 1988-89. This essay is being written from the field.

2. There is an organization called the Bethlehem Association in the United States that counts more than a thousand members as of this writing. Their newsletter includes information about people in the diaspora, which helps emigrants keep track of each other, but also provides historical notes and discussions concerning the present situation on the West Bank.

3. At the Vienna World Exhibition of 1873 the Ottoman Empire exhibited rosaries of olivewood, mother-of-pearl and glass from Jerusalem, Bethlehem and Hebron, as well as models of the holy city and other holy places (Scholch 1982:10).

4. See photographs of Muslim and Christian Palestinian women in Khalidi 1984:167, see also Al-Hout 1979, Lesch 1979).

5. Personal communication, Dr. Adnan Musallam, Bethlehem University.

6. In future publications I will describe this more fully. Not all were affluent, and it is apparent from the Honduran data that Bethlehemites outranked those from Beit Jala, who in turn felt themselves superior to those from Beit Sahur. The size of the community in question seems to have been a major determinant. In addition, however, family wealth, education, and kinship criteria (i.e., clan or *hamula* membership) all played a role.

7. Bananas were an unknown product and one that was easily perishable. It is significant that tobacco had been an important crop for some time in Palestine, so they must have felt more at ease with it (Zureik 1976:64). There is little remembrance today of their ancestors having dealt in tobacco, yet many of the earlier immigrants settled in El Salvador and along the Salvadoran-Honduran mountainous border. Cash for purchases of goods there would have been forthcoming primarily from sales of tobacco.

8. At various later times it was said (a) that they made their money by dealing in contraband, (b) that they burned their stores to collect the insurance, (c) that they take part in the international drug traffic. The specific mischief of which they are suspected is itself always a reflection of the times.

9. Their hemoglobinopathies are, unfortunately, totally unstudied.

10. This tends to contradict the view held by writers such as Garfinkle (1984:10) and espoused in this book by Rubenberg, that in the early years of this century the Arabs of Palestine did not think of themselves as Palestinians.

11. Marriages of Palestinians performed abroad were not automatically accepted under the laws of the Ottoman Empire or the British Mandate.

12. Later publications will outline the kinship system in some detail. As has frequently been noted in anthropological writings on the Middle East,

marriage with the father's brother's daughter was often preferred. This might be a first, second or third cousin, but she would most likely have the same surname as her husband. Hondurans found this custom incestuous and "primitive."

13. The Palestinian-Hondurans who have accepted permanent residency have largely built their new and luxurious houses in the same sections of town. Perhaps as a reaction to their parents' tendency to live above their stores in the business section, the succeeding generations established themselves in the "suburbs." One of these, perhaps the most desirable location in San Pedro Sula, is physically separated from the rest of the community by a bridge and it is said that perhaps 95% of its residences belong to Palestinians.

7

REFUGEES IN BELIZE:
A CAULDRON OF ETHNIC TENSIONS

Carolyn S. McCommon

Since the late 1970s, the stream of refugees and economic immigrants into Belize from Central America has had a profound impact on the country's political, social, and economic infrastructure. Although Belize has received international financial and technical assistance for their provision, the refugee presence has placed a burden on the fragile Belizean economy. The country is newly independent and struggling with its own identity as a state. As such, it is ill-pressed to meet the priorities of its own population, much less those of non-residents.

More significantly, Belize is a complex, multi-racial society with a delicate ethnic and racial balance. Historically, these relations have been good, but the rapid influx of Central Americans has accelerated the growth in the Mestizo population segment and threatened the traditional Creole domination.

The coincidence of the influx with the end of the colonial period and independence in 1982 also heightened debates concerning the definition of national identity. Traditionally the country's focus has been more Caribbean than Latin as a result of its colonial heritage. With waning British influence and increasing numbers of Creoles emigrating to the United States, many Belizeans saw this refugee influx as a force of 'latinization' which threatened to draw the country into the Central American sphere.

One approach to the refugee problem was the creation of a government liaison refugee office under the auspices of the United Nations High Commissioner for Refugees (UNHCR). The rising controversy over the refugee immigrant presence as well as the UNHCR's role has in a sense been a microcosm of the evolving and at times conflicting perceptions of Belizean national interest. This is reflected in a radical shift in immigration policy from the traditional open-door policy to a restrictive quota system.

This chapter describes and analyzes the impact of this conflict migration on Belizean society in relation to the changing dynamics of ethnicity. Following an overview on the historical dimensions underlying the ethnic diversity and dichotomy, the paper focuses on the refugee influx and the political and social reactions to this impact. The conclusion suggests that the impact of refugees not only intensified latent racial and ethnic conflict but has itself been intensified by this underlying dichotomy of Belizean society.

History, Immigration, and Ethnicity

"The blood of a true Belizean would have to include a substantial portion of African, Maya, and European blood. Also must be included would be a pint or two of Garifuna blood. Throw in a small portion of East Indian blood and mix it up. Surely, that's about as Belizean as it could get" (GIS 1987a:1)[1]

Belize is a small, sparsely populated nation of 165,000 occupying an area of 23,000 square kilometers. While its location places it in Central America, the country has experienced a different trajectory of social and economic development from those of its neighboring countries. As the former colony of British Honduras, it is distinguished by its small size, predominantly English speaking population, and pluralistic social structure. Among the distinct ethnic groups are Creole, Mestizo, Maya Indian, Garifuna, East Indian, Chinese, Mennonite, European, and Lebanese.[2] Ethnicity is at the same time reflected by a dichotomy between Caribbean and Latin American aspects which cross-cut and overlap ethnic distinctions. This can be broadly identified in terms of two complexes - an English-Creole speaking group of British and African descent, including Creole and Garifuna, and a Spanish-speaking group of Hispanic-Indian descent.[3]

The historical importance of migration in shaping this identity underscores the current concern over recent influxes of Central Americans. Immigration has been a central feature of Belizean society, providing the origins of the population, and through continued population flows, its ever-evolving identity. Central to this has been the colonial experience which not only fostered immigration as a tool to meet population needs but has also alternately blurred and reinforced ethnic distinctions.[4]

For over 300 years, Belize was a colonial enclave - a country whose economy was run primarily to produce wealth for Britain through the export of lumber (cf.Bolland 1986:69). The growth of this industry saw the evolution of Belize as a mono-economy, dependent on export crops and imported labor. The interplay of migration and chronic underpopulation in this development began with the coming of the first British adventurers in the early 17th century. These men were not interested in agriculture but in the extraction of timber and other forest products for sale in Europe. To the extent that they interacted with the local population, relations were far from cordial and sometimes hostile. They were completely unsuccessful in organizing or managing the Maya as a local work force and were forced to import African slave labor in their operations.

Through these and subsequent immigration schemes arose the present-day cultural diversity. The majority Creole element are descendants of African freedman and slaves imported from the West Indies during the 17th, 18th and 19th centuries and British loggers and merchants. Following abolition of the slave trade in 1838 and the emigration of over one-third the ex-slave population into Guatemala, other immigration schemes were promoted. These included the importation of indentured Chinese and East Indians during the late 19th century as well as less successful attempts to attract ex-Confederate soldiers from the United States.

At the same time, immigration has been a complex issue fraught with contradictions, particularly in regard to immigration from Mexico and Central America. While British loggers and merchants were successful in securing Great Britain's hegemony over the territory, disputes with Spain over the contested territory influenced domestic issues and heightened sensitivities over regional politics and immigration into Belize.[5] However, because of its geographical location, then, as now, the settlement was not immune to regional conflicts. Refugees from the nearby Spanish-speaking countries frequently sought refuge in Belize and runaway Belizean slaves found a haven in Guatemala.

These influxes of Hispanic groups laid the basis for the cultural dichotomy between Latin and Caribbean segments today. The large inflow of Mestizo and Yucatec Maya refugees fleeing the Yucatec wars during the mid-18th century was the first significant stream. The influx caused the population to double, and, for a brief time, established the Creole majority as a minority (Dobson 1977). Other immigrants during the same period included the Garifuna, a distinct black population of both African and Carib Indian descent who entered early in the 19th century looking for work. These were followed by more Garifuna from Honduras in the mid-19th century fleeing a local civil war.[6] In addition, groups of Guatemalan Kekchi and Mopan Maya Indian immigrants also entered and settled in the more remote southern and western regions (cf. Wilk 1985).

Among these groups, the emergence of a Creole elite has its roots in the efforts of British settlers to reinforce their own position. Fears over uncontrolled immigration, particularly from the Yucatec peninsula, underscored concerns of local settlers. The presence of large numbers of Hispanics with questionable loyalties was viewed with suspicion given the continued territorial claims by Spain. The settler minority maintained domestic political control by playing on its ambiguous relationship with the Creoles and cross-cutting relations with other ethnic groups. Power was shared with an emerging Creole elite who increasingly identified their future with that of the British. Notwithstanding official sanctions and practices that favored Europeans and people of light complexion, the Creole majority parlayed their allegiance into positions of economic and social dominance over those of Spanish and Indian descent, who were at a disadvantage because of their suspect allegiance (Ashdown 1987; Grant 1976).

Through successive immigration, these groups have reached what is perceived to be an equilibrium and by some, appropriate balance, with the Creole in the majority followed closely by the Mestizos. According to the 1980 census Creoles represented the majority group with 39.7% of the population compared to the Mestizos with 33.1% (Nicolait et al. 1980). However, in recent years, steadily increasing emigration to the United States by the two groups of African descent - Creoles and Garifuna - along with increasing immigration of Central Americans in comparable numbers is narrowing the gap (cf. Everitt 1984).

The Salvadoran Influx: The Refugee Problem

Magnitude and Characteristics

For many years, Salvadorans, along with Guatemalans, Hondurans, and Mexicans, have migrated to Belize for seasonal farm employment. Many arrived with work permits, sponsored by Belizean employers. While Guatemalans from the nearby border towns often remained, most of the Central Americans returned to their country of origin after the harvest. Beginning in the late 1970s, however, this pattern shifted from temporary seasonal migrations to large-scale flights of families and individuals. As in the rest of Central America, repression and violence became the immediate cause (Torres Rivas 1985).

This Central American influx into Belize presented the nation with a complex and rapidly escalating problem. Most were Salvadoran peasant refugees-"desperate and destitute migrants" arriving with few possessions or even official documents (Philip 1984:375). Many were what is often referred to as "crossfire refugees", people caught between the violence of various warring factions and forced to leave their homes for haven elsewhere. They arrived in Belize after an overland journey of over 600 kilometers through Honduras and Guatemala with a few hiring small boats to smuggle them into the country. As illegal aliens, they avoided contact with official authorities and deliberately settled in the remote jungle regions and near the western and northern areas where Spanish-speaking Mestizos have historically settled (Foster n.d.).

From only a few hundred arrivals in 1979, the immigrant stream escalated, reaching estimated figures of 7000 by 1982 and over 25,000 by 1984 (Asomani 1982; Palacio 1988).[7] The numbers, while small in comparison with other global refugee streams, were significant in a sparsely populated country of only 140,000. On this basis according to the 1984 World Refugee Survey, Belize ranked fifth in a global list of the ratio of refugees per native population (U.S. Committee for Refugees 1984).[8]

Their increasing presence presented a challenge for the government as most were semi-literate peasants with little technical, financial, or family resources to draw upon. Few spoke English. Often squatting on vacant land, they established simple, thatch huts, living in conditions of poverty and misery which shocked many Belizeans. Their pressing needs for emergency assistance and counselling along with their demands on public facilities such as health centers and bus transport confounded authorities.

Emergency Assistance and Durable Solutions

It is important to note that the initial influx of Salvadoran refugees occurred during the time when the country was realizing its independence from Great Britain. The government and public response to the refugee plight reflected the country's dilemma in reconciling its roots as an immigrant nation along with concern for the prior rights of native Belizeans and national security. As one official explained "Belize has traditionally been a haven for refugee people running from persecution and injustice, but this time the circumstances are taking on other profiles" (GIS 1981:5). From the outset, government concern with the refugees' impact on the ethnic balance and integration into society as "useful and productive members ... to contribute to the country's development" underscored the various courses taken (GIS 1983:10).[9]

As a new nation and developing country with few surplus resources, the definition and implementation of a refugee policy has been undertaken with assistance from various international, relief, and religious organizations including the UNHCR, the Refugee Apostolate of the Catholic Church, and the Mennonite Central Committee.[10] Of these, the UNHCR has had the central role, in which its relationship with the government of Belize has been a barometer of shifting attitudes.

An immediate focus on humanitarian aid was initiated in 1980 through an agreement with the UNHCR for provision of emergency assistance to newly arrived and other refugees in the form of clothing, medicine, and basic household needs. With increasing numbers and indications that the influx was of a long-term duration, the UNHCR and the government of Belize expanded their focus and in 1982 formally established a refugee office as a joint effort to provide refugee assistance. The refugee office was a provisional department of the Ministry of Home Affairs and responsible for all refugee matters: registration, legal assessment of refugee status, emergency assistance, counselling.[11]

In addition to emergency assistance, the government also opted to work with the UNHCR in finding a "durable" solution to facilitate the long-term integration of refugees into Belizean society. The policy was in accordance with the country's traditional "open-door" policy to allow entry to foreigners who could help in the country's development. Many of the Salvadorans were farmers, willing to work as casual labor for the sugar and citrus industries under conditions many Belizeans found unacceptable. With a large abundance of unused land, the government was anxious to develop a Belizean farming tradition to lessen its economic vulnerability and dependence on imported goods.

The "Valley of Peace" agricultural scheme was the first - and eventually only - joint venture of the Government and the UNHCR in resettling refugees in a pioneering farming project.[12] Initiated in 1982, the project was undertaken with the objective of providing homes and a farming livelihood for Belizeans as well as Salvadorans in a ratio of 1:2. Belizeans were to be selected from backgrounds similar to the Salvadorans and were to benefit from the same assistance as the Salvadoran refugees (Parvenu 1986).

The objective for the government was two-fold. In addition to facilitating self-sufficiency and the local integration of the refugee population, the government hoped the project would encourage Belizeans to develop a greater and broader involvement in agriculture. For its part, the government committed 15,000 acres, while the UNHCR in turn provided what was eventually to be a total of over $2,000,000 U.S. to develop infrastructure, including schools, roads, a health center, wells, latrines, and inputs for housing. Under the scheme, families received 50 acre holdings, initially on a lease with option to purchase after the land had been established with permanent crops.

The Valley of Peace resettlement project was the cornerstone of the government's refugee program, considered a model in its early stages - "a unique experience among mankind" according to one high government official (GIS 1982). It was a symbol of the nation's recognition of refugees and its humanitarian commitment to assist them in achieving viable self-sufficiency.

However, in many ways, it became a victim of its own promise. The network of communication between settlers with family and friends left behind in El Salvador and other refugees in Honduras portrayed Belize as a land of opportunity. Caught between economic and political violence, many Salvadorans found the lure of available land, land security, peace, and economic opportunity in Belize to be the final 'pull' in their decisions to leave El Salvador. Between 1981 and 1984, the flow of Central Americans into Belize, particularly to the Valley of Peace, increased dramatically. Within the community, the population swelled as extended kin of project settlers, new families, and single young men joined the community. One survey conducted in 1986 indicated a 40% increase in the number of households in only two years as many of these new arrivals remained, hoping to be considered for inclusion in the project (McCommon 1987).

Refugees or Aliens: The Immigration Issue

Immigration and the Social Crisis

Within the settlement, tension developed among Salvadorans and with fellow Belizean settlers over the limited resources and increasing number of squatters. Externally, resentment was expressed by Belizeans as well as by other Salvadoran refugees living in dispersed settlements on the degree of financial assistance and attention given the fledgling settlement.

The public debate over the rising number of Central American immigrants focused on the "explosive impact" of the uncontrolled immigration on Belizean society. Of particular concern was the increase in violent crimes such as robbery, murder, and drug trafficking which were attributed to illegal aliens. While it was recognized that drug barons were principally responsible for the activity, Belizeans felt that the Central Americans were easily lured into the cultivation of marijuana. Refugees and other immigrants were stigmatized as "violent" by nature (Foster n.d.) or as one women argued, "to have murder in their hearts" (McCommon n.d.).

At the same time, the press on social services, especially health and education, was overburdening public coffers. Schools, already overcrowded, were not equipped or trained to deal with the increasing numbers of children who seldom spoke English and were often poorly educated. Similarly, government supported hospitals and health clinics were overwhelmed with the numbers of patients, many of whom had different health needs from those of native Belizeans. In addition to malaria, medical authorities noted increases in dysentery and gastrointestinal diseases that were associated with the poor living conditions and lack of potable water and sanitation facilities.

The impact was particularly felt in rural areas where most immigrants settled. Natural resource management had never been a particularly pressing issue in Belize but the increasing numbers of scattered settlements concerned

Belizeans. Illegal land use along with indiscriminate land clearing and sharp rises in slash and burn cultivation threatened the environment.

In addition, the influx affected the local labor market both because of the numbers hired and the conditions under which they were employed. Unlike seasonal farmers who remained only temporarily, this influx of Central Americans made available a permanent, year-round source of cheap labor not only for agriculture but also for other industries. Further, non-Belizeans as undocumented workers were often exploited by employers to work under marginal and unsafe conditions unprotected by labor laws. This was seen as a threat for all workers, Belizeans as well as non-Belizeans.

Refugees, Immigrants, and Amnesty

The magnitude of the situation fueled speculations on the numbers of illegal immigrants with more frequent references made to the 'alien' problem than to the 'refugee' crisis.[13] The official immigration policy was perceived as ineffectual in light of the large numbers of undocumented foreigners entering the country.[14] Many feared that uncontrolled immigration might undermine national security as well as the prior rights of native Belizeans. According to Palacio (1988:4), some representatives of the local press incited national hysteria against the aliens. Some criticism also took on political tones, with indications that parties were splitting along racial lines in regard to the issue (cf. Philip 1984:375).

Faced with increasing numbers of Central Americans, the government announced a new policy in April, 1984, designed to establish control over the situation by legalizing the situation of all undocumented immigrants then in country. The government also hoped to stem further inflows of refugees and immigrants by giving notice that more restrictive immigration procedures would be employed in the future.

The amnesty achieved only limited success on both counts.[15] In relation to the numbers estimated to be in the country, fewer than half registered with the police. Of these, fewer than 30% were Salvadorans, who were thought to represent the bulk of recent arrivals, and over 50% were Guatemalans interested in legalizing their long-term undocumented status.[16] Many refused to register, while others were discouraged by the cumbersome bureaucratic procedures and required fees. Limited publicity along with inadequate preparation of immigration officials further hampered registration efforts. As for enforcement, officials found it difficult to locate and register immigrants given the fluidity of movement across borders and the widely dispersed settlements.

While the amnesty itself was only moderately effective, an important consequence was the collection of base-line data on undocumented immigrants residing in Belize, providing the first real appraisal of the situation. Of primary importance was the indication that clandestine immigration by Central Americans was far more extensive than believed, including not only political but also economic refugees. Over one-half the arrivals occurred between 1981-1984 during the height of the Central American economic and political crisis. For the government, the findings were ominous, suggesting that the recent influxes might become a permanent pattern of immigration if regional conflicts continued.

The data substantiated concerns about the long-term Latinization of Belizean society. Most registrants were rural and semi-urban people, considered culturally distinct not only from the Creoles but also the Spanish-speaking Mestizos. Further, most of the new arrivals were younger men and women (average age 30) who were at the peak of their child bearing phase (Palacio 1988).

Shift in Government Policy

At the conclusion of the amnesty period in July 1984, the government slowed the pace of the refugee program while it reviewed its immigration policy. The shift from its traditional open-door policy to a more restrictive program reflected a concern that immigration in general had "gotten out of hand". The policy shift became more evident during the election campaign six months later when the People's United Party (PUP), the political party which had dominated politics for over 30 years was voted out of office for the United Democratic Party (UDP). Indications of political polarization were seen in the PUP attracting a disproportionate share of the Hispanic vote while Creoles were drawn to the UDP.

In regard to the refugee situation, the official shift was dramatic. In 1985 over 1000 pending applications were put on hold and notice given that no further applications would be accepted. Of these, only two had been granted refugee status during the two years of this study. At the same time, administration of the program was transferred from the Ministry of Home Affairs to the Ministry of Foreign Affairs and Economic Development. For a period, the government initiated 'round-ups' of aliens, including highway check-points and harassments of rural Hispanics on the suspicion that they were undocumented aliens.

The government also declined to approve UNHCR requests for approval of diplomatic protocols regarding the rights of refugees. Further restrictions imposed by authorities frustrated UNHCR funding of a second phase of the Valley of Peace project. Subsequently, appropriations for these funds were considerably reduced and allocated to other country programs.

As part of a policy review, the government established the Immigration Advisory Committee in 1986. Composed of members from different ministries involved in refugee affairs, the committee reviewed existing documents, programs, and organizations working with refugees to provide guidelines for government policy. Release of these recommendations in an internal report to the government provided fuel for further debate on the refugee/alien issue.

Cabinet Paper #40 represented the synthesis of the recommendations approved by the government. Aimed at defining new laws on immigration policy, recommendations in this report included more rigorous control on work permits, citizen requirements based on knowledge of English, and a scaling down of UNHCR operations. Paramount in the government's concern was the perception that uncontrolled immigration was changing the existing ethnic balance. Adopting new restrictions on immigration was essential to "restore what had previously been in equilibrium...for the survival of Belize as we now know it" (GIS 1987b:1,2).

Central to the government's position were measures directed at the refugee influx. While the government asserted its willingness to accommodate 'legitimate refugee cases', it also expressed its concern that the refugee issue had become an alien problem over which the interests of the Belizean people had to take precedence (GIS 1987a). The decision to curtail the refugee process was seen by some as a major setback for the refugee program in Belize. Particularly affected were those Salvadorans who had entered the country after 1985 when the government placed its first hold on refugee applications. The resident Program Director for the UNHCR, whose relations with the government were already strained, described the report as "degrading refugees and degrading Belize" (GIS 1987b). Subsequently, the office was temporarily closed by the UNHCR and its programs put on further hold.

The Ethnic Dilemma: Conclusions

The core of the immigration debate is the shift in ethnic balance and, with this, the definition of national identity. Historically, Belize has been basically a black population and principally Creole in ethnic composition. With the influx of Central Americans, however, this majority was no longer certain, undermining the delicate balance that had accommodated the interests of the various ethnic groups.

The fear that this hegemonic order has been threatened by the Salvadoran immigration can be linked to the historical development of political, social, and economic power. The emergence of a Creole elite has its roots in the colonial period when the use of official sanctions and practices fostered subtle racial distinctions. These took on political overtones with the beginning of the nationalist movement in the late 1940s as party politics increasingly reflected a split between the two major ethnic groups, Creole and Mestizo. One of the central issues concerned whether Belize as a new nation should be affiliated with Central America or the Caribbean. While independence was eventually pressed on a strong anti-British platform that advocated a regional orientation, the issue has continued to have implications for ethnic relations. Over time, further political splits occurred, primarily among the Creoles over this affiliation. Often, as Grant (1976:76) has aptly pointed out, Creoles exploited different aspects of their cross-cutting ethnic affiliations "depending on the potentialities of the situation."

Underlying these political divisions were ethnic concerns related to the dichotomy of Caribbean and Latin American influences and subtle racial issues that have affected the evolution of Belizean society.[17] Previously, the salience of these factors had been muted principally by the shared colonial experience which mitigated differences between ethnic groups. With independence, however, this bond was erased and latent discriminations became more evident. As one Belizean official pointed out "...our ethnic groups have never been completely free of prejudices against each other" (Topsey 1987:3). The subsequent election of the

Creole-majority party in 1984 sharpened these divisions as Creoles further reinforced their social and political position.

The coincidence of timing of the influx of Central American refugees with independence heightened sensitivity to the salience of race and ethnicity in defining the power base. The Creole and the Garifuna - the two Black groups - saw their dominating position threatened by the immigration of individuals of Latin American descent. Their "major anguish" was based on their fears that the country "(was) slowly 'Latinizing'...The Blacks share a concern for their future in Belize if this process continues" (Everitt 1984:323). Consequently, ethnic differences between these two racial groups were muted as they forged a common allegiance.

The Central American influx accelerated the process of 'Latinization' long debated and rejected by those who consider Belize to be first and foremost a Caribbean nation. It brought to the surface underlying concerns of race and class that have often been suppressed. The further politicization of the refugee issue by some to reinforce and stabilize their own positions of power contributed to this tension.

While it is becoming increasingly obvious to Belizeans that their country can no longer continue to disassociate itself from regional Central American influences, there is still considerable debate on the implications of this for the social fabric of the nation. As they confront the issue of 'nationalism', Belizeans are going through an on-going process of self-examination for the emergence of a new 'Belizean' identity. The influx of Central Americans, and the consequent shift in demographic balances, power control, and social domination underlie the politics surrounding ethnic definitions and with it, the definition of what this ethnic identity is or will be.

NOTES

1. GIS will be used throughout the paper to refer to the Government Information Service which is the official government organization for providing news releases. One of the primary publications of this agency is a monthly newsletter presenting topical issues and official government positions.

2. This paper does not strive to present a full description of the various ethnic groups. The complexity of the social fabric deserves a more comprehensive treatment than can be addressed within the confines of this paper. Rather, this paper attempts to examine the impact of the refugee immigration on the two dominant groups, Mestizo and Creole.

3. Considerable debate has been given to the salience of race and ethnicity in defining these complexes and to the extent to which these produce a "cleavage" in Belizean society (Bolland 1977, 1986; Grant 1976; Smith 1965, 1984).

4. In a discussion of Mayan ethnicity, Wilk (1985) describes the impact of the colonial experience on the definition of ethnicity. He suggests that the growth of a common Belizean character has its roots in the shared colonial experience which provided a basis for different ethnic groups to forge a common identity.

5. Tension between Guatemala and Belize stems from a disputed 1859 treaty between Great Britain and Guatemala. Guatemala maintains a claim over the country, refusing to recognize Belizean statehood, and claims Belize as its 23rd department.

6. Gonzalez (1988) describes the ethnogenesis of the Garifuna in their settlements in Central America.

7. During the 1986 registration, over 8600 individuals registered. The figure fell far short of the number of illegal aliens estimated to be in country, but provided sufficient basis to extrapolate from additional police records an estimate of 25,000 arrivals, including women and children, between 1981 and 1984 (Palacio 1988).

8. Belize does not recognize as refugees Guatemalans fleeing the violence in their country. Historically, many Guatemalans, both Maya Indians and Mestizos, have moved back and forth between the two countries.

9. The UNHCR was set up on January 1, 1951 as a subsidiary organization of the United Nations General Assembly. Its main functions are the protection of refugees and the seeking of durable solutions to their problems through voluntary repatriation or integration into countries of asylum. For Belize, the UNHCR regional office is in San Jose, Costa Rica.

10. Other humanitarian aid was provided by the British and U.S. governments and the private sector through country-wide social and economic programs. It should be pointed out that neither the British nor the U.S. had an official input into the delineation of a Belize refugee policy.

11. It should be pointed out that at the government's stipulation, only Salvadorans could qualify for refugee status; specifically excluded were persons from Honduras, Nicaragua, and Guatemala.

12. Assistance from the U.S. Agency for International Development was provided for a pilot agricultural project in which the Valley of Peace site was chosen as one of two project sites in Belize by the Government of Belize. This project was known as the Accelerated Cocoa Development Project and was implemented by the Pan American Development Foundation (PADF) and Volunteers in Technical Assistance (VITA).

13. The term 'alien' is used by Belizeans to refer to Central Americans living in Belize.

14. Non-Belizeans qualify legally for three types of status - visitor, provisional/permanent resident, and refugee. Refugees are individuals who can prove to government authorities that they are fleeing for fear of violence to themselves or their families. Applications are made to the Refugee office where individuals are given provisional status while their cases are pending. A person applying for resident status must have been in residence for at least one year.

15. Information on the 1984 amnesty is drawn from an extensive report by Palacio (1988) on the implementation of the program and its impact on the refugee situation.

16. The preponderance of Guatemalan registrants - over half the total number - was surprising given the extent to which Guatemalan immigration is officially discounted. Their interest in legalizing status, particularly given their

long history of fluid movements across the borders suggests the permanence of their identification with the country.

17. Young 1978 provides a good overview of the ethnic base to Belizean politics. She argues that the history of party politics explains present-day relations between the Mestizo and Creole communities today. She points out that even within the Creole group racial distinctions exist noting that "...as Creoles climb the lightness ladder, which is usually the socioeconomic ladder, they try to forget their African roots."

8

LEBANON'S PROTRACTED CONFLICT: CAUSES AND CONSEQUENCES[1]

Cheryl A. Rubenberg

This chapter focuses on Lebanon's domestic conflict during the years 1958 through 1982. In 1958, only fifteen years after achieving independence, Lebanon experienced its first civil war. Subsequently, relative calm characterized the surface of Lebanese society until the conflict again exploded in 1975. However, even between the two periods of naked violence, Lebanon was rent with discord that involved the disintegration of the central government's authority and deterioration of the legitimacy of all national institutions including the military. During the second civil war which lasted from May 1975 through October 1976, the country was physically devastated. Even though open hostilities ceased, the conflict still persisted although its character was substantially transformed.

Lebanon's internal conflict was always aggravated by the intervention of foreign powers: for instance in 1958 the U.S. intervened to terminate the war and restore the status quo; in 1976 Syria performed the same function; and in the aftermath of the 1975-76 hostilities Syria occupied Lebanon's eastern Beqaa Valley and together with Israel (who invaded in 1978 and created a so-called "security zone" in the South), effectively partitioned the country. In 1982, Israel invaded again and imposed a three year occupation, triggering a renewal of the civil combat. The fighting in Lebanon continues unabated at this writing.[2]

The following analysis of the nature and causes of the 1958-82 conflict in Lebanon considers, among other factors, how ethnicity and migration have both affected and been influenced by this strife and illustrates the dialectical aspect of ethnicity in relation to the conflict. The analysis suggest that while ethnic groups (or what I will term "ethnic sects" -- i.e. religious-based ethnic aggregations) existed, and disputes were commonly expressed in religious symbols, other issues were more important than religious or ethnic-sect rivalry in generating the conflict and catalyzing war during 1958 and 1975. On the other hand, one result of the prolongation and intensity of Lebanon's post-independence discord was that it served to strengthen, reinforce, and reproduce ethnic-sect identities and tensions, and to transform the conflict, in the aftermath of 1976, into a more ethnically-based embroglio. Significantly, this reflects a pattern that originated in the nineteenth century wherein class conflicts generated by essentially economic issues were transformed into discord between religious communities. The circumstances and nature of these historic events (in addition to other factors and forces) contributed to the development of religious-based ethnicity in Lebanon, to the country's fragmented, hierarchical social structure and confessional-based political system, and to the eruption and transformation of the contemporary conflict.

Migration, in a variety of forms, also contributed to the Lebanese conflict. The most significant aspect of this issue was the migration from Palestine of approximately 128,000 refugees in 1948. By the mid-1970s the number of Palestinians in Lebanon had grown to between 350,000-400,000 - out of a population estimated at roughly 2.5 million (Rubenberg 1984a) In addition, internal migratory movements during the 1960s resulting from structural changes in agriculture had an effect on Lebanon's strife.

Ethnicity, Religion, and Social Organization

The question of ethnicity in an analysis of Lebanon is complicated and requires some elaboration. Within Lebanon religion is almost universally the primary basis of personal identity but in some denominations, religious considerations per se are not the sole, nor even the most important, attributes shared by affiliates. To varying degrees among them, factors of class, geography, kinship, political history, social organization, culture, and ideology constitute more significant aspects of social integration than do religious beliefs.

In examining the relationship between religious affiliation and social organization in Lebanon it is useful to distinguish between the concepts of "confession," "sect" and "ethnic-sect." A religion that functions as a "confession" comprises the least elaborate relationship; it constitutes a behavioral distinction essentially involving the preference of individuals for associating, e.g., marrying, socializing, etc., with other members of the same religion. A religion may be described as a "sect" (an organizational distinction) when its boundaries include social and political organizations that aggregate and articulate the economic, political, and social interests of the group. An "ethnic-sect" is an institution wherein religion, identity, class, and the whole panoply of cultural meanings are intimately and deeply fused. It usually involves sophisticated organizations but is marked above all by the complex cultural world view it provides its adherents (Farsoun 1988b). Such categories are arbitrary but they permit differentiation among the various denominations.

It is important to note, however, that the character of Lebanon's religious groups has not been fixed or static and it is essential to consider the historical unfolding of these groups as well as to examine how political, economic, and social forces have been involved in their development, reproduction and manipulation. Thus a discussion of the evolution of the three most important Lebanese ethnic-sects precedes, and provides the foundation for, the analysis of the contemporary factors that generated the post-1958 conflict.

Lebanon is a deeply fragmented society wherein political power is distributed on the basis of religious denomination according to an informal 1943 agreement known as the "National Pact" (see below). That formula enshrined Maronites as the dominant power and institutionalized a rigid confessional hierarchy grounded in Christian supremacy. However, while Maronites were assumed to be the numerically largest group in 1943,[3] the Shi'ia were the most populous denomination by the early 1970s and non-Christians constituted a majority against a minority of combined Christian churches. Nevertheless, the political structure remained wedded to the 1943 formula and this imbalance was a significant component of Lebanon's conflict. The most important of the seventeen religious groups constituting Lebanon's socio-political hierarchy are the Maronite, Greek Orthodox, Greek Catholic, Armenian Orthodox, Armenian Catholic, Sunni, Shi'ia, and Druze.

The Maronites, Druze, and Shi'ia have the most clearly defined characters as "ethnic-sects" or ethnic collectivities. There are, however, considerable differences in the historical periods and the circumstances in which they emerged as ethnic-sects. The Maronites developed an elaborate cultural identity in the mid-nineteenth century; the Druze followed, though more slowly, and in part in reaction to Maronite coalescence and group ascendance; Shi'ia ethnicity did not crystallize until the early 1970s. The Maronite, Druze and Shi'ia denominations are also "sectarian" and the dates at which they began to develop political and social organizational structures are likewise widely separate, roughly corresponding to their development as ethnic-sects. Most important in terms of the contemporary Lebanese conflict, are the mid-nineteenth century circumstances that transformed the Maronites and Druze into ethnic collectivities and created and reproduced a pattern of confessional-based political and social relations. Some of the most devastating consequences for post-independence Lebanon were: a weak central government, institutionalized factionalism, the failure to develop a Lebanese "national" identity or loyalty, and the generation and perpetuation of confessional-based conflict. Among Lebanon's other major religious denominations, the Armenians -- both Orthodox (Gregorian) and Catholic -- also constitute an ethnic-sect but they have been less significant in the development of contemporary Lebanon than the aforementioned groups and will not be considered herein. The Sunni, Greek Orthodox, and Greek Catholic are primarily "confessions" though there has been some social organization -- i.e., "sectarian" development -- in all three.

Several factors explain the historical elaboration of ethnic identities among the Maronites, Druze, and Shi'ia (explained further below.) One involves their schismatic or heterodox origins as "off-shoots" of mainstream Christian and Islamic denominations. They have thought of themselves, and have been thought of, as apart from the majority -- unique, original, and/or infidel, heretical, and blasphemous, and thus have striven to maintain their distinctiveness. Another reason involves their tribal origins and the long-standing inter-tribal conflicts and intra-tribal loyalties that mark their internal relations and external associations. A further reason is related to the geographical contiguity of these denominations: the Maronites have been located almost exclusively in Mount Lebanon, the northern area of the Lebanon Mountain range (hereafter referred to as "the Mountain"); the Druze are congregated in the southern parts of the Mountain -- an area known as the Shouf; and the Shi'ia are concentrated in

Mount Amil' in southern Lebanon and in the Hirmil district of the northern Beqaa Valley. All three groups migrated to these areas from distant places in the Arab world between the fifth and eleventh centuries A.D. The Lebanese historian Kamal Salibi has analyzed the significance of several of these factors:

> ...[these] sects are in fact tribes, not only in social behavior but also by historical origin...all of them perpetuate to this day Arab tribal loyalties and conflicts...[and] all...have historical roots in a particular geographical territory...[In the fifth and sixth centuries] Arab tribalism insinuated itself into the politics of the Christian church...Islamic sectarianism remained for the most part an Arab tribal phenomenon... religious doctrines, mostly of little relevance to daily life, somehow managed to graft themselves onto tribes, and to transform them into and perpetuate them as sects... (Salibi 1988: 15,16,21,26)

The impact of foreign powers -- especially France -- and the political, social, and economic effects of foreign relations and associations also contributed to the elaboration of ethnicity among these groups. Finally, a particularly important aspect of their development as ethnic-sects involves an interlocking of class transformations with confessional affiliation that served to solidify their character as all-encompassing cultural collectivities.

During the nineteenth century a combination of internal and external economic and political factors resulted in the decay of feudalism within the Maronite community and in the Maronites becoming economically dominant while in simultaneous and related processes the Druze declined economically. In the mid-twentieth century major economic transformations profoundly altered the economic situation of the Shi'ia -- both absolutely and relative to other Lebanese denominations -- and gave rise to its emergence as an ethnic-sect. Moreover, in the context of these changes each denomination developed a generalized class orientation: the Maronites as bourgeois; the Druze as a mainly "middle class" of family farmers; and the Shi'ia as a peasant class (Farsoun 1988a, 1988b).

The historical experience of Lebanese who identify as Sunni, Greek Orthodox, and Greek Catholic has been considerably different. Lebanese Sunni are part of a much larger community that has dominated the Arab world since the spread of Islam in the seventh century. Ninety per cent of all Muslims are Sunni and many tribes, clans, and families are subsumed within Sunnism. In all Arab countries except Lebanon, Sunnis control the political, economic, and social institutions.[4] Therefore the Sunni do not have the particularistic character or the dissident aspect of Shi'ia and Druze. Lebanon's Sunni community appears to have identified with the regional position of its co-religionists even though it has not been politically powerful in Lebanon. In addition, the Sunni are geographically fragmented: some, the urban trading elites, live in various coastal cities including Beirut, Tripoli, and Sidon, while others, the peasants, have until the 1960s mostly lived in the Beqaa Valley in eastern Lebanon and in the northern plain of Akkar. The Sunni are also divided in terms of class: in Beirut,

Tripoli, and Sidon there is a wealthy (absentee) land-owning elite and a commercial elite plus an urban proletariat, while in the Beqaa and in Akkar they have been primarily an impoverished peasant class (Farsoun 1988a). It is noteworthy that in Lebanon no Sunni oligarch ever organized a political party in any viable sense of the term (not even one confined to his sect), nor did any ever clearly or consistently identify himself with an overall political or social program or vision (Khalidi 1979).

Similarly, the Greek Orthodox and Greek Catholic are part of the two major historic churches in the Christian world; unlike the Maronites they have co-religionists throughout the Middle East cutting across tribal, kinship, and geographical boundaries. The sense of uniqueness and particularism is much less in these denominations than in the Maronite. Moreover, they have not been geographically contiguous in Lebanon. The Greek Orthodox are spread throughout the Kura district of northern Lebanon, the southern Beqaa, and in Beirut and Tripoli while Greek Catholics are found in and around the city of Zahleh in the Beqaa and throughout the southern part of the Mountain. Both the Greek Orthodox and Greek Catholic communities have considerable class cohesiveness as bourgeois and petit-bourgeois but this has not been enough, by itself, to transform them into ethnic-sects.

An analysis of the Lebanese conflict requires consideration of the role of Palestinians and the question of Palestinian ethnicity which presents a somewhat different picture than that of the Lebanese ethnic-sects. The development of Palestinian ethnicity is a twentieth century phenomenon related to the Zionist settlement and colonization of Palestine; the processes of dispossession, deinstitutionalization, and dispersal in 1948 resulting from the creation of Israel; the transformation of Palestinians from a class of mainly peasant farmers into landless, destitute refugees; and their experience as "foreigners" in Lebanon. (The Maronite-dominated Lebanese government was exceedingly hostile to Palestinians, fearing that the mostly Muslim refugees posed a threat to continued Christian supremacy. Many non-official Lebanese were hostile for other reasons.) The development of Palestinian ethnicity was also related to specific efforts on the part of the Palestine Liberation Organization (PLO) to produce a Palestinian "national" identity. Palestinian ethnicity has little religious content: there are Sunni Muslims (the majority) and a variety of Christian denominations among them. However, as with the relationship between Lebanese ethnic-sects and the conflict in Lebanon, there is a dialectical aspect to Palestinian ethnicity and that conflict. Palestinians have been victimized by the conflict but they also contributed to it and Palestinian ethnicity was deepened as a result of the conflict.

The Historical Development of Lebanese Ethnic Sects and Palestinian Ethnicity: The Dialects of Conflict and Ethnicity

Feudal Society in the Lebanon Mountain

A number of characteristics of the traditional *iqta'* (feudal) system on the Mountain including the nature of the feudal hierarchy, the kinship basis of status, and the personalistic character of patron-client relationships affected the evolution of contemporary Lebanese society. Similarly, the character of post-independence Lebanon was shaped by several nineteenth century transformations that occurred in the *iqta* system e.g., the status reversal between the Maronite and Druze communities, the decomposition of capitalism in Maronite society, the evolution of Maronite ethnicity, the integration of the Mountain into the European economic system, and the development of communal conflict between the Maronites and Druze. Especially notable as regards the latter were three periods -- the 1820 peasant revolt, the 1840 uprising against the Egyptian occupation, and the 1858 peasant uprising in the Kisrawan, each of which began as class-based or economic conflict but took on a confessional character. The transformations in the *iqta* system are analyzed below in the context of Maronite and Druze ethnic-sect development.

Until the early nineteenth century the Mountain was a feudal society not unlike European feudal systems. It enjoyed a special status within the Ottoman Empire as an "emirate" with relative autonomy from the Turkish sultan. From 1517 to 1697 Druze held the title of "emir" and were the dominant power in the Mountain. In 1697, power passed to the Shihab family, at the time Sunni but later converted to Christianity. The last of the Shihab emirs, Bashir II, governed until 1842 when the Ottomans, under pressure from European governments, imposed a new form of administration -- the dual *qa'immaqamiyyah* -- based on partition between the Maronite and Druze communities.[5] In 1861 the European powers imposed their own "Special Regime." During the nineteenth century the fortunes of the Druze declined while those of the Maronites rose and the Maronite community became the dominant power in the Mountain.

The rigid feudal hierarchy that characterized the Mountain during the emirate was notable for the cross-confessional affiliations that existed among the elites of the various denominations. At the top of the hierarchy was the Ottoman sultan; directly under him, the emir. Below these two were a few *muqata'jis* (hereditary chiefs of geographical districts); eight to twelve sheiks; and at the bottom of the hierarchy, the *'ammiyyah* (peasants) including both small farmers and sharecroppers. There were splits and rivalries between feudal families -- conflicts among *muqata'jis* and sheiks -- but these were predominately partisan or kinship in character and almost never took the form of confessional conflict (Khalaf 1987; Odeh 1985). However, during the nineteenth century internal and external forces acted to strengthen confessional identification among Maronites and Druze, transforming it into sectarian ethnicity. Nevertheless, the cross-confessional interests of the elites did not vanish. In fact these interests were reflected and reproduced in the 1943 agreement (the "National Pact") that formed the governing structure of the new state. Moreover, until well into the 1975-76 civil war class-based affiliations continued to characterize relations among the traditional elites of all confessions except Druze (though most communities were shaken by the emergence of new elites).

In the *iqta* system property itself was not the principal factor in determining the social position of the *muqata'jis* and sheiks; instead their status reflected a continuity of traditional considerations grounded in kinship while the social honor and prestige they enjoyed did not vanish with diminished wealth. Thus, as noted by Lebanese sociologist Samir Khalaf: "Given this association between kinship and social status it is little wonder that the family survived as the fundamental socioeconomic and political unit in society" (Khalaf 1987:28). And, indeed, contemporary Lebanon has been characterized by the primacy of the family as the most important unit of social organization and agent of political socialization. Post-independence Lebanon has also been marked by another legacy of the Mountain's feudal society -- the nature of its patron-client relationships which persist in the institution of fealty (the recognized obligation of a leader in return for the loyalty and unquestioned allegiance of a follower). The endurance of patronage is related to the non-military character of the Mountain's social system, the fact that political legitimacy resided in personal loyalty, and in the personal (non-confessional) nature of political allegiances (Khalaf 1987:76-80).

The following examines the factors and historic forces that contributed to the development of the Maronites, Druze, and later the Shi'ia as ethnic sects. It considers the religious, ideological, tribal, and political-historical basis of each sect's distinctiveness as well as the internal, local, and international political, economic, and social dynamics that contributed to the transformations in each. The evolution of Palestinian ethnicity is also analyzed.

Maronites

There are conflicting accounts concerning the origin of the Maronites;[6] however, one plausible explanation suggests that they were originally Gnostic Christians from Yemen who, sometime in the sixth century, fled persecution there and established themselves in northern Syria and the adjacent parts of Mount Lebanon. Once in Syria they associated themselves with the cult of a fifth century local saint, Marun, taking their name from him, and calling their first patriarch Yuhanna Marun (Salibi 1988: 20). According to Salibi:

> As Arab tribal newcomers there, the Maronites strove to maintain their tribal distinctness from the established Ghassanid and other Syrian Arabs, not only by maintaining themselves as an independent sect, but also by organizing themselves as an independent church. That the Maronite sect actually conceived of itself as a tribe is reflected by the term *sha'b Marun* (the people of Marun), used by a Maronite poet to describe his community as late as the fifteenth century (Salibi 1988: 20).

The Maronites participated in the Crusades in the eleventh and twelfth centuries, earning the distrust of their Muslim neighbors. In the sixteenth century (consummating a process begun in the twelfth) they submitted to the authority of Rome in exchange for being permitted to retain their special rites which include conducting their liturgy in Syriac and the marriage of parish priests.

Until the mid-seventeenth century the Maronite community was weak, disorganized, torn by clan factionalism, and had little social or political influence in the life of the Mountain. The majority were serfs in the service of Druze feudal overlords. However, between 1590 and 1634, the Maronites began to expand into the Shouf, the Beqaa Valley, and most important, into the Kisrawan where they displaced almost all the Shi'ia residents (Cobban 1985; Odeh 1985). In the Kisrawan Maronites founded monasteries, cleared the valleys of stones, terraced the land, and established large feudal estates. In addition, the community began to engage in the production of raw silk as a commercial product for export thus providing an economic outlet for the landless peasantry. By the nineteenth century nearly 200 silk-reeling factories provided employment for about half the total number of Maronite families in Mount Lebanon. Moreover, the silk industry, based on wage work and tax payments in cash, introduced capitalist relations of production alongside the feudal relations, acting as a counter to feudalism and contributing to its erosion (Petran 1987; Randal 1983; Farsoun 1988a; Owen 1988).

Throughout the eighteenth and nineteenth centuries the Maronite church itself acquired great tracts of land and by the nineteenth century it had become the largest, most organized, and wealthiest institution in the Mountain (Harik 1968:125). As the Church gained power (at the expense of the feudal aristocracy), it became the dominant institution in the organization of the Maronite community.[7] The ability of the Maronite church to develop social institutions -- schools, hospitals, philanthropic associations, and other community organizations -- derived from its economic strength and independence (resulting from its own resources plus those it acquired thorough its linkages with Christian Europe) and was exceedingly important in the evolution of the Maronites as a sectarian organization. The extent and sophistication of Maronite social institutions created, in effect, an autonomous "civil society" for the Maronite community. More important, especially in the development of Maronite ethnicity, was the role of Maronite clergymen as "articulators and carriers of a new Maronite ideology and communal consciousness that challenged the sense of personal allegiance and kinship ties, which were the hallmarks of feudal society" (Khalaf 1987:32). All of these elements contributed to the bonding of the community, its development of a "nationalist" ideology and a Maronite "ethnicity," and to the evolution of the Maronites as an ethnic-sect. In turn, all were important in the evolution of Maronite power in the Lebanon Mountain (Farsoun 1988a; Petran 1987; Moosa 1986; Randal 1983; Odeh 1985; Khalaf 1987).

The progression of the Maronite community was also greatly facilitated by the assistance of external powers. For instance, French economic penetration of the Ottoman Empire in the early eighteenth century and French-Maronite

"Christian" affiliation resulted in Maronites gaining employment as interpreters, clerks, and commercial agents in French consulates and in the trading stations of French companies. It also led to their winning French consular protection since the community was placed under the "guardianship" of France and French kings chose their consuls from among Maronite notables (Moosa 1986). At the same time, various other European (Christian) powers increasingly penetrated the Mountain, extending protection and favoritism to all sectors of the Maronite community -- merchants, usurers, brokers, the Church, and even peasants as well as to other Christian communities in the Mountain. Together the European connections gave the Maronites (and other Christians) a distinct advantage over the Druze and Muslim communities. Sociologist Samih Farsoun points to one aspect of such advantage: "...only three out of a total of 29 Beirut merchant houses trading directly with England were Muslim; the rest were Christian" (Farsoun 1988a:118). In addition to expanding and deepening economic ties between the West and the Maronites, the European linkages provided an opening for Christian missionaries to stream into the Mountain where they set up hospitals, schools, and other facilities as well as churches. The consequences of this are evident, in one example, by the fact that at the end of the nineteenth century, of 650 primary schools in the Mountain only 13 were Muslim or Druze (Petran 1987:31). The ability of the Maronites to avail themselves of the education provided by the missionaries -- education far superior to what was available to most Shi'ia, Sunni, or Druze -- explains in considerable measure the marked differences in occupation and socio-economic status between the religious groups in the twentieth century. In addition, as a result of their close and lengthy association with France, many Maronites adopted French as either their primary or exclusive language. This contributed to the Maronite sense of separateness from the Arab world, produced and reproduced a "Western" (Occidental) orientation, and played a role in the development of Maronite ethnicity. As one analyst commented, Maronite "spiritual and cultural Meccas were Rome and Paris...Their mythology stressed their non-Arab or pre-Arab ancestry -- they were *from* but not *of* the Near East" (Khaladi 1979:34).

In both subtle and striking ways European penetration combined with the internal attributes of and transformations in Maronite society to catalyze further change among the Maronites as well as in the social fabric of the Mountain. In 1820 the first of several important nineteenth century upheavals occurred. It was a peasant uprising (known as the *ammiyyah*), essentially a tax revolt, initiated by peasants in the Kisrawan and Matn districts. Significantly, it was backed by Maronite clergy, and despite its origin in objective economic issues that affected all peasants, the *ammiyyah* remained a fundamentally Maronite phenomenon. In fact, in Khalaf's judgement its most significant effect was "to initiate the transition from the traditional ties of kinship, status, and personal allegiance to a more communal form of social cohesion where the sources of political legitimacy were defined in terms of ethnicity and confessional allegiance" (Khalaf 1987:35).

Between 1831-40, Egypt, with French backing, occupied Syria and control of the Mountain passed from the Ottoman sultan to Ibrahim Pasha (son of Mohammed Ali, ruler of Egypt). Emir Bashir II administered the area in the service of the Egyptians. The Egyptian occupation was highly beneficial to the Maronites: it enforced equal rights for Christians and Jews, employed Maronites throughout the administration, exempted them from certain taxes, conscripted Druze, and permitted the Maronites alone to retain their arms. At the same time Ibrahim Pasha reoriented the Mountain's foreign trade from Asia to Europe, expanding it enormously, and making Beirut the principal port of the eastern Mediterranean and the center of increasing European merchant, trading, and banking houses (Petran 1987:25). The expansion of trade was primarily advantageous to Maronites (and other Christians). In addition, Emir Bashir systematically confiscated the lands of Druze lords, forced them and some of their more loyal peasants to flee, and in turn, encouraged Maronite peasants to take over those lands. Some of the Druze landholdings also found their way into the hands of Maronite monasteries and merchants. As a consequence, the Maronite peasantry, merchants, and Church gained at the expense of the Druze, contributing to a radical alteration in the status of the two communities: Maronites who had been the serfs of Druze sheiks before the arrival of the Egyptians were the chief moneylenders of these same sheiks by the time they departed as well as holding a sizeable portion of Druze land (Polk 1963; Odeh 1985; Petran 1987; Farsoun 1988a; Khalaf 1987).

An announcement by Ibrahim Pasha in 1840 that Christians would no longer be exempt from conscription sparked a revolt by the Maronites. Soon they were joined by Druze, Sunni, and Shi'ia in a widespread insurgency against the Egyptians. Druze fighters played the major role in the actual combat; however, as with the 1820 uprising, initiative and leadership were in the hands of Maronite peasants and clergy. The initial revolt failed and the intervention of outside powers as well as conflict over land soon fragmented the local alliance. A British-Ottoman military expedition entered the Mountain, drove out the Egyptians, and restored Ottoman power.

With the defeat of Ibrahim Pasha and Emir Bashir, exiled Druze returned to the Mountain and their attempts to reacquire their lost property led to armed conflict with the Maronites. In 1842, under pressure from the Europeans, the Ottomans administratively separated Mount Lebanon from the Shouf, imposing a partition called the double *qa'immaqamiyyah* (district presidency) -- drawn up by the Austrian Chancellor, Prince Metternich (Cobban 1985). Two of the most lasting effects of the partition were to sharpen communal cleavages and to catalyze a second outbreak of fighting in 1845. That strife led to a revision of the *qa'immaqamiyyah* but as with the first partition, it served mainly to reinforce the power of the leading families and the religious heads of both groups, contributing to the reproduction of religious-based loyalties and enmities (Petran 1987). The second partition provided the governing structure for the Mountain until the European powers imposed the "Special Regime" in 1861. Another effect of the *qa'immaqamiyyah* was the further deepening and strengthening of relations between the French and the Maronites including reinforcement of the Maronites' perception of themselves as part of the Occident and "non-Arab".

In 1858 a second peasant revolt, again backed by Maronite clergymen, erupted in Kisrawan. It was essentially a rebellion against feudal abuses with the participants demanding agrarian reform, a decrease in the exploitation of the peasants, increased taxation of feudal families, and a decrease in the notables' privileges. However, despite the class issues and the broad economic orientation of the movement in Kisrawan (as with the 1820 insurrection), its base did not broaden beyond the Maronite community. Druze peasants who initially joined the struggle did not have the backing of their religious leaders; indeed the *uqqal* (religious elite) specifically counselled them to "avoid sedition." (Khalef 1987: 40). Moreover, in order to deflect the class questions in their own community, Druze sheiks incited sectarian fears among the peasantry. In the end the conflict was transformed into a sectarian war (Petran 1987; Farsoun 1988a).

During its course, the Druze recaptured most of the land in the Shouf they had earlier lost to the Christians but the communal strife intensified confessional hostilities and provided a pretext for European intervention. In 1860 the French sent an intervention on behalf of the Maronites and in 1861 the European powers established the Special Regime, a joint authority through which they ruled the Mountain for sixty years. The Special Regime created a provincial governorship, established a unique economic arrangement marked by *laissez-faire* practices and low taxes, and legally united the Mountain with Beirut by bringing its commercial transactions under the jurisdiction of Beirut courts (Owen 1988; Cobban 1985). The new administration brought stability to the Mountain, European penetration increased, and the Maronites prospered.

Combined European control over the Mountain was transformed into unitary French domination in 1920 when, at the San Remo Conference, France assumed "mandates" for Syria and the Lebanon. The mandates formally separated the Mountain from Syria and created the *Grand Liban* -- an area slightly more than twice the size of the Mountain which in 1943 became the geographical territory of the independent Republic of Lebanon.

French rule too proved highly advantageous to the Maronites including: (1) the continuing educational opportunities through French missions; (2) permission for remittances from Maronite emigrants to flow into the community without the burden of taxation (remittances that were second only to silk as a source of income); (3) French contributions for the improvement of infrastructure development in Maronite districts; (4) French subsidies for housing and other living conditions in Maronite areas which contributed to the survival of small and medium peasant farmers in the Mountain and in general elevated the already privileged status of the community; and (5) the allotment of public posts and favors to the Maronites in numbers greatly disproportionate to the size of their community (Petran 1987:28-32).

Moreover, largely as a result of French backing, the Maronites were able to institutionalize themselves as the dominant power in the 1943 "National Pact" that established the political structure of the newly independent Lebanese state. Indeed, as early as the mid-nineteenth century, the French had begun to encourage the Maronites to articulate explicitly the goal of a separate (from Syria), politically united, "Lebanon" under Maronite leadership (Petran 1987). However, the creation of a political system based on religious affiliation with the enshrinement of the Maronites as the dominant power reproduced religiously-based identifications and loyalties and fanned the fire of communal conflict.

In sum, several unique forces shaped the development of the Maronite community as an ethnic-sect: (1) the peculiarities of Maronite experience and ideology; (2) the virtual monopoly of the Maronites over the silk industry in Lebanon from the seventeenth century on; (3) transformations in the organization and nature of the Maronite church; (4) alignments between the Maronites and various European powers, in particular the French; and (5) the geographic identity of the Maronites with Mount Lebanon which merged with its religious, social and economic distinctiveness to produce the sense of an "historic homeland" (Petran 1987:24). Together these factors and forces contributed to the transformation of the Maronites from a religious confession to a sectarian organization and a complex ethnic aggregation.

The Druze

The Druze are an out-growth of the Isma'ilis, a heretical branch of Shi'ism, itself a minority within Islam.[8] They originated in Cairo in 1017 when a small group of Isma'ilis formulated a doctrine in which the Fatimid Caliph of Egypt, al-Hakim, was recognized as not only the infallible "imam" of his time but as the *mawla* (or lord) in whose human person the unity of the five *hudud* (emanations) of God were made manifest. A Shi'ia missionary, Muhammad al-Darazi, was the first to convert to the belief in al-Hakim's divinity and it is from him that the name Druze is derived.[9] Shortly after emerging they were driven out of Egypt and fled to Syria where they settled in three areas: the Hawran mountains south of Damascus (today Jabal Druze), the southern part of the Lebanon Mountain range (the Shouf), and in the Galilee (today northern Israel) (Salibi 1988; Randal 1983).

The Druze allied with Muslims in the wars against the Crusaders giving rise to a warrior aristocracy. In 1517 the Ottoman Sultan Selim conferred status and recognition on the community by confirming Sheik Fakhr al-Din, of the Ma'n clan, emir of the Mountain. That act established the institution of the emirate as the administrative structure for governing the feudal social order on the Mountain and established the Druze as its leading power. The Druze maintained that position until the Ma'n family died out in 1697 at which time the Junblats became the leading clan among the Druze but the title of emir passed to the Shihabs. From the thirteenth through the seventeenth centuries the Druze were large land owners, managing great feudal estates; they developed a strong social organization and refined their military prowess. Between 1585 and 1635 an outstanding Druze leader, Fakhr al-Din II, expanded the area under the control of the emirate, advanced the political life of the Mountain (in particular, elevating the Maronites to the same civil status as Druze), and contributing significantly to the development of a distinct Druze world view (Cobban 1985:22-23,38; Odeh 1985:29). However, during the eighteenth and nineteenth centuries the political and economic situation of the Druze declined. This was the consequence of a number of factors (many already discussed) including inter-clan conflict that sapped Druze power (Petran 1987:23). Nevertheless over the centuries the Druze retained a strong sense of the importance of the family in their social life and of the uniqueness of their particular socio-political traditions which include an enduring stress on military values as well as maintaining the geographical contiguity of the community in the Shouf. Several characteristics of the Druze which have contributed to their sense of ethnicity including their "profound moral cohesion" and the history of the emirate, the "princedom" and "the hierarchy of families beneath whose authority different families can live together..." (Hourani 1988:9).

Several aspects of nineteenth century conditions as they affected the Druze warrant further comment: When Emir Bashir II assumed the emirate in 1788, he attempted to consolidate his personal power by curtailing the power of the Druze *muqata'jis* and sheiks. Then during the Egyptian occupation (1831-1841) Ibrahim Pasha demanded conscription of Druze to serve for fifteen year terms in the Egyptian army while Bashir continued to dispossess and force into exile prominent Druze feudal families. Egyptian rule and Bashir's administration combined to turn Druze land over to Maronites; to undermine the authority and privileges of the remaining feudal families (i.e., taking away their right to collect taxes, maintain law and order, or exercise judicial authority); and granted Druze none of the preferential treatment accorded Christians (Khalaf 1987:57). Indeed, as Khalaf argues: "[The]...growing disparity between religious groups, a feature that has had a lasting impact on Lebanese society, was one of the byproducts of Egyptian occupation" (Khalaf 1987:49).

The Druze did not benefit from the penetration of the European powers into the economic and political life of the Mountain or from its integration into the European economic system. The absence of religious ties between them and the Europeans stands in marked contrast to the extensive pattern of Maronite linkages and the benefits derived from such connections. Correlatively, the Druze community did not experience the profound socio-economic transformations that accompanied the decay of feudalism and the emergence of capitalism among the Maronites. Nevertheless, the confiscation of Druze feudal estates resulted in the break-up of traditional land concentrations and when the Druze recovered their land during the upheavals of 1858-60, many families acquired farms of smaller size than had previously existed. Thus while the basis of Druze social relations remained essentially feudal in character (until well into the mid-twentieth century) the economy of the community underwent some alteration from a latifundista-arrangement to a more "middle-class" form of family farms. The declining fortunes of the Druze together with the forces that rocked the community in the eighteenth and nineteenth centuries increased the Druze sense of communal solidarity and loyalty, deepened its belief in its separateness and distinctiveness, and reproduced the Druze inclination toward communal self-reliance. Together, these factors contributed to the growth of Druze ethnicity and the transformation of the denomination from a confession to an ethnic-sect.

The Shi'ia[10]

Lebanese Shi'ia are part of a sub-sect within Shi'ism known as the "Twelver's" who acknowledge twelve imams beginning with Ali. They believe that the twelfth disappeared and remains concealed, leaving the community with the hope of his "return" as the *Mahdi* (a messianic term, roughly, "the rightly guided one") who will establish justice and peace on earth. After the defeat and death of Husayn in 680, the *Shi'at Ali* scattered widely, suffering oppression from Sunni rulers wherever they settled. The Lebanon Mountain (as it did for other dissidents) provided an attractive refuge and several Shi'ia clans settled there. Between 969 and 1099 the Shi'ia enjoyed a period of prosperity and independence; however, subsequently their fortunes declined relative to those of both the Druze and Maronites'. Their distinctive aspects have helped maintain the communal solidarity and identity of Shi'ia across the centuries.

In contrast with their minority status in Islam and among Arabs, the Shi'ia community in Lebanon is larger than the Sunni. Indeed, since the early 1970's it has constituted the largest of all Lebanon's religious denominations. However, until the mid-1950s the Shi'ia were an insignificant force in Lebanese society and politics. Such political representation as the community had was virtually monopolized by six prominent land-owning families. This situation was related to the fact that the Shi'ia comprised the lowest economic strata in Lebanon, having been historically a collective of peasant farmers and to the fact that the traditional elite in the Shi'ia community identified more closely with Maronite elites than with Shi'ia masses, accepting Lebanon's socio-economic system and political framework as long as the personal interests of the elite were served. None of the forces that impacted on the Maronite and Druze communities in the nineteenth century affected the Shi'ia; however, in the 1950s the fortunes of the community declined precipitously in response to profound changes in Lebanon's economy. In turn, the Shi'ia community was transformed internally, emerged as an ethnic-sect, and took its place alongside the Maronites and Druze in the dynamics of the Lebanese conflict.

The most important of the economic and social pressures affecting the Shi'ia in the period from 1950-75 were related to changes in the nature of agriculture, in particular the growth of the export sector, which had severe negative consequences for the Shi'ia peasantry. Export agriculture resulted in the virtual disappearance of sharecropping, with farmers increasingly specializing in the production of fruit trees and poultry for export. These changes resulted in a permanent state of indebtedness for the peasantry and led to its exploitation by merchants, moneylenders, and small local banks. Eventually thousands of destitute Shi'ia sharecroppers and peasant families were uprooted by financial obligations and bankruptcy, and were forced to sell what property they had. This led, in turn, to their migration to Beirut and other cities in search of work. By 1975 more than 40 percent of Lebanon's total rural population had migrated -- from the South alone the figure was 60 percent -- and the vast majority of these internal migrants were Shi'ia. Most ended up in the miserable slums of Beirut where life was even worse than in the countryside but where they were readily susceptible to political mobilization (Nasr 1985:10-11).

During this time, many Shi'ia emigrated to the Arab oil-producing countries in the Gulf in search of employment. When they returned home, they came with new wealth that facilitated the purchase of land and orchards, the establishment of new commercial networks, and the carving out of new spheres of social influence. This altered traditional power relations, shifting influence to the returning migrants and away from the traditional notables and religious families.

Thus a new Shi'ia bourgeoisie emerged followed by a radicalized intelligentsia, a layer of middle-level salaried workers in the cities, and an industrial proletariat. Eventually a new Shi'ia elite appeared that included religious figures, politicians, and financiers (Nasr 1895).[11]

Growing out of these social and economic transformations, the *Barakat al-Mahrumin* (Movement of the Dispossessed) was born in the early 1970's in the slums of Beirut. Organized by the Shi'ia clergyman Imam Musa Sadr, this movement focused on the development of social institutions, the articulation of economic grievances, and political mobilization but it drew heavily on the unique symbolism of the Shi'ia religious heritage -- the special rituals, values, heroes, emphasis on social protest, and tradition of revolt against illegitimate authority. The movement attempted to reinterpret traditional symbols with a contemporary meaning, in particular utilizing them to legitimize political action and to evoke the collective memory of the community (Nasr 1985).

The main constituents of the *Barakat al-Mahrumin* were landless Shi'ia urban migrants, the poverty-ridden Shi'ia peasantry, the growing Shi'ia petty bourgeoisie (whose advancement was blocked by the existing economic structures), and the new Shi'ia bourgeoisie (that was excluded from the political system). In the words of analyst Salim Nasr:

> The main purpose of the movement...[was] to achieve 'equality' with other [religious] communities within the Lebanese confessional system, including a share in the administration, the national budget, and the economy...He [Musa Sadr] formed a multi-class bloc whose goal was to bring together all parts of Shi'ia society (Nasr 1985:12).

And, in fact, the movement served primarily as a point of Shi'ia political identity and mobilization, contributing significantly to the evolution of Shi'ia ethnicity and the transformation of the confession into an ethnic-sect.

In sum, the most important factors and forces that crystallized Shi'ia ethnicity include: (1) the historic uniqueness of Shi'ia ideology and experience; (2) the collective condition of the Shi'ia in Lebanon as a peasant class occupying the lowest socio-economic position and excluded from participation in the political process; (3) economic transformations in Lebanon during the 1950s and 60s; and (4) the movement of Imam Musa Sadr. In addition, the extent of the institutionalization of Lebanon's religiously-based political and social system by the time the Shi'ia became mobilized contributed to their pursuing their interests within an ethnic-sect framework as opposed to a secular basis.[12]

The Palestinians

Palestinian ethnicity contrasts with that of the Lebanese ethnic-sects in that it is not centered in religion and has to a greater extent been the product of powerful external political, economic, and social forces that have buffeted Palestinian society. Palestinian ethnicity has arisen primarily (though not exclusively) in reaction to the effects of Zionism, a colonial-settler movement that originated in nineteenth century Europe and involved the emigration to Palestine of world Jewry for the purpose of establishing an exclusive Jewish state. However, even given the enormity of the pressures and forces acting on Palestinian society, the evolution of Palestinian ethnicity has not been linear or without contradictory aspects. Traditional forms of Palestinian social organization, identity, and values (i.e., kinship, village, and honor) have worked against the development of a broad "Palestinian" cultural world view.

Palestinians migrated to Lebanon because of the conflict in Palestine which grew out of the incompatibility between Zionist objectives for a Jewish state in Palestine and Palestinian interests.[13] Massive Jewish migration to Palestine totally transformed the demographic and socio-political character of the area (J.Abu-Lughod 1971). This conflict erupted into violent hostilities several times in the twentieth century -- 1920, 1921, 1929, 1936-39, and 1947-48. In the latter period the fighting resulted from the United Nations General Assembly resolution that recommended the partition of Palestine and from Zionism's success, in May 1948, in creating the state of Israel. In the course of this violence, many Palestinians fled to neighboring countries seeking temporary refuge but expecting to return to their homes when the hostilities ceased.

Israel, however, never permitted their return thus creating the permanent Palestinian refugee problem. As a consequence of events in 1947-48, some 770,000 Palestinians, over half the indigenous population, lost their land, homes, and property; were transformed into stateless persons, impoverished refugees, and unwanted "guests" in foreign countries; and experienced the destruction of their villages and the disruption of their family life -- the traditional bases of Palestinian society. Approximately 128,000 of these made their way to Lebanon. By the early 1970s the number of Palestinians in Lebanon had grown to between 350,000 and 400,000 persons. The increase was the result of additional migration after Israel's capture of the West Bank (and Gaza) in the June 1967 war, King Hussein's forced eviction of Palestinians from Jordan in 1970-71 following a coup attempt, and natural increase (Rubenberg 1984a).[14]

One of the elements that affected the development of Palestinian ethnicity was the negative experiences of Palestinians in Lebanon. Traditional Palestinian identity was composed both of particularistic aspects -- kinship and village -- and a more universal dimension, involving the sense of being "Arab" and an integral part of the Arab nation. When other Arabs treated Palestinians with hostility, this contributed to a feeling of separateness and distinctiveness as "Palestinians."

While accounts differ on the treatment of Palestinians by the Lebanese people (as distinct from the negative government attitude discussed later in this paper), most analysts agree that over time the majority of the Lebanese became exceedingly hostile toward Palestinians.[15] Amongst Lebanese Muslims, especially the Shi'ia of the South, reactions to the plight of the refugees involved both initial hostility and, more commonly, initial hospitality that was later transformed to hostility.

However, the reasons for the hostile attitudes appear to involve cultural values and economic conditions rather than "ethnic" conflict (i.e., "Lebanese" vs. "Palestinian," or "Shi'ia" vs. "Sunni" -- Palestinian Muslims were Sunni). The most important norm in all Arab societies is honor which is expressed in males through the ability to provide sustenance for their families; in the meeting of social and economic obligations in the hierarchy of age and gender relations; loyalty; the ownership of and attachment to land; and generosity in the provision of hospitality to others. Lebanese peasants knew little of the Palestinians' actual experience with Zionism and tended to view their leaving their land, destituteness, and refugee status as something for which the Palestinians themselves were responsible and had brought upon themselves. Such attitudes in turn caused them to look upon Palestinians as dishonorable, shameful, cowardly, lacking in self-respect, and as a symbol of the humiliation of all Arabs. One Palestinian woman recalled this experience in Lebanon: "When we left the camp, they used to follow us pointing and laughing. Often we would return weeping." An early form of mockery often shouted at Palestinians, was: "Where are your tails?" (Sayigh 1979:108-25). It is also the case that the Palestinians' sense of loss and shame made them turn inward, shunning contact with non-Palestinians, who, in the words of Sayigh:

> at best did not share their abnormality and at worst would taunt them with having sold their country or fled in cowardice. And with the establishment of the camps, the 'otherness' of the Palestinians was concretized in a particularly humiliating way. Now they were marked out as 'different' by a special identity (refugee), special areas of residence (camps), special restrictions on movement, special schools, and -- most humiliating of all -- U.N.R.W.A. ration (Sayigh 1979:125).

It seems likely that insofar as they were treated negatively, Palestinians were despised not because they were "Palestinian" but because they were perceived as having violated fundamental cultural norms. Indeed, the role of differing perceptions of behavior and experiences in the context of shared patterns of meanings and symbolic systems with regard to honor should not be minimized. Nevertheless, the consequences of such bitter experiences had lasting effects and contributed to the development of a Palestinian ethnic identity.

Economic factors were also important in generating conflict between Lebanese and Palestinians. Lebanese peasants often refused to share scarce food or other provisions with Palestinians who recount stories of having to pay for water for thirsty children and of being refused water when they could not pay (Sayigh 1979:104-5.) One explanation for such behavior resides in the extreme poverty of the peasants in the South. Yet in spite of the poverty such behavior so contradicts the traditional Arab norm of generosity that it seems explicable only in the context of the perception of Palestinians as having transgressed the normative parameters associated with honor and therefore not deserving of generosity.

On the other hand, the economic behavior of middle and upper class Lebanese (of all religious denominations) toward Palestinians was essentially exploitative, and "culture" does not appear to have been an issue. Henry Edde, nephew of former Lebanese president Emile Edde, commented on this aspect:

> We did not welcome the Palestinians with open arms or take
> them to our hearts. We did not make available to them the
> most basic necessities of life -- neither water, nor electricity,
> nor drainage facilities, nor roads, nor social services. It is we
> who deliberately put them near the urban areas and not on the
> frontiers, in response to the wishes of the businessmen for
> cheap labor...It was the Lebanese bourgeoisie, to which I
> belong, that advised this so that the Palestinians could be
> exploited in Beirut and in agriculture on the coast (Petran
> 1987:74).

The utilization of Palestinians as the cheapest possible source of labor over
time buttressed a persistent labor surplus and held down wages for poor Lebanese
which further contributed to their hostility. Finally, while there were middle and
upper class Palestinians among the refugees, the vast majority had been peasant
farmers -- small holders or sharecroppers. The collective experience of
transformation from a self-sufficient peasant class to a group of destitute,
dependent refugees contributed to the evolution of Palestinian ethnicity.

While cultural considerations militated toward the development of
Palestinian ethnicity, at the same time aspects of culture also worked against the
formation of Palestinian ethnic identity. Traditional Palestinian identity is, as
noted, centered in the family and village and, intimately related to both, is the
paramount social value of honor. As discussed by sociologist Rosemary Sayigh:

> Peasant culture, particularly the concept of family honor,
> depended for its maintenance on a community whose ancestors
> had lived together, and whose descendants would continue to
> live together for all foreseeable time. The key to the
> preservation of values lay in each family's need for the respect
> of its neighbors (Sayigh 1979:14).

Palestinians resisted the transfer of personal identity from the particularism
of kinship and village to the more universal concept of nationalism. Indeed
Palestinians re-created villages and kinship formations in the refugee camps by
settling in communal arrangements that reflected traditional patterns of
association. Moreover, while the traumas of dispossession, dispersion,
deinstitutionalization, and transformation acted to produce a "Palestinian"
consciousness, they also worked in the reverse as well:

> Dispersion had both centrifugal and centripetal effects upon
> Palestinian social structure and consciousness. By scattering
> them and exposing them to different political systems and
> influences, it increased their tendency to form small groups and
> factions. Yet at the same time, it constituted a condition that
> all suffered from, even if not equally, and against which most
> would ultimately rebel. It did not create unity, but it did create
> a pressure for unity as a means of changing a situation that

was intrinsically threatening. In no region of the dispersion could a Palestinian feel completely free or secure (Sayigh 1979:101).

The final factor in the evolution of Palestinian ethnicity was the explicit efforts of the Palestine Liberation Organization (PLO) to mold and develop it. The PLO acquired an independent status in Lebanon in 1969 and thereafter engaged in the processes of institution-building and nation-building. A fundamental objective of the PLO -- a goal that was reflected in every PLO institution in Lebanon (hospitals, clinics, factories, schools, unions, etc.) -- was the strengthening, deepening, and solidifying identification of the Palestinian people with the idea of a Palestinian nation. This nation-building effort was fostered through conscious attention to the preservation, creation, and transmission of Palestinian culture. Each PLO institution, in addition to its functional work, drew on the cultural heritage of traditional Palestinian society and juxtaposed that with the cultural experience born of living in exile (e.g., deprivation of a homeland and the struggle to return to that homeland), to imbue each Palestinian with a definitive "Palestinian" ethnic identity (Rubenberg 1983).

Palestinian ethnicity is still in the process of formation. Most Palestinians feel a sense of being "Palestinian" although this is probably more a nationalist ideological framework rather than an all-encompassing cultural identity. Palestinian ethnicity is fractured by kinship and village identities which have been reproduced in the diaspora in spite of dispersion, as well as by religious and class differences. This contrasts with the development of ethnic identities among the Maronites, Druze, and Shi'ia which have been produced and reinforced by the intersection of family and confessional allegiances as well as by class associations, geographical contiguities, and "tribal" (denominational) experiences and ideologies. On the other hand, the sense of "Arab" cultural identity in the context of hostile attitudes and behavior from other Arabs sharpened Palestinian ethnicity as did the experience of being transformed from a class of (mostly) peasants into destitute refugees. The objective situation of Palestinians in Lebanon (the discrimination, hatred, and hostility they experienced) forced them to organize socially, politically, and militarily to protect themselves and to meet their basic needs. Such organization contributed to the development of Palestinian ethnicity but it also added to the hostility of the Lebanese toward the Palestinians and to the production and reproduction of conflictual relations between them. That conflict in turn also furthered the evolution of Palestinian ethnicity.

The Nature of the Contemporary Conflict in Lebanon

The 1958 civil war was the first violent challenge to Lebanon's post-independence socio-political system. The actors were less clearly defined and the violence less sustained than in the 1975-76 strife but the weaknesses of the system were unmistakable (Odeh 1985:98-102). Fighting was quelled as a result of the United States' dispatching of Marines to Lebanon -- an intervention that briefly cast the domestic issues in an international "cold war" framework and temporarily shored up the status-quo. In the aftermath of 1958 Lebanon experienced a proliferation of parties and movements of various orientations and ideologies and for a time the kinship and confessional character of the system was muted in the play of "secular" politics. The issues that were debated between 1958 and 1975 were clearly economic and political in nature; yet confessional attachments, though often obfuscated, were never far from the surface. An analysis of the two main "sides" in the 1975-76 war -- the Lebanese National Movement (LNM) and the Lebanese Front (LF) -- illustrates the persistence of confessional affiliations.

The various groups that emerged during the 1950s and '60s included pan-Arab/Arab-nationalist, socialist, marxist, Marxist-Leninist, pro-Syrian, Nasserite, and Ba'athist tendencies. The leadership and cadres of some groups cut across confessional lines but others, despite secular trappings, were grounded in confessional politics. The most important of these was the Progressive Socialist Party (PSP). Ideologically the PSP was pan-Arab, anti-confessional, democratic, and championed social and economic reforms in the Lebanese system. However, the party was organized in 1949 within the Druze community by Kemal Junblat who, while professing socialist and progressive ideas was at the same time, the feudal leader of the Junblat clan, the family that had dominated the Druze since the seventeenth century. And while the PSP later gained members from all confessions except Maronite, its constituency remained overwhelmingly Druze. In addition, Junblat and the party played highly significant roles in Lebanon's burgeoning political life. In August 1970, as Minister of the Interior (the government position designated by the 1943 National Pact for Druze), Junblat secured legalization of three parties -- the Communist Party of Lebanon (CPL), the Arab Ba'ath Socialist Party, and the Syrian Social Nationalist Party (SSNP) -- then united them with the PSP in a coalition -- the Lebanese National Movement -- of which Junblat assumed, and retained, leadership. By 1975 the LNM was an umbrella for five major parties (the PSP, the CPL, the Organization for Communist Action (OCA), the SSNP, and the Independent Nasserite Movement (INM)) and another six minor ones.

The PSP was not the only confessional-based organization in the LNM; its second largest affiliate, the INM, was identified with lower and middle class sectors of the Sunni community and the LCP, originally led by a Maronite, drew its major support from the Greek Orthodox community. On the other hand, the SSNP was more genuinely secular, having members from the Greek Orthodox, Shi'ia, Druze, Maronite, and Sunni denominations, and the Arab Ba'ath Socialist Party drew recruits from the Sunni, Shi'ia, and Greek Orthodox communities. However, in 1975 the LNM formed an alliance with Musa Sadr's *Barakat al-Mahrumin* whose confessional character was never in question. Thus at one level it is fair to observe the LNM broke down into Druze, Sunni, Greek Orthodox, and Shi'ia components.

The LNM did not articulate a program until the summer of 1975, *after* the start of the civil war. Then it called for reform of the Lebanese system, abolition of political sectarianism, and democratic, popular, non-confessional representation. The platform also included demands for balance in the distribution of power among the executive, legislative and judicial branches of government; reform of the civil administration and the army; protection of the basic rights of individuals; and the formation of a constituent assembly. The LNM was also not committed to armed struggle; indeed, it consistently sought to utilize the political process to achieve its objectives. In fact, so weak was its interest in military affairs that the LNM relied on the PLO to provide it with military protection and assistance (though by 1975 several parties in the coalition had spawned militias).[16]   The other "side" in the civil war was the Lebanese Front (LF), a much more homogeneous alliance than the LNM, composed of three main parties all representing Maronite clans, as well as numerous smaller parties, almost all Maronite, plus the Maronite clergy.[17] Each party had a fully armed militia; these were collectively known as the Lebanese Forces. By the early 1970s their expressed primary objectives were to suppress by force the LNM and its constituent groups, preventing their participation in the political process, and denying their realization of any of their reformist structural goals.

The PLO fought with the LNM during the civil war (though at several crucial points it pursued strategies that contradicted the interests of the LNM)[18] while the Palestinian question intersected with all the domestic Lebanese issues and was an important catalyst to the coalescence of both the LF and the LNM. The emergence of the PLO in the post-1967 period as the symbol of Palestinian nationalism and of the unresolved Palestine conflict reignited the long-standing contention among Lebanese over the identity of the country: was it an Arab state, part of the Arab world, and therefore bound to support the Palestinian cause as a matter of Arab national honor; or, was it a Western country, separate from the Arab world, with no intrinsic relationship to the fate of the Palestinians? The LNM considered Lebanon Arab, supported the Palestinians, and sought basic structural change in the Lebanese socio-political order; the LF considered Lebanon Western, did not support the Palestinian cause, and strove to maintain the domestic status quo.

Confessionalism contributed to the cohesiveness of the LF and conversely to the ineffectiveness of the LNM as a political (and military) force. Moreover, despite the various issues, ideologies, groups, and coalitions involved in the 1975-76 confrontation, viewed from one angle, it bore an unmistakable resemblance to nineteenth century Druze/Maronite confessional discord and reflected a continuing effort by the disadvantaged confessions and ethnic-sects to improve their social, economic, and political statuses relative to the Maronites (whose dominance since the nineteenth century was related to the subordination of the others). Further, in the aftermath of the war, Lebanon's conflict shed all pretensions of secular politics, resuming the character of purely inter-confessional strife -- the only real change being the addition of the Shi'ia as a major actor. The persistence of confessional (and kinship) attachments underlies the Lebanese conflict and constitutes the most important reason for the failure of secularization.

To comprehend further the complex ways in which confessionalism (and kinship) insinuated themselves in Lebanese state and society and contributed to Lebanon's protracted conflict it is necessary to dissect the causes of the 1975-76 war. These are found in a series of interconnected internal and external conditions that affected post-independence Lebanon as well as in the country's prior lengthy history. Most of the relevant history has been discussed above; the remainder of the paper examines the contemporary conditions that gave rise to the civil war. The most important internal variables were: the social framework of Lebanese society -- its fragmented, hierarchically arranged groups; the pyramidal class structure; the weak and corrupt central government; the rigid political system based on religious affiliation; and a prevailing condition of anomie that was generated by the dynamics of Lebanon's laissez faire economic system. The most significant external factors included the presence of the Palestinians and Israel's continuous violations of Lebanon's sovereignty (Barakat 1979:3-20).

Internal Variables

1. Social Structure
    The Lebanese social system is made up of a multiplicity of allegiances and loyalties of which kinship, confessional affiliation, and fealty are the most significant. These connections also constitute the most important sources of identity, ideology, and social organization.
    In the 20 or so years preceding the 1975-76 war kinship had grown less significant in Lebanese society, with the family beginning to lose some of its conventional functions. Nevertheless, the patriarchal extended family, with its hierarchical organization based on age and gender, remained the primary unit of social organization, and a very prominent determinant of status, class, and power. Even more significant was that the family remained the principal agent of political socialization and indoctrination. Thus, kinship ties and confessional allegiances reinforced each other, and this explains, in considerable measure, why denominational affiliation took precedence over national loyalty (Barakat 1979). In addition, kinship rivalries and competitions permeated every aspect of social life, at times even fracturing the cohesion of strong ethnic-sects such as the Maronites. An example occurred in the 1978 mafia-style massacre of Tony Franjieh and his family in their home (together with 34 other individuals) by Bashir Gemayel, illustrating one dimension of the discordant relations between two of the three most powerful Maronite families.
    Lebanon is composed of seventeen different religious communities, each organized hierarchically on the basis of sacred and secular authority and socio economic status. The elites (religious and secular) in each community promote their own self-interest as well as the concerns and conflicts of members of their group. Not infrequently the interests of the elites and masses within a given denomination diverge considerably; nevertheless, both the interests and enmities have been typically articulated as confessional rivalry. The traditional elites of the various denominations have been responsible for the perpetuation of the confessional-based system -- primarily because it serves their personal gain. Most important, the Lebanese political system (discussed below) is structured so as to consecrate confessional ties, preying upon and encouraging the continuation of confessional and ethnic-sect loyalties.

In addition to the kinship and religious foundations of Lebanese society is the persistence of the feudal institution of fealty with its characteristic patron-client relationships and its various forms of patronage. Khalaf notes that fealty is "still very much alive in both form and content in contemporary [Lebanese] political life...There is hardly a phase of the political process untouched by it" (Petran 1987:30 quoting Khalaf). The present-day *za'im* (the leader who functions as a mediator or "fixer"), continues to capitalize on kinship, personal, and religious connections to cement and expand a web of reciprocal loyalties and obligations -- dispensing jobs and favors, intervening in the bureaucratic and judicial processes on behalf of clients, and demanding in return gratitude, allegiance, and a willingness to take up arms when called upon (Khalaf 1987). However, not all modern *zu'ama* are connected to religious or kinship groups. As a result of socioeconomic and political transformations after World War II (including rapid urbanization, the growth of political parties and "pseudo-ideological" groups, and other factors) a new type of *za'im* emerged -- popular political activists and self-made businessmen -- who offered new sources of patronage that were often politically oriented and occurred within the context of a political party or movement, a labor organization, or even a benevolent voluntary association (Khalaf 1987; Eickelman 1981). Kemal Junblat was an archetypal modern *zu'ama*. Eickelman argues that the new *za'im* have a class affiliation that cuts across traditional informal groupings of kinship and religion, stating that "class conflict has become the root of current Lebanese political unrest, not locally held ideologies concerning how that society is divided" (Eickelman 1981, 164-65).

Significantly, however, there is a striking similarity between the modern cross-confessional *zu'ama* ties and the connections among *muqata'jis* and sheiks that existed in the Lebanon Mountain's pre-nineteenth century feudal system. New elites have indeed emerged but the basic structures of the system have remained essentially unchanged. Whatever the basis of *zu'ama* patronage, the institution of fealty is perpetuated and maintained on an almost exclusively *personal* (rather than ideological, institutional [formal], or programmatic basis) and this has contributed powerfully to the ongoing fragmentation in Lebanese polity and society, and to the fostering and perpetuation of conflict rather than cooperation at the national level.

In sum, as a consequence of the persistence and dominance of kinship, confessional, and fealty affiliations serving as the primary sources of identity, ideology, and social organization, post-independence Lebanon suffered from the institutionalization of factionalism and the absence of development of a Lebanese national identity or a sense of loyalty to the country. Conflict was thus fostered and its resolution impeded.

2. Pyramidal Class Structure

It is estimated that in the early 1970s approximately four percent of the Lebanese population received 32 percent of the GNP while 82 percent received 40 percent (Barakat 1979:10-11). Moreover, the greatest proportion of the national wealth was in the hands of Maronites while the overwhelming majority of Muslims, in particular the Shi'ia, were extremely poor. Thus there was, as noted earlier, an important overlap between class and confession (although there were always some very wealthy non-Christians and some poor Christians of various, including Maronite, denominations.) But in the absence of an overriding Lebanese nationalism, and given that the elites encouraged the perpetuation of the confessional prism for viewing economic as well as all other issues, the masses often perceived class antagonisms as confessional conflict. An important consequence was that the secular organizations that did emerge (e.g., the CPL, the OCA, the SSNP, the INM, and others) advocating aggregation based on class or interest affiliation, failed to win and *sustain* significant popular support. The failure of the LNM and of the process of secularization was but the most striking result. In addition, economic issues intersected with confessional ties and contributed to the evolution of ethnic-sects as well as to the production and reproduction of conflict in the framework of ethnic discord (Barakat 1979; Farsoun 1988a, 1988b).

3. Weak Central Government

From the outset of Lebanon's post-independence history local leaders, established families, and religious authorities held greater influence over their followers than did the central government while several "states" (religious cantons) always existed within the Lebanese state. The existence of hierarchically arranged kinship and religious groups, autonomous confessional cantons, the institution of fealty, and the personalistic basis of authority all served to impede the development of a strong central government and to contribute to its extraordinary corruption.[19] That such a system would dissolve into violence seems virtually inevitable.

4. The Rigid Religiously-Based Political System

In 1943 (based on the results of a dubious 1932 census), an informal "National Pact" for sharing power was agreed upon by the elites of Lebanon's various religious groups. The National Pact apportioned political power according to the numerical strength of each group, enshrining Christians, in particular Maronites, as the dominant party in a consociational arrangement. Allotment of parliamentary seats was on the basis of a six-to-five Christian-non-Christian ratio broken down roughly as follows: Maronites 30 percent; Greek Orthodox 11 percent; Greek Catholic 6 percent; Armenian Orthodox 4 percent; and Armenian Catholic, Protestants, and other Christian minorities one percent each, totalling 3 percent, i.e., 54 percent Christian: Sunni Muslims 20 percent; Shi'ia Muslims 19 percent; and Druze 6 percent, i.e., 45 percent non-Christian. All government offices were permanently assigned according to denomination: the president -- the kingpin of the system and holder of extraordinary powers -- was always a Maronite; the prime minister a Sunni; the Speaker of the Chamber of Deputies a Shi'ia; the Deputy Prime Minister/Deputy Speaker a Greek Orthodox, and so on. Likewise Cabinet portfolios were carefully distributed among Christians and non-Christians and key ministries were reserved for particular denominations, although these formal institutions were relatively powerless and ineffectual in the play of Lebanon's politics. The National Pact was also intended as a "compromise" between the Maronite desire for a complete separation from the Arab world and a formal affiliation with France, and the Muslim-Druze desire for a reintegration of Lebanon with Syria and an Arab identification. However, it merely obscured the issue temporarily, contributing to its reemergence later as a fundamental aspect of Lebanon's conflict.

Maronites may have been numerically dominant in 1943 but by early 1975 the Shi'ia had become the largest community, representing approximately 30 percent of the population. By that time the total non-Christian population stood at about 60 percent Christian population, with Maronites constituting around 23 percent of the Christian minority. Nevertheless, the rigid confessional balance established by the National Pact remained unchanged and became by itself a major source of conflict (Cobban 1985; Nasr 1985). Two processes contributed to Lebanon's demographic transformation. The most important was the significantly higher birth rates within the Muslim communities relative to the Christian, particularly Maronite, denominations (Druze, however, have the lowest fertility rates among all denominations.) The differences in fertility between the two groups appear to be related to social and structural factors such as the educational levels of women, urbanization, and participation of women in the labor force rather than to religious motives *per se* (Chamie 1977). There is a considerable body of literature to substantiate these assertions regarding fertility; however a second factor, the emigration of Maronites as an aspect of the demographic transformation, is far less well documented and it is only possible to speculate as to its influence. It is thought, however, that Maronites emigrated in higher numbers than Muslims or Druze (Petran 1987:31). In addition, internal migratory changes played a role in transforming Lebanon's social landscape and contributing to the outbreak of civil war. During the 1960s the structural changes in agriculture that affected the South, the Akkar, and the Beqaa resulted in the pauperization and proletarianization of some 40 percent of Lebanon's rural labor force and catalyzed major migratory movements. An additional factor in the migration of Lebanese from the South to Beirut was the terrible pressure which the Israelis maintained against South Lebanon from 1968 on, through their constant military assaults (Cobban 1985:115). The displaced peasants then became the cadres of the new parties and movements that constituted the LNM (Nasr 1985; Farsoun 1988a).

5. Social Unrest and Anomie

Within a very short time after its independence Lebanon became the business, financial, and administrative capital for all the economic activities of the Middle East. Enormous amounts of money flowed into the country, but prosperity was confined to a few areas and a few families. Moreover, despite the fact that Lebanon became the financial center for the whole Middle East, profits were not invested there and few compared to only 40 percent for the total developmental projects were undertaken. These factors, combined with the rigidity of the political system, the extreme disparities in access to the wealth and resources of the society, the willingness of the privileged to employ force to protect their standing, and the absence of any overriding sense of Lebanese nationalism, all contributed to an ever-deepening feeling of anomie within the population, intensifying conflict and giving impulse to the use of violence on a mass scale. Worse, as the country spiraled downward into its violent ferment, the laissez faire economic system encouraged the emergence of a class that was able to become rich from the conflict itself -- through looting, smuggling, and the arms trade (Barakat 1979; Nasr 1978).

External Forces

1. The Palestinians

From the outset of the Palestinian migration in 1948, the Lebanese government viewed the refugees with hostility. When Israel made known its prohibition on their return to Palestine, the government objected to their settlement in Lebanon. One reason for this attitude was the Maronite fear that Palestinians constituted a threat to continued Christian supremacy under the terms of the National Pact. (The majority of Palestinians who came to Lebanon were Muslim.) The government's antagonism was also related to the fact that the refugees were natural allies of the various Lebanese secular and pan-Arab nationalist organizations (who also represented a potential threat to the perpetuation of the *status quo*). Additionally, the government was apprehensive about the possibility of future discord with Israel, given the Zionist-Palestinian conflict.

The Palestinian refugees were eventually permitted to remain; however, the hostility of Lebanese officials became an institutionalized fact of their existence. The majority were prevented from integrating into Lebanese society; instead they were forced to reside in seventeen camps (set up by the United Nations Relief and Works Agency for Palestinian Refugees -- UNRWA) wherein they were repressively controlled by the Deuxieme Bureau (the Lebanese secret police). In the early 1950s the camps were put under a state of emergency, described in the words of one observer as being sheer "terror":

> It [the state of emergency] completely oppressed the camps, turning them into ghettos and quasi-concentration camps. Movement into and out of the camps was restricted; curfew was imposed at sunset; informers infiltrated every quarter. Political police dominated the whole life of the camps; the commander had almost a free hand. Humiliation of men, collection of "gifts," and "protection fees," imprisonment for long periods without trial, beatings, and other means of intimidation and oppression were very common practices (Sharif 1978:15).

Christian Palestinians were able to obtain Lebanese citizenship with a fair amount of ease, but Muslims rarely so, unless they secured the personal connections and money necessary to "facilitate" the status change. Muslim women were allowed citizenship if they married a Lebanese Christian man -- a relatively rare event. By 1978 only 40,000 Palestinians had citizenship. Those who did not were forbidden to work without procuring special work permits which were very difficult to arrange and were valid only for specified jobs at specified places. By 1969 only 2,362 Palestinians had work permits. The government also prohibited Palestinians from attending public schools at any level and most refugees were too poor to attend Lebanon's private schools (Gordon 1983; Petran 1987; Faris 1981).

As the power and control of the Lebanese government declined during the 1960s, official Lebanese repression of Palestinians decreased, although Palestinians remained confined to camps, citizenship was still withheld, and employment and education opportunities were not opened. On the other hand, in the post-1967 period when the Palestinians organized themselves and the PLO became an armed and powerful group within the Lebanese context, new antagonisms and hostilities emerged. In 1969, the Lebanese government and the PLO signed the Cairo Accord, which granted the PLO the right to an autonomous political and military status in Lebanon as well as the right to carry out raids against Israel from Lebanon's soil (Khalidi 1979).[20] Subsequently, the hostility of the Lebanese was intensified as a result of Israel's military attacks, for which the Palestinians were held responsible. The presence of the Palestinians served to reignite the dispute among various groups about the identity of the country while the autonomous, armed status of the PLO after 1969 contributed to the drive by Maronite parties to arm themselves, take law and order into their own hands, and to join together in a united front -- the LF. This in turn was a major factor contributing to the erosion of the national military and to the ripening of conditions for civil war. The PLO/LNM alliance during the civil war resulted in further animosity toward the Palestinians from both their LNM allies and their traditional Maronite enemies (Deeb 1980; Odeh 1985; Petran 1987; Khalidi 1979; Rabinovich 1979).

2. Israel's Involvement

Israel's continuous violations of Lebanon's sovereignty were another major factor aggravating the Lebanese conflict and contributing to its eruption into civil war. From 1968 on Israel engaged in a policy of ground and air attacks against Lebanon in reprisal for Palestinian guerrilla activity against Israel. Typically, however, the attacks bore little relation to Palestinian operations originating in Lebanon; moreover, they were always massively disproportionate to Palestinian actions. For example, in December 1968 Israel raided Beirut's International Airport and destroyed thirteen civilian planes of Lebanon's Middle East Airlines - allegedly in retaliation for an attack on one El Al plane at Athens International Airport. In mid-April, 1973, thirty-five Israeli commandos entered West Beirut, assassinated three top PLO leaders, and killed nine Lebanese civilians. A good summary of Israel's involvement is provided by analyst Tabitha Petran:

> In the seven years from May 1968 to April 1975 Israel committed more than 6,200 acts of aggression against Lebanon: nearly 4,000 aerial and artillery bombardments of villages, towns and refugee camps; more than 350 military incursions, large and small, employing hundreds -- on occasion

thousands -- of troops equipped with tanks, helicopters, and planes; as well as continual violations of airspace and territorial waters. The year 1972 alone saw a four-day Israeli occupation of the Arquob in January, a devastating two-day land and air invasion in September, heavy air raids the same month against Palestinian refugee camps throughout Lebanon and Syria which left hundreds dead, as well as frequent bombardments of Lebanese villages. Forty percent of the actions took place in the seventeen months between the October 1973 war, when the resistance officially halted incursions from Lebanon into Israel, and the outbreak of the Lebanese civil war (Petran 1987:142).

In addition to the deaths of civilians (Lebanese as well as Palestinian) and the destruction of property, the on-going Israeli violations of Lebanese territory and sovereignty were a major drain on Lebanon's already thin governmental legitimacy: the inability of the Lebanese armed forces to defend the country and its people was a glaring testament to its impotence. During the 1975-76 war Israel openly assisted the Lebanese Front (Snider *et al.* 1979; Khalidi 1979; Rubenberg 1986a). Barakat summarizes the effect of Israel's intervention:

> Simply, the Israeli raids contributed to the intensity of Lebanese internal conflicts. The raids divided the Lebanese themselves, turned many Lebanese against the Palestinians, and acted to further polarization. Once the civil war started, Israel began directly to support the rightists, helped to keep the war going, and indirectly pressured Syria towards siding with the rightists (Barakat 1979:19).

The civil war terminated in October, 1976, but within seventeen months, in March, 1978, Israel invaded Lebanon in a major land, sea, and air campaign. It occupied southern Lebanon until June, during which time it created a so-called "security zone" with a Lebanese surrogate, Saad Haddad, in charge. Thereafter Israel continued its land and air raids into Lebanon, marked by a particularly intense two-week period of aerial bombardment in July, 1981, that was capped by the bombing of a residential sector of Beirut in which 300 civilians were killed. Following that aggression, the U.S. mediated a truce between Israel and the PLO, but Israel continuously violated the agreement (the PLO observed it), culminating in Israel's June 1982 invasion of Lebanon. That three-month long war resulted in more than 20,000 civilian deaths, the destruction of much of South Lebanon and West Beirut, and marked the beginning of a three year occupation. In addition, as a result of its alignment with one Maronite faction, Israel enshrined the Phalange as the dominant power in Lebanon, installing Bashir Gemayel as president, and after his assassination, installing his brother, Amin. These and other Israeli policies contributed to the renewal of civil war. In 1985 Israel withdrew from most of Lebanon; however, it continued to bomb and invade the country at will.

Conclusion

The analysis of Lebanon's contemporary conflict affords insight into the dialectical tension in the interactions among migration, ethnicity, and conflict. The consequences of these have resulted in the fragmented fabric of Lebanon's social order having shared in its formation, deformation, reformation, and disintegration.

Numerous historical forces and factors contributed to the segmented, stratified, hierarchically arranged political, social, and economic system that characterized post-independence Lebanon. These included migrations from the sixth through the eleventh centuries, the legacy of feudalism, political and economic interventions by the European powers, communal economic transformations, and the development within its boundaries of several autonomous systems of social meaning. These same forces and factors had a share in bringing about the production, development, reinforcement, and reproduction of ethnicity in Lebanon. For instance, the circumstances surrounding the migration of Maronite, Druze, and Shi'ia to the Lebanon Mountain combined with their heterodox ideologies to affect the evolution of ethnicity in these groups. Feudalism contributed to the endurance of personalism, patronage, and fealty and to the survival of the family as the fundamental unit of social organization. Kinship in turn intersected with confessional affiliation and added to the development of ethnic-sects. Third, the European penetrations of the Lebanon Mountain served to bolster the fortunes of the Maronites as a community -- initially through their Christian religious affiliations, later by more direct economic and political linkages (including facilitating the Maronites' enshrinement as the dominant power in the National Pact) -- and to reinforcing the Maronites' perception of themselves as distinct and separate, "non-Arab", and "Western". Fourth, nineteenth century migrations -- e.g., the expansion of the Maronite community and the exile and return of the Druze -- contributed to the development of Maronite and Druze ethnicity. Finally transformations in the Maronite community, its bonding and prospering, and its development of social institutions, contributed to its emergence as an ethnic-sect. In turn, those factors increased conflicts and tensions between the Maronites and Druze. As a consequence, Maronite and Druze ethnic identities were reinforced and a framework was established for viewing future conflicts in the context of ethnic rivalries.

Lebanon's social and political fragmentation and the generation of its post-independence conflict were also intimately related to the governing structure of the state -- the 1943 National Pact -- that was based on confessional affiliation. That arrangement served to bolster the traditional leadership of each confessional group, institutionalized factionalism, and impeded the development of a "Lebanese national" identity. The political system spawned by the Pact resulted in numerous negative consequences including: reinforcing kinship, confessional, and fealty affiliations; manipulating and intensifying ethnic or "ethnic-sect" loyalties; working against the emergence of a transcendent Lebanese identity; impeding accommodation or responsiveness by failing to accommodate demographic changes or demands for political reform (i.e., disregarding calls for power-sharing from new economic groups such as the emerging liberal bourgeoisie or from new ethnically-based political movements such as the *Barakat al-Mahrumin)*; producing and reproducing discord; and promoting the use of violence as a means of improving their position by those who were excluded from political and economic privilege.

Post-independence migrations also played a role in spawning the fragmentation and conflict in Lebanon. These included internal rural to urban movements resulting from changes in the nature of agriculture, the migration and return of some Shi'ia to Gulf countries, the movement of peasants from the South to Beirut resulting from Israeli military attacks, and Maronite emigration. These migrations had multiple effects that included the emergence of new elites, the catalyzation of Shi'ia ethnicity, the provision of cadres for the various secular parties, demographic transformations that shifted the population balance to a clear majority of non-Christians and erosion of support for the National Pact.

This inherently unstable socio-political milieu was further strained by the migration of Palestinians to Lebanon -- itself a consequence of conflict (in Palestine) and migration (the immigration of European Jewry and its transformation of Palestine into a Jewish state). Palestinians contributed to the Lebanese conflict by reigniting the dispute among Lebanese over the identity of the country i.e., whether it was Arab or Western; by becoming an armed and powerful political and military presence in Lebanon (illustrating and aggravating the impotence of the Lebanese government); by intersecting with domestic Lebanese issues such as the question of power sharing based on secular determinants rather than confessional affiliation, economic disparities, etc., and thus contributing to the sharpening of cleavages among Lebanese; and by alignment with the LNM, including military support in the civil war.

Lebanon's instability and fragmentation were further aggravated as a result of the constant military assaults by Israel whose disregard for Lebanese sovereignty and territorial integrity and disdain for the lives and circumstances of Lebanese and Palestinian civilians were major factors in catalyzing the 1975-76 civil war and in the perpetuation of the post-war conflict.

The evolution of ethnicity among the Maronite, Druze, Shi'ia, and Palestinian communities has illustrated the dynamic mix of forces and factors involved in the production and reproduction of ethnic identity. It suggests that ethnicity is not static or fixed, rather that it is socially produced in the process of historical actions and interactions that create, maintain, transform, and reproduce it. Several universal aspects of ethnicity have been illustrated in the Lebanese case.[21] For instance, the multifaced ways in which ideological beliefs assume organizational expression -- e.g. the Lebanese ethnic-sects, Palestinian "villages" in the refugee camps, and the PLO. Secondly, the politically volatile aspects of cultural notions of self and community which were illustrated in several circumstances: (1) the ways in which the associations between the Maronites and France reinforced, contributed to the definition of, and reproduced the Maronite sense of separateness and uniqueness; (2) the confessional -- "ethnic" -- basis of Lebanon's political system and the contribution of the system to conflict; (3) the various ways in which Lebanon's conflict emerged from the clashes between ethnic-sects and the fact that their presence impeded the development of a "national" community that may have been able to transcend the conflict; and (4) the development of Palestinian ethnicity and "nationalism" -- both arising from and contributing to situations of conflict.[22] Third, the interrelationship between class transformations and the evolution of ethnic identification, particularly notable in the relationship between the decomposition of feudalism and the emergence of capitalism and the development of Maronite ethnicity. Finally, the dynamic between "society" (i.e. the context of general cultural assumptions concerning the nature of the social world and social relationships) and ethnic identity which was strongly apparent in the experience of the Shi'ia, whose ethnic identification evolved in and was partly determined by a social system organized on the assumption that confessional allegiances should serve as the basis of political organization.

Lebanon's protracted conflict demonstrates that conflict both results from and contributes to ethnicity as well as being a cause and a consequence of migration. It also suggests that even though the objective basis of a conflict may involve economic issues, the presence of ethnic collectivities affect how the conflict is defined and perceived by the participants, and can serve as a catalyst to its transformation from economic competition to ethnic rivalry.

So polarized, intense, and complicated is Lebanon's conflict that it is difficult to be optimistic about a future for Lebanon as a viable, sovereign socio-political entity. At this historical moment Lebanon's conflict could not be resolved without a prior resolution of the conflict over Palestine: the Lebanese social fabric could not be repaired so long as 350,000 to 400,000 Palestinian refugees remain in Lebanon. However, a solution to the Palestine conflict that would be acceptable to Palestinians as well as durable entails an independent Palestinian state which, given the present regional power configuration, does not appear in the offing. Moreover, even considering such a possibility, Lebanon would still be faced with the legacy of almost 150 years of confessional ("ethnic") conflict, the depth of ethnic affiliations in the context of virtual anarchy in post-1976 -- and especially post-1982 -- Lebanon, and the continuous refusal of Maronite elites to accept any agreement for increased power-sharing with other groups.[23] Lebanon's future thus appears to portend continued internal fragmentation and conflict aggravated by external interventionism including Syrian penetration and domination and continued Israeli occupation in the self-proclaimed "security zone" it holds in the south, together with its continued military assaults.

NOTES

1. I would like to thank Samih Farsoun and Elaine Hagopian for their time and assistance in clarifying several of the issues in this paper in the course of several lengthy discussions. Remaining conceptual or factual errors are entirely my responsibility.

2. While the post-1982 situation does not readily lend itself to analysis, the basic components of this period are a legacy of the 1958-82 conflict and of the forces and factors that gave rise to it.

3. The issue of Maronite numerical supremacy in 1943 is considered questionable and is based on a 1932 census that has never been repeated.

4. In Iraq, Shi'ia constitute the majority of the population but control of the political apparatus is and always has been in the hands of Sunni. (In Iran, which is *not* an Arab country, Shi'ia -- of the "Twelver" sect -- make up the majority of the population and control the government which, since 1979, has been an Islamic Republic.)

5. The Shihab clan re-emerged as the dominant power in post-independence Lebanon from 1958 to 1970 -- an era known as "Shihabism" during which Fuad Shihab was president from 1958 to 1964 and his disciple, Charles Helou, occupied the Presidency from 1967 to 1970.

6. Many Maronites claim that they are descendants of the Phoenicians (attempting to demonstrate both an indigenous presence in the Mountain and their "non-Arab" lineage). However, all independent historical evidence indicates that they were immigrants to the Mountain and that they were originally Semitic speakers (i.e., Arabs).

7. The importance of the Maronite Church is attested to by Khalaf (1987:33):

> The Church, early in the nineteenth century and particularly in North Lebanon, was in a favorable position to assume the intellectual and political leadership necessary for changing the world view or political outlook of the peasants. The priest was doubtlessly the most ubiquitous and central figure in the village. He was not only entrusted with the task of attending to the spiritual needs of his community and administering sacraments at various stages of the life cycle, he was also authorized to resolve family disputes and marital problems and was often sought as mediator in factional conflict and village rivalry.
>
> The enterprising priests were also a source of employment to the surplus manpower of the village. They were active in establishing voluntary associations and religious societies. But most important, they virtually monopolized the school system and the printing press -- the only media available at the time.
>
> In short, there was hardly an aspect of the secular life of the community that remained untouched or unaffected by the omnipresence of clerics or clerical education. Second to the family, no other group or institution figured as prominently in the daily lives of individuals...

8. The Isma'ilis came into being in 765 after the death of Ja'far Ibn Muhammad the sixth Imam. They recognize his eldest son, Isma'il, as the seventh imam and hence are known as "Seveners" as well as Isma'ilis. (The Druze consider Ja'far's younger son, Musa, as the seventh imam and acknowledge his successors through the twelfth imam.) Isma'ilis are mainly associated with the Fatimid Caliphate in Egypt. The Fatimids (who came from Tunis) conquered Egypt in 969 and ruled until 1171 when they were overthrown by Saladin. The end of the Fatimids was the end of Isma'ili rule in Egypt; however, the sect survived though divided (one branch became known as the Assassins and was

found in Syria and Iran though it has now died out; the other branch emerged in India and in the contemporary period it is headed by the Aga Khan and has numerous followers.

9. The Druze believe that Hakim is not dead, but departed, and that he will reappear. They believe in transmigration of the soul and emanations of the Deity. Not all Druze know the secret doctrines of their sect. They are divided into two groups -- the *uqqal*, the sages who are initiated into the secret teachings of the *hikmah* (the Druze religious doctrine), and the *juhhal*, those who are ignorant of the *hikmah*. Nevertheless, all Druze are united by a religious covenant and have a religious duty to help one another, especially against non-Druze.

10. Shi'ism grew out of a dispute among Muslims over who was the rightful successor to the Prophet Mohammed. After the Prophet's death the first three caliphs (successors) were elected by the notables of the Islamic community. However, during the rule of the third, Uthman, some in the community argued that the line of succession should henceforth pass through Uthman's heirs. Uthman's cousin Mu'awia, governor of Syria, encouraged the idea of dynastic succession through his family -- the Umayyads. When Uthman died, Muhammad's cousin and son-in-law, Ali, was elected as fourth caliph. Mu'awia gave Ali tacit recognition but the Islamic community was split between those who recognized Ali -- the *Shi'at Ali* (Party of Ali) -- and those who thought that rightful succession should pass through Mu'awia and the Umayyads. Subsequently Ali was murdered and Mu'awia immediately proclaimed himself caliph. Eventually Ali's youngest son, Husayn, challenged the legitimacy of Umayyad rule and was killed fighting the Umayyad army. The majority of Muslims, the Sunni, accept Umayyad dynastic governance (661-750) as legitimate. The Shi'ia, who today constitute only some nine per cent of Muslims, believe that Ali and Husayn were the rightful successors and moreover that governance of the Islamic community must pass through the Prophet's family (thus Ali is considered by Shi'ia as the first rightful successor -- in Shi'ism, "imam").

In addition, Shi'ia consider Ali and Husayn martyrs, and in particular commemorate Husayn's martyrdom as a symbol of continuous struggle for justice and righteousness against illegitimate authority. The martyrdom of Husayn also has a redemptive aspect: his challenge to the politically powerful and numerically superior Umayyads is believed to have carried the message that the Shi'ia were to strive for a righteous society no matter how small their number.

11. Of these changes in Lebanon's Shi'ia community Albert Hourani writes:

The Shi'ia of southern and eastern Lebanon have been slow to find their voice, partly because of the slowness of educational advance among them, and partly because of the system of landownership. The landlords grew stronger between 1860 and 1920, and the peasants became sharecroppers; some of the lords became part of the national elite, prepared to accept the existing order so long as their interests were protected by it. For a time they were able to speak for the community but that time is now passed. The traditional leadership has declined, old land-owning families have given way to new ones and land itself has become less important as a basis of power. Emigration...has changed the structure and popular consciousness of the community... (Hourani 1988: 9).

12. For a period in 1975-76 the *Barakat al-Mahrumin* articulated its goals in the ideology of secularism but that was related to its alliance with the Lebanese National Movement in the context of the civil war. The movement was never secular.

13. The majority -- some eighty per cent -- of the Palestinians who migrated to Lebanon were Muslim. All Palestinian Muslims are Sunni. There are several denominations among the Christian Palestinians including Greek Catholic, Greek Orthodox, and others.

14. The Palestinian experience in Lebanon, while unique in some respects, was in the main -- especially in the hostility accorded Palestinians -- typical. The major exception to this was in Jordan where all Palestinians were offered citizenship. However, that policy was directly related to the Hashemite monarchy's expressed objective of absorbing into the territory of Jordan, East Jerusalem and the area of Palestine known as the West Bank (i.e. the West Bank of the Jordan river, which since 1967 has been under Israeli occupation and from 1950 to 1967 was under Jordanian occupation).

15. Some analysts argue that Palestinians were treated badly from the outset of their arrival in Lebanon (Sayigh 1979; Faris 1981) while others suggest that they were initially well received and harbored with warmth and hospitality (Farsoun 1988b; Hagopian 1987). The truth of the matter is very difficult to ascertain at this historical juncture and in the absence of extensive independent field work. The best judgement of this writer is that both kinds of treatment occurred depending on the area to which a Palestinian went, the socio-economic status of the Palestinian and of the Lebanese with whom he/she came into contact, and the religion of both. However, since the dialectical interaction between negative attitudes and the development of ethnicity (plus the additional dynamic of conflict) is most relevant for this analysis, the text seeks to explain why Palestinians were treated negatively.

16. The INM spawned a Sunni militia known as al-Murabitun while the *Barakat al-Mahrumin* gave rise to a Shi'ia militia Amal.

17. The Maronite clans included the Phalangist Party (of the Gemayel family), the National Liberal Party (of the Chamoun family) and the Zghartan Liberation Army or the Marada Brigade (dominated by the Franjieh family). The LF also included numerous smaller parties, almost all Maronite, plus the Maronite clergy led by Father Sharbel Kassis, who played an important role in the conflict.

18. In particular the PLO did not support an LMN initiative in March 1976 and declined to fight Syria when in June 1976 it intervened to bolster the Lebanese Forces against the LMN. The reasons are related to the PLO's precarious position vis-a-vis all the Arab governments. Since it has no independent (Palestinian) territorial base, the PLO is ultimately dependent on the good graces of the Arab regimes for its existence and survival. In the post-1973

period there was a consensus, led by Saudia Arabia and agreed to by Syria, concerning the nature of a regional Arab-Israeli settlement. Given its weakness vis-a-vis the Arab regimes, the PLO had no choice but to go along with the Arab state consensus. For a variety of reasons, an LMN victory in Lebanon would have threatened this Arab state strategy. In addition, the LMN posed a threat to the Arab governments with its pan-Arab, secular, democratic ideologies (Rubenberg 1986b, 1988).

19. Sociologist Halim Barakat describes some of the specific attributes of the Lebanese system that reflected the government's weakness and corruption:

> protection of outlaws by political leaders...; (2) settlement of feuds and conflicts...without interference of court or central authorities; (3) smuggling by political elites...with full knowledge of authorities...; (4) widespread evasion of taxation by businesses, professionals, and others to the extent that taxation was almost limited to salaries and custom duties...; (5) establishment of private militias; (6) direct interference by foreign powers in Lebanese internal affairs and free movement of foreign agents including those of Israel and other enemies of Arab countries; (7) use of Lebanon as a stage for conflicting Arab groups, governments and movements...; (8) greater importance of informal than formal roles...; (9) the playing of conflicting roles [such as holding a position in the national government at the same time that an individual was heading a private militia]...; (10) lack of authority on the part of the government to collect data or conduct census...; (11) difficulty of enforcing laws and imposing solutions even when solutions were reached (Barakat 1979:12-13).

20. Of course, the accord itself was a testament to the weakness of the Lebanese government.

21. The theoretical aspects of ethnicity discussed here are drawn from Eickelman 1981:157-74.

22. The political volatility of ethnicity is also apparent in the protracted conflict over Palestine which has resulted from the idea of Jewish "ethnicity" and the belief in the "right" to its expression through a "Jewish" state in Palestine--both created by the ideology of Zionism and the Zionist movement.

23. Several such accords have been worked out in the past several years, ratified by every other group, but negated by Maronite political and/or military opposition.

9

CONFLICT, MIGRATION, AND ETHNICITY: A SUMMARY

William H. Durham

The papers in this volume provide a valuable and diverse set of case studies on the dynamics of ethnic identity and mobilization in contemporary state societies. Spanning a broad range of geographic settings -- from Central and North America to Europe and the Near East -- the papers focus on inter-ethnic conflict in an impressive spectrum of social, political, and economic contexts. Before turning to consider points raised by specific papers, let me highlight a few general themes that emerge from this collection.[1]

First, the studies offered here remind us that ethnicity is more than a matter of identification and affiliation with a given cultural system or "style" (as in Royce 1982:18); it is also a matter of strategy, of the active *use* of that system or style by its adherents. The papers here are sometimes subtle about this aspect, as indeed they are on the whole subject of ethnicity`s definition. Yet the point is made repeatedly and forcefully in the case studies: ethnicity is both an identity and an instrument; it is at once a statement of cultural membership and a tool or weapon by which members attempt to negotiate improved standing within a social system. As one author, Martin Diskin, put it, "The essence of ethnicity is its tactical importance within a context of conflict" (p.26).

Second, the studies offered here remind us that ethnicity is also a statement of political and economic asymmetry within a society. Ostensibly, of course, ethnicity is a declaration of *cultural* position, an oath of allegiance to a particular conceptual system or "set of descent-based cultural identifiers" (as in Cohen 1978:387). But in stratified state societies like those discussed here, ethnicity is effectively a declaration of *social* position as well. This is because dominant groups readily define -- and frequently impose -- their own symbol and value systems as normative; in such a context, ethnicity is then a statement, whether submissive or defiant, of subordinant status. The point is well illustrated by Ruth Mandel's paper on migrant guestworkers in West Berlin: "reproducing the Germans' perception, the many nationalities [of guestworkers] place themselves within a hierarchically ordered scheme" (p.64). Ethnicity thus reveals the contour of power relations and social status in complex societies.

Third, the papers of this collection emphasize that ethnicity flourishes in conflict situations. While this is neither a new nor unexpected finding (see, for example, Despres 1975), these case studies help to clarify some of the main reasons for the association, particularly in the context of large-scale intercultural migration. Such migration, we see here, has two key consequences with regard to ethnicity: first, it brings into daily contact -- and often into sudden and unanticipated contact at that -- what may be two very different and unfamiliar cultural systems; second, it initiates this experiment in culture-contact in a setting guaranteed to produce at least the perception of competition. Real or imagined losses may be economic (as in competition for farmland or jobs), political (as in competition for power or social position), or some combination of the two. But the result is the same: intercultural education takes place in a charged atmosphere. Sooner or later, the students all learn that "other" also means "threat." As Carolyn McCommon tells us, such was the lesson taught (with irony) at the "Valley of Peace" in Belize; certainly it was also taught in Lebanon, as Cheryl Rubenberg emphasizes, particularly to Maronites and Palestinians.

Once "other" is identified as "threat," a renewal or strengthening of ethnic identity becomes a logical and strategic response in several respects. First, it can serve to broaden and generalize the issues. By appeal to a common cultural heritage, what may well begin as a very specific contention, affecting only a few individuals on either side, or even as a seemingly trivial dispute, can be magnified into a matter of global or systemic concern. The "other" can be convincingly portrayed as a threat to a whole society and way of life. Second, ethnicity helps to legitimize responsive action. As a declaration of cultural difference, it provides a ready opportunity to accentuate distinctions and promote categorical "we/they" thinking. In extreme cases, reactive expression can reach levels of ridicule and dehumanization which surely make it easier to fight and harm an opponent. Third, ethnicity also helps to organize a response. Through appeals to salient cultural symbols and parallel historical threats, group leaders can use ethnic affiliation to build social cohesion and allegiance to a cause. But once unified, activated, and organized via ethnicity, rivals may then appear to be more of a threat; this, of course, may serve to stimulate further response, additional threat, and so on. The potential for feedback is endless. For these reasons and others alluded to in chapters above, ethnicity blossoms in conflict situations.

One final theme deserves mention, reflecting its prominence in the title of this compendium. Migration plays a key role in many of the cases explored here, generally as a consequence of conflict in the homeland and generally, but not always, a cause of conflict in the host country. In essence, migration is a common mechanism by which "other" comes to be "threat." But though migration is often to "blame," in some formal sense, for the ensuing conflicts, the overall message of these papers is certainly *not* a condemnation of the down-trodden refugees of war-torn lands. It is, if anything, an appeal for empathy, for understanding, and for social scientific aid to those refugees; displaced victims of belligerence at home, they are often the unwitting seed-bearers of new conflict abroad.

Specific Contributions

Let me now turn to discuss briefly each of the papers assembled in this volume. Diskin's paper, to begin with, traces the emerging ethnic identities of peoples in Nicaragua's Atlantic Coast region to the last ten years of "interaction between the greater political context and the [region's] cultural structure" (p.12). In particular, it argues that the early efforts of the Sandinistas to consolidate a new form of state hegemony over the region were quickly viewed as a threat to the desires of local populations -- particularly Miskitu and Sumu Indians -- for regional autonomy. The threat prompted a groundswell of political activism, abetted in no small measure by U.S. efforts to overthrow the Sandinistas, including self-conscious efforts by the Miskitu and Sumu to express their ethnic heritage and "prior right" to political autonomy and regional lands. As Diskin points out, these claims are based upon a highly idealized and romanticized view of the past. At the same time, the Sandinist leadership tended to view Indian demands as counter-revolutionary regional separatism.

Diskin's analysis is noteworthy for its succinct summary of complex events, for its inclusive treatment of all ethnic groups in the region (up to and including Mestizos, who are often overlooked despite their great numbers), and for its identification of the multiple interacting forces that have contributed to the "shaping" of ethnic identities in the region. The one thing missing -- and understandably so in a work of this length -- is discussion of Indian identities and their evolutionary dynamics in pre-Sandinist times. It seems to me possible that events since 1979 could simply have intensified and accelerated changes in self-conception and expression that were initially set in motion much earlier, perhaps during the colonial period. In that case, the U.S. threat and the Sandinista's "learning process" might best be credited with a quantitative, rather than qualitative, impact on the dynamics of ethnic expression.

The paper by McCommon is, in subject and content, a model of analysis for the themes of this volume. The study describes the rapid build-up of inter-ethnic tensions in Belize following the arrival of more than 25,000 Salvadoran refugees between 1979 and 1984 -- or what amounted to more than 1 person of every 6 by the time the country ended its open-door policy. The example is paradigmatic: Belize initially welcomed Salvadorans (as well as other outsiders) as seasonal migrant laborers, only to find by 1980 that many were staying on. As "cross-fire refugees" from the incipient civil war in their homeland, they had neither the intention nor the option of returning home. When the Belizean government teamed up with the U.N. High Commissioner for Refugees to provide emergency assistance for these destitute souls, they only succeeded in making matters worse. The relief effort became a classic case of unforeseen consequences: offering not only a "Valley of Peace" to the refugees but also land -- to the tune of 50 acres with purchase rights, a deal beyond the wildest dreams of most rural Salvadorans in my experience -- they essentially *baited* a far greater influx of Salvadoran poor. As McCommon notes, the project quickly became "a victim of its own promise" (p.96).

As if all of this were not serious enough, the Valley of Peace project coincided with the formalization of political independence for Belize in 1982.

Historically, as McCommon points out, the population of the country has been predominantly black and Creole in ethnic orientation. But by 1982, people perceived that the "ethnic balance" was shifting and that the country was in danger of "Latinizing." In other words, the migrants had unwittingly brought with them a sizeable political threat, at just the time that Creole power was finally about to be legitimized. Not surprisingly, the government responded by closing the country's "open door" migration policy as of 1984, and by blocking U.N. funding for a second phase of the so-called "Peace" project. Again, one could hardly imagine a more fitting tale for the themes of this volume. All ingredients are there: cross-fire refugees, migration, political threat, host-country conflict, ethnic affiliation and mobilization, etc.

The consequences of cross-fire migration of a different scale are described in the paper about Kanjobal Mayans by Allan Burns. Seeking to "illustrate how [their ethnic] identity has changed through the Kanjobal experience as unofficial refugees in the U.S." (p.47), Burns looks at five aspects of their new life in Indiantown, Florida: residence patterns, work, leadership, religion, and communication. The case supports the general themes of the volume concerning ethnic conflict. At the same time as housing, schools, and public services become "overwhelmed" by the influx of migrants, and neighbors complain that their property values have dropped, we learn that the public image of the Kanjobal has "shifted from one of victims undergoing culture shock to one of sometimes dangerous migrant farmworkers" (p.55) -- in short, the immigrants are now viewed as a threat.

Despite obvious differences in time, place, and context, Nancie Gonzalez's case study of Christian Palestinians in Honduras comes to strikingly similar conclusions. Fleeing the hardships of the Ottoman Empire earlier this century, many of the *"Turcos,"* we are told, began life in Honduras as frugal, itinerant merchants, plying dry goods to a captive market of banana workers on the coast. Between business acumen, kin ties, and a legendary passion for saving money, the Palestinians prospered even as their numbers grew, to the point where they dominate today the hardware, furniture, and clothing industries of the country. Notes Gonzalez, "only as the Palestinian group became numerous and their success apparent did the Hondurans become nervous and resentful of them" (p.82). In addition, time and continued immigration have made it clear that theirs is a case of "permanent removal" from the homeland. Now that the economic loss to Hondurans is more apparent, and so is the tendency of the newcomers to isolate themselves in an ethnic enclave, Gonzalez finds evidence for increased prejudice and inter-ethnic hostility. Once again, the stage is set: "other" has been identified as "threat."

But while the Honduran case shows structural similarities to other examples in this volume, there is also an important difference: in contrast to the Salvadorans in Belize for example, or the Mayans in Indiantown, Palestinians in Honduras have enjoyed "phenomenal" economic success. In fact, many have been able to negotiate their way into the ranks of the business elite of the country, thereby compounding issues of ethnic identity with those of social class; in such a context, class antagonism surely adds weight to any expression of bigotry and ethnic prejudice. Significant in its own terms, the economic success of the *Turcos* also provides an unusually sharp lens through which to view the detailed evolution of inter-ethnic relations. For example, Gonzalez notes that certain features of Arab tradition and social organization -- for example, the custom of hiring kin at the cost of their keep -- gave the immigrants a ready-made "competitive advantage" over the locals. But many of these features were subtle and inobvious to Hondurans, who then came up with explanatory theories of their own -- such as the belief that the Palestinians must have formed secret pacts with the Devil. The case emphasizes that ethnic hostilities are fueled not simply by perceived inequities in resources and opportunities, but also by the folk theories that locals use to understand and interpret those inequities.

A second and already more serious conflict involving Palestinians is explored in the paper on Lebanon by Cheryl Rubenberg. As one of the more complex and provocative contributions of the set, the paper begins with concise historical sketches of the evolution of ethnicity within each of the main groups involved in the Lebanese conflict: Maronites, Druze, Shi'ia, and Palestinians. Noteworthy in the analysis are several points of particular relevance to this volume. First, Rubenberg shows that there are striking differences in the circumstances and time course of emerging ethnic expression within each of the four groups. Unlike the Maronites and Druze, for example, Shi'ia ethnicity did not "crystallize" until the last few decades, at which point sharecroppers and small farmers were especially threatened by export agriculture; in a similar vein, Palestinian ethnicity is the only one of the four not focused on religious affiliation. Rubenberg's point is that even in a complex cultural mosaic, ethnicity evolves in response to a "dynamic mix of forces and factors,... actions and interactions" (p.132) that are unique to each population. Second, Rubenberg argues convincingly that, in the nineteenth century, "class conflicts generated by essentially economic issues were transformed into discord between religious communities" (p.104), thus promoting the separate and rivalrous ethnicities of Maronites and the Druze. Key among those conflicts were tax revolts, peasant uprisings, and land grabs which, despite their broad class-based orientation, consistently favored the former at the expense of the latter. So drastic was the transformation that Maronites who had been the serfs of Druze sheiks went on to become their moneylenders in the course of just a few years. Needless-to-say, "confessional allegiances" blossomed. Third, Rubenberg emphasizes the role of external powers in these historical transformations. In particular, she notes that historical discord between Lebanese religious groups originated as "byproducts" of French and Egyptian interventions in the area, interventions which facilitated the demise of feudalism, the rise of capitalism, and thus the ascendancy of the Maronites. In this case, "other" was no particular threat until outsiders made them one.

Following these historical sketches, Rubenberg's analysis of the conflict in Lebanon itself offers a number of important and germane contributions. First, it emphasizes the importance of internal social organization -- especially the patriarchal family, pyramidal class structure, and rigid political system which froze sectarian representation at 1943 levels -- to the virtual institutionalization of the conflict. Among other things, these features explained why, "denominational affiliation took precedence over national loyalty" (p.124); they continued to hide class antagonism behind religious dispute; and they helped make the central government singularly unresponsive to the demands of minority confessionals for political and economic reform. Here, too, Rubenberg's arguments are persuasive: there *is* more involved than simple "ethnic sect rivalry." Tragically, however, the system is so sectarian that nearly all of the issues are at least perceived in those terms.

Rubenberg also provides revealing analysis of external forces that have added still further fuel to the fire. Chief among these are the continued interventions of external powers -- such as the repeated bombings and intrusions by the Israelis -- and the problematic Palestinian immigration. But these, too, are viewed locally through the infamous "confessional prism." For example, the Palestinian presence greatly intensified the internal debate over the identity of Lebanon: "was it an Arab state," as the Muslim Druze and Shi'ia desired, "and therefore bound to support the Palestinian cause as a matter of Arab national honor; or was it a Western country," as the Christian Maronites wished, "with no intrinsic relationship to the fate of the Palestinians?" (p.123). In this way, says Rubenberg, it was again *not* some primordial ethnic antagonism that generated the conflict between Lebanese and Palestinians so much as the perception that Palestinians constituted yet another threat to the established social order.

Thus I view Rubenberg's paper as fitting illustration, in a highly complex setting, of the themes of this collection. For each of the major rival groups in Lebanon, we see that contemporary ethnic identity is a historical product of repeated conflictive interactions. Curiously, the one exception is the case of the Sunni who do not appear to have formed a cohesive ethnic identity in this context. Rubenberg suggests that this may be because "Lebanon's Sunni community appears to have identified with the [dominant] regional position of its co-religionists" (p.106), but I am not fully persuaded. As a look at the Sunni in Mandel's paper confirms, this exception certainly warrants closer study.

Ruth Mandel's analysis of ethnicity among migrant guestworkers in West Berlin provides colorful illustration of her point: migration does "open the door to radically different possibilities for expression" (p.72). In her study, we are treated to two especially powerful examples: the "blooming of alternative expressions of Islamic identity" (p.67) in the case of the Sunnis and Alevis, and the marvelous story of the Akropolis restaurant operated by ethnic Turks. The former is apt illustration that ethnic expression is "a dynamic, flexible construct, grounded within the confines of historical, ideological, social, and political-economic structures" (p.71). In the Turkish homeland, Alevis are an oppressed minority group -- "a dangerous, secret cabal, replete with mysterious beliefs and rites"(p.68) in the eyes of the Sunni. In West Germany, their status reflects a significant transposition: seen as the more progressive and democratic of the Muslims, their "dissociation from the Sunnis abroad renders them superior, not inferior, in the eyes of mainstream German society" (p.68).

The restaurant story tells a similar tale, but shows by example the instrumental side of ethnic affiliation. In their homelands, Mandel notes, Greeks and Turks have historically served as one another's "salient other"; in Germany, by contrast, both groups have come to see that they have much more in common, just as Gonzalez noted in the case of Palestinians and Jews in Honduras. But because "Greek" is more familiar and less threatening to Germans than is "Turkish," the choice in advertising is then easy for the restauranteur: "to represent himself as the unmarked ethnic rather than the marked, thus assuring himself a more lucrative outcome" (p.72). The story reminds us that migrants find ample room for maneuvering in a novel situation. As this example illustrates, Mandel's analysis is clear and convincing, and certainly there is support in anthropology these days for her attempt "to situate a symbolic approach to culture within a historical and political domain" (p.72). It would be useful to have more data on the transposition of the Alevis that resulted from their "adopting symbols and practices thought of as German."

The political use and manipulation of symbols is also a prominent theme in the final paper to be discussed, Alexander Moore's chapter on "Symbolic Imperatives for a Democratic Peace in Guatemala." In contrast to Mandel's analysis, however, Moore's primary concern is with the use of symbols at the level of the state: the current government of Guatemala, he suggests, "shall very much need common symbols in order to orchestrate the consensus [it] desires" (p.39) in the aftermath of the civil war in the early 1980s. In particular, he recommends that the Guatemalan government undertake conciliatory "definitional ceremonies" and "redressive ritual action," basing his argument on both some "exemplary national symbols" used in the U.S. and Mexico, and on the "local immobilism" he observed during fieldwork in a Guatemalan village in the 1960s.

To my mind, the real value of Moore's paper lies not so much in its prescription for new symbols in Guatemala's future as in its implication for understanding the dynamics of ethnicity, class, and conflict in Guatemala's past. To take one good example, Moore describes the "veritable explosion of traditional ritual" (p.34) during the 1960s in the Indian community he calls "Atchalan," and relates that resurgence of ethnic expression to the violent overthrow of the reformist Arbenz regime in 1954. He convincingly portrays both the formal political exploits at the time of local leader Cesar Reyes and the impressive, if less formal, resurgence of local power among the Indian elders or *principales*. Having united disparate, even dissident, factions within the revitalized cargo system, the *principales*, says Moore, were in "full control of the suddenly burgeoning ritual life of the local Indian community... Ostensibly all were agreed on common symbols" (p.35, 36).

With this case material, Moore adds to the volume a striking Guatemalan example of evolving ethnic expression. Here, too, it is clear that ethnicity blossoms in a conflictual context; however, that context -- the counterrevolutionary "liberation" of the Armas regime and its successors -- and the Indian response could be analyzed further. To me, the activities of Atchalan seem like much more than a "local immobilist settlement" following the violence of 1954 -- "splendid, baroque, florescent, expensive, and absorbing" but also "inadequate to the task of political integration and consensus" (p.34). Instead, they look a lot like the other cases we have seen in this volume -- cases in which ethnicity blossoms as part of a continuing attempt to negotiate improved position within a social system. With the end of the Arbenz regime and the collapse of its bold land reform program, this resurgence of Indian tradition and identity may simply have been part of an attempt to regain a measure of local agency. The attempt was evidently unsuccessful, and thus perhaps "immobilist" in effect. But surely that, too, was mainly because of external forces and the intransigence of the state.

Be that as it may, Moore's example of a "local explosion" of Indian ethnicity adds a valuable dimension to this collection. Indeed, it brings me back to wondering about the search for integrative, nationalist political symbols in the first place. As long as conflict in Guatemala - and other nations as well - is organized along the lines of both ethnicity and class, it could be that the search for universal "primordial symbols" (p.39) -- "those that are immediately recognized as signifying the identity of a people [as a whole]" -- is largely in vain. Instead of trying to find new, all-encompassing identities and symbols, perhaps we should simply learn to live with and respect the diversity of old ones.

NOTES

1. This paper is based on comments originally prepared for the session, "Conflict, Migration, and the Definition of Ethnicity," at the 1987 Annual Meeting of the American Anthropological Association. Because new papers have been added for publication, and the original ones reordered, I discuss the papers in a different sequence than in the table of contents.

BIBLIOGRAPHY

Abu-Lughod, J.L.
1971 "The Demographic Transformation of Palestine." In *The Transformation of Palestine*. Ibrahim Abu-Lughod, ed., pp. 139-64. Evanston: Northwestern University Press.

Aguirre Beltran, G.
1967 *Regiones de Refugio: El Desarollo de la Comunidad: El Proceso Dominical en Mestizo America*. Mexico: INI. Akwesasne Notes
1987 "MISURASATA Proposes Peace Treaty." Late Spring. Rooseveltown, New York. pp. 18-20.

Al-Hout, B.N.
1979 "The Palestinian Elite during the Mandate Period."*Journal of Palestinian Studies* 9:85-111.

Ammar, N.
1970 "They Came from the Middle East." *Jamaica Journal* 4(1):2-6. Americas Watch.
1979 *Human Rights in Guatemala: No Neutrals Allowed*. New York: Americas Watch.
1983 "Creating a Desolation and Calling it Peace: May, 1983." Supplement to the 1982 Report. New York: Americas Watch.
1984 *Guatemala: A Nation of Prisoners*. New York: Americas Watch.
1986 *With the Miskitos in Honduras*. New York: Americas Watch. Amnesty International
1981 "Guatemala: a Government Program of Political Murder." London: Amnesty International.
1982 Report, (February). London: Amnesty International.

Ashabranner, B., and P. Conklin.
1986 *Children of the Maya: A Guatemalan Indian Odyssey*. New York: Dodd, Mead and Co.

Ashcraft, N.
1973 *Colonialism and Underdevelopment: Processes of Political Economic Change in British Honduras*. New York: Teachers College Press.

Ashdown, P.
1987 "The Problem of Creole Historiography." In *Readings in Belizean History*, Lita Krohn, *et al.* eds. Belize: Belize Studies.

Ashdown, P.
1985 "The Growth of Black Consciousness in Belize 1914-1919: The Background to the Ex-Servicemen's Riot of 1919." *Journal of Belizean Affairs* 2(2):1-5.

Asomani, K.
1982 "Belize Settlement Project." *Refugees Magazine* Sept. 1982, pp.22.

Azar, E.
  1980 "The Conflict and Peace Research Data Bank (COPDAB) Project." *Journal of Conflict Resolution* 3(1):143-152.
  1986 "Protracted International Conflicts: Ten Propositions." In *International Conflict Resolution: Theory and Practice*. Edward E. Azar and John W. Burton, eds., pp. 28-39. Boulder: Lynne Rienner.
Barakat, H.
  1979 "The Social Context." In *Lebanon in Crisis: Participants and Issues*. P.Edward Haley and Lewis W. Snider, eds., pp. 3-20. Syracuse: Syracuse University Press.
  1988 *Toward a Viable Lebanon*. Halim Barakat, ed. London: Croom Helm.
Birge, J.K.
  1937 *The Bektashi Order of Dervishes*. London: Luzac and Co.
Black, G.
  1984 *Garrison Guatemala* (with Milton Jamail & Norma Stoltz Chinchilla). New York: Monthly Review Press.
Blumberg, A., ed.
  1980 *A View from Jerusalem, 1849-1858: The Consular Diary of James and Elizabeth Anne Finn*. Rutherford: Farleigh Dickinson Press.
Bohannan, P., ed.
  1967 *Law and Warfare*. Garden City: Natural History Press.
Bolland, O.N.
  1977 *The Formation of a Colonial Society*. Baltimore: John Hopkins University Press.
  1986 *Belize: A New Nation in Central America*. Boulder: Westview Press.
Boothby, N.
  1986 "Children and War." *Cultural Survival Quarterly* 10(4).
Burns, E.B.
  1980 *The Poverty of Progress: Latin America in the Nineteenth Century*. Berkeley: University of California Press.
Camposeco, J.
  1987 Personal interview, June, 1987.
Chaliand, G., ed.
  1980 *People Without a Country: The Kurds and Kurdistan*. London: Zed Press.
Chambers, R.
  1985 "Hidden Losers? The Impact of Rural Refugees and Refugee Programs on Poorer Hosts." *International Migration Review* 20(2):245-263.
Chamie, J.
  1977 *Religion and Population Dynamics in Lebanon*. Ann Arbor: Population Studies Center, University of Michigan. CIDCA/Development Study Unit
  1987 *Ethnic Groups and the State: The Case of the Atlantic Coast in Nicaragua*. University of Stockholm, Department of Social Anthropology.

Clay, J.
1983 *Voices of the Survivors: the Massacre at Finca San Francisco, Guatemala.* Cambridge, Mass: Cultural Survival, Inc., and Anthropology Resource Center.
Clay, J., ed.
1983 "Death and Disorder in Guatemala." *Cultural Survival Quarterly* 7(1):1-63.
Cobban, H.
1985 *The Making of Modern Lebanon.* Boulder: Westview Press.
Cohen, A.
1965 *Arab Border Villages in Israel.* Manchester: Manchester University Press.
Cohen, R.
1978 "Ethnicity: Problem and Focus in Anthropology." *Annual Review of Anthropology* 7:379-404.
Consejo Mundial de Pueblos Indígenas
1984 "Declaración de Principios." Presented at the Bogotá negotiating session with the Sandinista government, Dec. 9, 1984.
Davis, S.H.
1970 *Land of Our Ancestors: A Study of Land Tenure and Inheritance in the Highlands of Guatemala.* Ph.D. Dissertation, Harvard University.
De Vos, G. and L. Romanucci-Ross.
1982 *Ethnic Identity: Cultural Continuities and Change.* Chicago: University of Chicago Press.
Deeb, M.K.
1980 *The Lebanese Civil War.* New York: Praeger.
1984 "Lebanon: Prospects for National Reconciliation in the Mid-1980's." *The Middle East Journal* 38(2):267-84.
Dennis, P.A.
1981 "The Costeños and the Revolution in Nicaragua." *Journal of Interamerican Studies and World Affairs* 23(3):271-96.
Dennis, P.A, and M.D. Olien
1984 "Kinship among the Miskito." *American Ethnologist* 11:718-730.
Despres, L.A., ed.
1975 *Ethnicity and Resource Competition in Plural Societies.* The Hague: Mouton.
Dib, G.
1975 *Law and Population in Lebanon.* Law and Population Monograph Series No. 29, Medford, MA: Fletcher School of Law and Diplomacy.
Diskin, M.
1987 "The Manipulation of Indigenous Struggles." In *Reagan Versus The Sandinista.* Thomas W. Walker, ed., pp.80-96. Boulder: Westview Press.
Diskin, M., T. Bossert, S. Nahmád, and S. Varese.
1986 "Peace and Autonomy on the Coast of Nicaragua." A Report of the LASA Task Force on Human Rights and Academic Freedom. Pittsburgh: Latin American Studies Association.

Dobson, N.
1977 *A History of Belize*. Trinidad and Jamaica: Longman Caribbean, Ltd.
Dozier, C.L.
1985 *Nicaragua's Mosquito Shore*. Alabama: University of Alabama Press.
Dunbar Ortiz, R.
1984 *Indians of the Americas: Human Rights and Self-Determination*. Praeger: New York.
1984a "Miskito in Nicaragua: An Information Packet." *Indigenous World/El Mundo Indígena*. San Francisco.
Economist Intelligence Unit
1987 *Country Profile: Belize, Bahamas, Bermuda*. Great Britain: The Economist.
Eickelman, D.F.
1981 *The Middle East: An Anthropological Approach*. Englewood Cliffs: Prentice Hall.
Epp, F.
1970 *Whose Land is Palestine?*. Grand Rapids: William B. Erdmans Publishing Co.
Everitt, J.C.
1984 "The Recent Migrations of Belize, Central America." *International Migration Review* 18(2):319-325.
Fagoth, S.
1982 "A Witness to Genocide." *AFL-CIO Free Trade Union News* 7(3):1-3. Department of International Affairs, AFL-CIO.
n.d. "La Moskitía: Autonomía." Ms.
Falla, R.
1975 "La Conversión Religiosa: Estudio sobre un Movimiento Rebelde a las Creéncias Tradicionales en San Antonio Ilotenango, Quiche, Guatemala (1948-1970)." PhD. dissertation, University of Texas.
1978 *Quiche Rebelde*. Guatemala: Editorial Universitaria.
Faris, H.A.
1981 "Lebanon and the Palestinians: Brotherhood or Fratricide." *Arab Studies Quarterly* 3(4), pp. 352-370.
Farsoun, S.
1988a "E Pluribus Plura or E Pluribus Unum? Cultural Pluralism and Social Class in Lebanon." In *Toward A Viable Lebanon*. Halim Barakat, ed., pp. 99-132. London: Croom Helm.
1988b Interview.
Ferris, E.G.
1987 *The Central American Refugees*. New York: Praeger.
Flapan, S.
1987 *The Birth of Israel: Myths and Realities*. New York: Pantheon Books.
Foster, M.L., and R.A. Rubinstein, eds.
1986 *Peace and War: Cross-cultural Perspectives*. New Brunswick: Transaction Books.

Foster, B.
   n.d. "Dispersed Refugee Communities in Belize: A Social Diagnosis." Report submitted to the Refugee Office, Government of Belize.
Frente Sandinista de Liberación Nacional
   1981 "Declaración de Principios de la Revolucion Popular Sandinista sobre las Comunidades Indígenas de la Costa Atlántica." Ms. Managua, Nicaragua.
Fried, M., M.Harris, and R. Murphy, eds.
   1968 *War: the Anthropology of Armed Conflict and Aggression.* Garden City: Natural History Press.
Friedlander, J.
   1975 *Being Indian in Hueyapan: a Study of Forced Identity in Contemporary Mexico.* New York: St.Martin's Press.
Gamst, F.C.
   1986 "Conflict in the Horn of Africa." In *Peace and War: Cross-cultural Perspectives.* Mary Foster and Robert Rubinstein, eds., pp. 133-151. New Brunswick: Transaction Press.
Garfinkle, A. M.
   1984 "Chapter I." In *Genesis in the Arab-Israeli Conflict: Perspectives.* Alvin Z. Rubinstein, ed., pp.1-39. New York: Praeger.
Gökalp, A.
   1980 *Têtes Rouges et Bouches Noire: Une Confrérie Tribal de l'ouest Anatolien.* Paris: Société d'Ethnographie.
Gonzalez, N.L. (Solien de)
   1961 "Family Organization in Five Types of Migratory Wage Labor." *American Anthropologist* 63:1264-8.
   1969 *A Heritage of Pride: the Spanish-Americans of New Mexico.* Albuquerque: University of New Mexico Press.
   1988 *Sojourners of the Caribbean: Ethnogenesis and Ethnohistory of the Garifuna.* Urbana: University of Illinois Press.
Gordon, D.C.
   1983 *The Republic of Lebanon: Nation in Jeopardy.* Boulder: Westview Press.
Gordon, E.T.
   1987 "History, Identity, Consciousness, and Revolution:Afro-Americans and the Nicaraguan Revolution." In *Ethnic Groups and the Nation State: The Case of the Atlantic Coast in Nicaragua.* CIDCA/Development Study Unit, ed., pp.135-168. University of Stockholm, Department of Social Anthropology.
Government Information Service
   1980 "Our Brother's Keeper." *The New Belize* September 1980, p.2.
   1981 "Asylum: An Update on the Refugee Situation in Belize." *The New Belize* December 1981, pp.4-6.
   1982 "The Valley of Peace: An Example in Resettling Refugees." *The New Belize* September 1982, pp. 5-6.
   1983 "Anglican Church Studies Refugee Problem." *The New Belize* November 1983, pp.8-11.
   1983b "A Refugee's Story." *The New Belize* November 1983, p.13.

1987a "The Blood of a True Belizean." *Belize Today* August 1987, p.2.

1987b "The Immigration Issue." *Belize Today* July 1987, pp.2- 4.

Grant, C.H.

1976 *Making of Modern Belize: Politics, Society, and British Colonialism in Central America.* London: Cambridge University Press.

Gurdian, G.

1987 "Autonomy Rights, National Unity and National Liberation: The Autonomy Project of the Sandinista Popular Revolution on the Atlantic Coast of Nicaragua." In *Ethnic Groups and the Nation State: The Case of the Atlantic Coast in Nicaragua.* CIDCA/Development Study Unit, ed., pp.171-189. University of Stockholm, Department of Social Anthropology.

Hadowi, S.

1967 *Bitter Harvest: Palestine between 1914-1967.* New York: The New World Press.

Hagopian, E.

1978 *South Lebanon.* Elaine Hagopian and Samih Farsoun, eds. Special Report No. 2. Detroit: Association of Arab-America University Graduates.

1987. Interview.

Hale, C.R.

1987a "Inter-Ethnic Relations and Class Structure in Nicaragua's Atlantic Coast: An Historic Overview." In *Ethnic Groups and the Nation State: The Case of the Atlantic Coast in Nicaragua.* CIDCA/Development Study Unit, ed., pp. 33-57. University of Stockholm, Department of Social Anthropology.

1987b "Institutional Struggle, Conflict and Reconciliation: Miskitu Indians and the Nicaraguan State (1979-1985). In *Ethnic Groups and Nation State: The Case of the Atlantic Coast in Nicaragua,* CIDCA/Development Study Unit, ed., pp.101-28. University of Stockholm, Department of Social Anthropology.

Hale, C.R. and E.T. Gordon

1987 "Costeño Demography: Historical and Contemporary Demography of Nicaragua's Atlantic Coast." In *Ethnic Groups and the Nation State: The Case of the Atlantic Coast in Nicaragua.* CIDCA/Development Study Unit, ed., pp.7-31. University of Stockholm, Department of Social Anthropology.

Hamilton, G. G.

1985 "Temporary Migration and the Institutionalization of Strategy." *International Journal of Intercultural Relations* 9:405-25.

Handler. R. and J. Lineken

1984 "Tradition, Genuine or Spurious." *Journal of American Folklore* 97(385):273-290.

Harik, I.

1968 *Politics and Change in a Traditional Society, Lebanon, 1711-1845.* Princeton.: Princeton University Press.

Helms, M.W.
1971 *Asang: Adaptations to Culture Contact in a Miskitu Community.*
Gainesville: University of Florida Press.
1986 "Of Kings and Contexts: Ethnohistorical Interpretations of Miskito
Political Structure and Function." *American Ethnologist* 13:506-23.
Herzfeld, M.
1982 *Ours Once More: Folklore, Ideology, and the Making of Modern
Greece.* Austin: University of Texas Press.
1987 *Anthropology Through the Looking-glass: Critical Ethnography in the
Margins of Europe.* Cambridge: Cambridge University Press.
Heusner, K.
1987 "Belizean Nationalism: The Emergence of a New Identity." *Belizean
Studies* 15(2):3-24.
Homans, G.C.
1950 *The Human Group.* New York: Harcourt, Brace & World. Hourani, A.H.
1988 "Visions of Lebanon." In *Toward A Viable Lebanon.* Halim Barakat, ed.,
pp.3-14. London: Croom Helm.
Incer, J.
1985 "Toponomías Indígenas de Nicaragua." In *La Prensa Literaria,* August
10, 1985, Managua, pp. 1, 5-7.
Jenkins Molieri, J.
1986 *El Desafío Indígena en Nicaragua: El Caso de los Miskitos.* Mexico
City: Editorial Katún.
Jones, S., E. McCaughan, E.S. Martinez, eds.
1984 *Guatemala: Tyranny on Trial: Testimony of the Permanent People's
Tribunal.* San Francisco: Synthesis Publications.
Kamke, J.
1982 "Special Report: Refugees in Belize." Inter-American Council on
Refugees, *Refugee Report* No. 6, May 1982.
Karpat, K.H.
1985 "The Ottoman Emigration to America, 1860-1914." *International
Journal of Middle Eastern Studies* 17:175- 209.
Kayyali, Abdul A.W.
1978 *Palestine: A Modern History.* London: Croom Helm.
Kerr, M.
1959 *Lebanon in the Last Years of Feudalism, 1840-1866.* Beirut: Catholic
Press.
Khalaf, S.
1987 *Lebanon's Predicament.* New York: Columbia University Press.
Khalidi, W., ed.
1979 *Conflict and Violence in Lebanon: Confrontation in the Middle East.*
Cambridge: Center for International Affairs, Harvard University.
1984 *Before Their Diaspora: a Photographic History of the Palestinians, 1876-
1948.* Washington, D.C.: Institute for Palestine Studies.
LaFarge, O.
1947 *Santa Eulalia: The Religion of a Cuchumatan Indian Town.* Chicago:
University of Chicago Press.

Leach, E.R.
   1954 *Political Systems of Highland Burma*. Cambridge: Harvard University
      Press.
Lesch, A.M.
   1979 "Israeli Deportation of Palestinians from the West Bank and the Gaza
      Strip, 1967-1978." *Journal of Palestinian Studies* 8(2):101-131.
Levine, R., and D. Campbell
   1972 *Ethnocentrism: Theories of Conflict, Ethnic Attitudes, and Group
      Behavior*. New York: Wiley and Sons.
Linton, R., and A. Linton
   1949 *We Gather Together: The Story of Thanksgiving*. New York: Henry
      Schuman.
Lovell, W. G.
   1985 *Conquest and Survival in Colonial Guatemala: A Historical Geography
      of the Cuchumatan Highlands, 1500-1821*. Kingston: McGill Queen's
      University Press.
Mandel, R.
   1988 *"We Called for Manpower but People Came Instead:" The Foreigner
      Problem and Turkish Guestworkers in West Germany*. Ph.D.
      Dissertation, University of Chicago.
   n.d. "Shifting Centers, Emergent Identites: Turkey and Germany in the Lives
      of Turkish *Gastarbeiter*." Forthcoming in *Movement and Exchange in
      Islam*, D. Eickelman and E. Piscatory, eds.
Manz, B.
   1988 *Refugees of a Hidden War: The Aftermath of Counterinsurgency in
      Guatemala*. New York: SUNY Press.
Ma'oz, M.
   1968 *Ottoman Reform in Syria and Palestine 1840-1861: the Impact of the
      Tanzimat on Politics and Society*. Oxford: Clarendon Press.
McCommon, C.
   1986 "Valley of Peace Census and Evaluation." Report submitted to the
      Ministry of Foreign Affairs, Government of Belize.
   n.d. Internal Project Reports, Accelerated Cocoa Development Project,
      VITA, Arlington, Virginia.
Mélikoff, I.
   1982 "Recherches sur les composantes du syncrétisme Bektachi-Alevi." In
      Studia Turkologica memoriae Alexii Bombaci dicata, pp.379-95.
      Napoli.
Melville, T., and M.Melville
   1971 *Whose Heaven, Whose Earth?* New York: Knopf.
Migdal, J. S.
   1980 *Palestinian Society and Politics*. Princeton: Princeton Uiversity Press.
Miralles, M.
   1986 *Health Seeking Behavior of Guatemalan Refugees in South Florida*.
      Masters Thesis, University of Florida.

Misurasata
1981 "La tenencia de la tierra de las comunidades indígenas y criollas de la costa atlántica." Ms. Managua.

Mogannam, M.
1937 *The Arab Woman and the Palestine Problem*. London: Herbert Joseph.

Moore, A.
1963 *The Guatemalan Plantation System in Historical Perspective*. Masters Thesis, Columbia University.
1966 *Social and Ritual Change in a Guatemalan Town*. Ph.D. Dissertation, Columbia University.
1973 *Life Cycles in Atchalan: the Diverse Careers of Certain Guatemalans*. New York: Teachers College Press.
1984 "From Council to Legislature: Democracy, Parliamentarianism and the San Blas Cuna." *American Anthropologist* 86:28-42.

Moosa, M.
1986 *The Maronites in History*. Syracuse: Syracuse University Press.

Morris, B.
1986a "Operation Dani and the Palestinian Exodus from Lydda and Ramle in 1948." *The Middle East Journal* 40(1):82-110
1986b "The Harvest of 1948 and the Creation of the Palestine Refugee Problem." *The Middle East Journal* 40(4):671-86. Myerhoff, B.
1978 *Number Our Days*. New York: Dutton.

Naff, A.
1983 "Arabs in America: a Historical Overview." In *Arabs in the New World*. Sameer Y. Abraham and Nabeel Abraham, ed., pp. 9-29. Detroit: Wayne State University Press.

Nash, J.
1967 "Death as a Way of Life: the Increasing Resort to Homicide in a Mexican Indian Town." *American Anthropologist* 69(5):455-70.

Nash, M.
1958 *Machine-age Maya: The Industrialization of a Guatemalan Community*. Glencoe, Illinois: Free Press.

Nasr, S.
1978 "Backdrop to Civil War: The Crisis of Lebanese Capitalism." *MERIP Reports*, No. 73, December:3-13.
1985 "Roots of the Shi'i Movement." *MERIP Reports*, No. 133, June 10-16.

Nettleship, M.A., R.D.Givens, and A. Nettleship, eds.
1975 *War: Its Causes and Correlates*. The Hague: Mouton.

Nicolait, R., and Associates.
1980 *Environmental Profile: Belize*. Belize: U.S. Agency for Internationl Development.

Nietschmann, B.
1979 *Caribbean Edge*. Indianapolis: Bobbs-Merrill.
1987 "Militarization and Indigenous Peoples. Introduction: the Third World War." *Cultural Survival* 11(3):1-16.

Odeh, B. J.
1985 *Lebanon: Dynamics of Conflict*. London: Zed Press.

Olien, M.D.
1983 "The Miskito Kings and the Line of Succession." *Journal of Anthropological Research* 39(2):198-241.
Otterbein, K.F.
1970 *The Evolution of War.* New Haven: HRAF Press.
Owen, R.
1988 "The Economic History of Lebanon, 1943-1974: Its Salient Features." In *Toward A Viable Lebanon.* Halim Barakat, ed., pp. 27-41. London: Croom Helm.
Palacio, J.
1988 "Illegal Aliens in Belize: Findings from the 1984 Amnesty." In *When Borders Don't Divide: Urban Migration and Refugee Movements in the Americas.* Paticia Pesser, ed., Center for Migration Studies, New York.
Parvenu, M. A.
1986 *Refugee Migration and Settlement: Belize -- The Valley of Peace Project,* M.S. Thesis, University of Wisconsin, Madison.
Peretz, D.
1958 *Israel and the Palestine Arabs.* Washington, D.C.
Perez, C.
1987 "Coming to the United States." Ms. Indiantown, Florida, Indiantown Middle School Thunderbird Thoughts.
Perez, L.
1986 "Cubans in the United States." *Annals of the American Academy of Political and Social Science* 487:126-137.
Petran, T.
1987 *The Struggle Over Lebanon.* New York: Monthly Review Press.
Philip, G.
1984 "Belize: The Troubled Regional Context." *The World Today* 40:370-376.
Platt, D.C.M.
1972 *Latin America and British Trade 1806-1914.* London: Adam and Charles Black.
Polk, W.
1963 *The Opening of South Lebanon, 1788-1840.* Cambridge: Harvard University Press.
Porath, Y.
1966 "The Peasant Revolt of 1851-61 in Kisrawan." *Asian and African Studies* 2:77-157.
Press, R. M.
1985 "Mayan Refugees in Florida." *The Christian Science Monitor,* May 28, 1985.
Rabinovich, I.
1979 "The Limits of Military Power: Syria's Role." In *Lebanon in Crisis.* P. Edward Haley and Lewis W. Snider, eds., pp. 55-74. Syracuse: Syracuse University Press.
Rahman, F.
1979 *Islam.* Chicago: University of Chicago Press.

Randal, J.C.
1983 *Going All the Way: Christian Warlords, Israeli Adventurers, and the War in Lebanon.* New York: The Viking Press.

Rangel, C.
1977 *Del Buen Salvaje al Buen Revolucionario.* Caracas: Monte Avila Editores.

Ressler, E., N. Boothby, and D. Steibock.
1988 *Unaccompanied Children: Care and Protection in Wars, Natural Disasters, and Refugee Movements.* New York: Oxford University Press.

Riggs, F.W., ed.
1985 "Ethnicity: Concepts and Terms Used in Ethnicity Research." *International Conceptual Encyclopedia for the Social Sciences,* Vol. I. Honolulu: International Social Science Council.

Roett, R., ed.
1985 *Report on Guatemala: Findings of the Study Group on United States-Guatemalan Relations,* SAIS Papers in International Affairs, Denver: Westview Press.

Rosenfeld, H.
1978 "The Class Situation of the Arab National Minority in Israel." *Comparative Studies in Society and History* 20:374-407.

Ross, M.H.
1985 "The Limits to Social Structure: Social Structural and Psychocultural Explanations for Political Conflict and Violence." Paper presented at the 87th Meetings of the American Anthropological Association, Washington, D.C.

Royce, A.
1982 *Ethnic Identity: Strategies of Diversity.* Bloomington: Indiana University Press.

Rubenberg, C.A.
1983 *The Palestine Liberation Organization: Its Institutional Infrastructure.* Belmont, MA: Institute of Arab Studies.
1984a "Palestinians in Lebanon: A Question of Human and Civil Rights." *Arab Studies Quarterly* 6(3):194-221.
1984b "The Israeli Invasion of Lebanon: Objectives and Consequences." *Journal of South Asian and Middle Eastern Studies* 8(2):3-28.
1986a *Israel and the American National Interest: A Critical Examination.* Champaign: University of Illinois Press.
1986b "Conflict and Contradiction in the Relations between the Arab States and the Palestine National Movement." In *Palestine: Continuing Dispossession.* Glenn E. Perry, ed. Belmont, MA: Association of Arab-American University Graduates Press.
1988 "The Structural and Political Context of the PLO's Changing Objectives in the post-1967 Period." In *The Arab-Israeli Conflict: Twenty Years After the Six Day War.* Yehuda Lukacs and Abdalla Battah, eds. Boulder: Westview Press.

Rubenstein, H.
  1983 "Remittances and Rural Underdevelopment in the English-speaking
    Caribbean." *Human Organization* 42(4):295-306.
Runciman, S.
  1968 *The Historic Role of the Christian Arabs of Palestine*. London:
    Longman.
Sahlins, M.
  1961 "The Segmentary Lineage: an Organization of Predatory Expansion."
    American Anthropologist 63(2):332-345.
Salibi, K.
  1988 "Tribal Origins of the Religious Sects in the Arab East."In *Toward A
    Viable Lebanon*. Halim Barakat, ed., pp. 15-26. London: Croom Helm.
Sayigh, R.
  1979 *Palestinians: From Peasants to Revolutionaries*. London: Zed Press.
Scholch, A.
  1982 "European Penetration and the Economic Development of Palestine,
    1856-82." In *Studies in the Economic and Social History of Palestine
    in the Nineteenth Century*. Roger Owen, ed., pp. 10-87. Oxford: St.
    Antony's College.
Scudder, T. and E. Colson
  1982 "From Welfare to Development: a Conceptual Framework for the
    Analysis of Dislocated Peoples." In *Involuntary Migration and
    Resettlement*, Anthony Oliver-Smith and Art Hansen, eds. Boulder:
    Westview Press.
Segev, T.
  1986 *1949: The First Israelis*. New York: The Free Press.
Sereseres, C.D.
  1985 "The Guatemalan Legacy: Radical Challengers and Military Politics." In
    *Report on Guatemala: Findings of the Study Group on United States-
    Guatemalan Relations*. Riordan Roett, ed., SAIS Papers in International
    Affairs, Denver: Westview Press.
Sharif, H.
  1978 "South Lebanon: Its History and Geopolitics." In *South Lebanon*. Elaine
    Hagopian and Samih Farsoun, eds. Special Report No. 2. Detroit:
    Association of Arab-American University Graduates.
Sharif, R.
  1977 "Latin America and the Arab-Israeli Conflict." *Journal of Palestinian
    Studies* 7:98-112.
Smith, C.
  1978 "Beyond Dependency Theory: National and Regional Patterns of
    Underdevelopment in Guatemala." *American Ethnologist* 5:574-617.
Smith, M.G.
  1965 *The Plural Society in the British West Indies*. Berkley: Univ. of
    California Press.
  1984 *Culture, Race, and Class in the Commonwealth Caribbean*. University
    of the West Indies: Dept. of Extra-mural Studies.

Snider, L.W., P.E. Haley, A.R.Wagner, and N.J.Cohen,
  1979 "Israel." In *Lebanon in Crisis*. P. Edward Haley and Lewis W. Snider,
    eds., pp. 91-112. Syracuse, Syracuse University Press.
Stavrianos, L.
  1958 *The Balkans Since 1453*. New York: Holt, Rinehart and Winston.
Stephens, J.L.
  1949 *Incidents of Travel in Central America and Yucatan*. Richard L.
    Predmore, ed., New Brunswick, N.J.: Rutgers University Press.
Stillman, Y.K.
  1979 *Palestinian Costume and Jewelry*. Albuquerque: University of New
    Mexico Press.
Stork, J.
  1985 "The War of the Camps, the War of the Hostages." *MERIP Reports*,
    No. 133, June: pp. 3-7.
Swartz, M.J., et al..
  1966 "Introduction." In *Political Anthropology*. M. J. Swartz et al.., eds.,
    pp.1-42. Chicago: Aldine.
Tibi, B.
  1981 *Arab Nationalism: A Critical Enquiry*. (ed. and translated by Marion
    Farouk-Sluglett and Peter Sluglett), New York, St. Martin's Press,
    (first published in Germany in 1971).
Topsey, H.
  1987 "The Ethnic War in Belize." Ms., Department of Archaeology, Gov. of
    Belize.
Torres-Rivas, E.
  1985 *Report on the Condition of Central American Refugees and Migrants*.
    Occasional Paper Series, Center for Immigration Policy and Refugee
    Assistance, Georgetown University and the Intergovernmental
    Committee for Migration.
Tsimhoni, D.
  1976 *The British Mandate and the Arab Christians in Palestine 1920-1925*.
    Ph.D. Dissertation, University of London.
  1978 "The Greek Orthodox Patriarchate of Jerusalem during the Formative
    Years of the British Mandate in Palestine." *Asian and African Studies*
    12:77-121.
Turner, V.
  1957 *Schism and Continuity in an African Society*. Manchester: Manchester
    University Press.
  1974 "Hidalgo: History as Social Drama." In *Dramas, Fields, and Metaphors:
    Symbolic Action in Human Society*. V.Turner, ed., pp. 98-155, Ithaca:
    Cornell University Press.
Turney-High, H.H.
  1949 *Primitive War: Its Practice and Concepts*. Columbia: University of
    South Carolina Press.
United Nations High Commissioner for Refugees
  1986 "Fact Sheet: Belize." Ms., UNHCR.

United States Committee for Refugees
1984 *World Refugee Survey 1984*. Washington, D.C.: United States Committee for Refugees.

Valencia, E.
1984 *Guatemalan Refugees in Mexico, 1980-1984*. New York: Americas Watch Committee.

Van Bruinessen, M.
1978 *Agha, Shaikh and State: On the Social and Political Organization of Kurdistan*. Netherlands.

Vilas, C.M.
1987 "Revolutionary change and Multi-Ethnic Regions: the Sandinista Revolution and the Nicaraguan State." In *Ethnic Groups and the Nation State: The Case of the Atlantic Coast in Nicaragua*. CIDCA/ Development Study Unit, ed., pp. 61-100. University of Stockholm, Department of Social Anthropology.

Vogt, E.V. and S.Abel.
1977 "On Political Rituals in Contemporary Mexico." In *Secular Ritual*. Sally Falk Moore and Barbara Myerhoff, eds., pp. 173-188. Assen: van Gorcum.

Volney, Constantin F.C. de
1787 *Travels through Syria and Egypt in the Years 1783, 1784, and 1785*. 2 vols. London: C.G.J. and J. Robinson.

Warner, W. L.
1961 *The Family of God*. New Haven: Yale University Press.
1962 *American Life: Dream and Reality*. rev. ed. Chicago: University of Chicago Press.

Wedge, B.
1986 "Psychology of the Self in Social Conflict." In *International Conflict Resolution: Theory and Practice*. Edward E. Azar and John W. Burton, eds., pp. 56-62. Boulder: Lynne Reinner.

Wilk, R.
1985 "History and Mayan Ethnicity in Belize." *Journal of Belizean Affairs* 2(1):12-16.

Wolf, E.R.
1982 *Europe and the People without History*. Berkeley: University of California Press.

Young, A.
1978 "Ethnic Politics in Belize."*Caribbean Review* 7(3).

Zureik, E. T.
1976 "Transformation of Class Structure among the Arabs in Israel: from Peasantry to Proletariat." *Journal of Palestine Studies* 6:39-60.

INDEX

About the Contributors

Allan F. Burns is an Associate Professor of Anthropology at the University of Florida. He has worked in Central America and Mexico and, presently, in Micronesia, where he has assisted the local university in developing skills in anthropological video-filming.

Martin Diskin is Professor of Anthropology at Massachusetts Institute of Technology. A specialist in Central American affairs, he has written extensively on agrarian and economic policy making in developing societies.

William H. Durham is Professor of Anthropology at Stanford University. A Mesoamericanist, he has been especially interested in the relationship between biological and cultural phenomena, and has made contributions to our understanding of population dynamics in different kinds of societies.

Nancie L. Gonzalez is Professor of Anthropology at the University of Maryland, College Park, where she is also an Associate of the Center for International Development and Conflict Management. She has worked among various ethnic groups in Central America, including Cakchiqueles, Garifuna, Ladinos, and, most recently, Palestinians.

Carolyn S. McCommon is the Rural Development Adviser for Volunteers in Technical Assistance (VITA), a U.S. non-governmental organization involved in international development programs. She has worked in various aspects of program design, implementation, and evaluation for the World Bank and the U.S. Agency for International Development.

Ruth Mandel received her Ph.D. in Anthropology at the University of Chicago in 1988. Since then she has been a post-doctoral fellow at the Berlin Program for Advanced German and European Studies, The Free University.

Alexander Moore is Professor and Chair of Anthropology at the University of Southern California. He has worked extensively in several Latin American countries, with a special interest in political systems and the behavior patterns associated with them.

Cheryl A. Rubenberg is Associate Professor of International Relations in the Political Science Department of Florida International University. She has written numerous articles and books on the PLO, Palestinian human rights and U.S. policy in the Middle East.